Managing Business Performance

*Where there is balance and harmony
there is performance*

Managing Business Performance

Performance

The Science and the Art

Umit S. Bititci

This edition first published 2015
© 2015 John Wiley & Sons, Ltd

Registered office
John Wiley & Sons Ltd, The Atrium, Southern Gate, Chichester, West Sussex, PO19 8SQ, United Kingdom

For details of our global editorial offices, for customer services and for information about how to apply for permission to reuse the copyright material in this book please see our website at www.wiley.com.

Wiley publishes in a variety of print and electronic formats and by print-on-demand. Some material included with standard print versions of this book may not be included in e-books or in print-on-demand. If this book refers to media such as a CD or DVD that is not included in the version you purchased, you may download this material at http://booksupport.wiley.com. For more information about Wiley products, visit www.wiley.com.

Library of Congress Cataloging-in-Publication Data

Bititci, Umit S.
　Managing business performance : the science and the art / Umit S. Bititci.
　　pages cm
　Includes bibliographical references and index.
　ISBN 978-1-119-02567-2 (cloth)
　1. Performance technology.　2. Performance.　3. Organizational effectiveness.
4. Management.　I. Title.
　HF5549.5.P37.B57 2015
　658.4′013—dc23　　　　　　　　　　　　　　　　　　　2015018007

A catalogue record for this book is available from the British Library.

ISBN 978-1-119-02567-2 (hardback) ISBN 978-1-119-02568-9 (ebk)
ISBN 978-1-119-02569-6 (ebk)　　　ISBN 978-1-119-16654-2 (obk)

Cover design: Wiley
Cover image: © Irur/Shutterstock

Set in 10/12pt Times by Aptara Inc., New Delhi, India
Printed in Great Britain by TJ International Ltd, Padstow, Cornwall, UK

"Not everything that can be counted
counts ... and not everything that counts
can be counted."

Albert Einstein

Contents

PART THREE
The Art

Preface

Ultimately, a manager's job is to manage the performance of their organisation. Just as a CEO is responsible for the overall performance of their company, a team leader with two staff is responsible for the performance of their team. In management education, although we teach people about strategy, finance, operations, human resources, sales, marketing and so on, we rarely educate them about how to manage the performance of organisations.

Organisations are complex systems; understanding how to manage each part of the system is important, but does not provide us with a comprehensive understanding of how these parts interact and why organisations behave the way they do. In my view, the measurement and the management of business performance provide a complementary lens which helps executives and management students alike to develop a more holistic understanding of the complex systems they are responsible for managing. With this, I strongly support the view that measurement and management of business performance should feature as a core subject in the curricula of management education at all levels, undergraduate, postgraduate and executive.

Acknowledgements

Although I am the sole author of this book, the knowledge, experiences and insights contained within are fruits of a real team effort over several years. Thus, I cannot solely claim credit for this book without acknowledging the contribution of others.

First, a big thank you to my wife, Maggie, and daughters, Yasmin and Melissa, for being such a fantastic, supporting family, enabling me to focus on this work over the past 25 years. I hope all the days when dad was travelling and working late at night was not too big a sacrifice.

Second, my wide and prolific research team, starting with my mentor and friend, Professor Allan Carrie, and including the fantastic and dedicated people listed below. Some of them worked in my team as research associates, some were PhD students and some were collaborators from other institutions, some were visiting researchers and some were just friends, but they all played a key role in my work. All of this would not have been possible without your contributions. Many thanks to you all.

- Aylin Ates, now assistant professor in Glasgow, UK
- Carsten Begemann, now professor in Hannover, Germany
- Catherine Maguire, now research administrator in Glasgow, UK
- David MacKay, now consultant in Glasgow, UK
- Denis Kearney, CEO of Tsunami, Ireland
- Garry Smith, CEO of Sirius Ltd, UK
- Gilad Tiefenbrun, MD of Linn Products
- Ian Laird, serial CEO, now CEO of Moorebrook Textiles
- Ihssan Jwijati, previously experienced manager in the Middle East, now researcher in Edinburgh, UK
- Ivor Tiefenbrun, founder of Linn Products
- Janice Rodger, administrator, Glasgow, UK
- Jillian MacBryde, now professor in York, UK
- Joniarto Parung, now vice-principal in Surabaya, Indonesia

- Katherine Davis, now consultant in London, UK
- Kepa Mendibil, now associate professor in Stirling, UK
- Liam McDevitt, now working in industry in the USA
- Nuran Acur, now associate professor in Istanbul, Turkey
- Paola Cocca, assistant professor in Brescia, Italy
- Patdono Suwignjo, now professor in Surabaya and advisor to the Indonesian government
- Patricia Garengo, now associate professor in Padua, Italy
- Pavel Albores, now associate professor in Aston, UK
- Peter Ball, now reader in Cranfield, UK
- Sai Nudurupati, now associate professor in Manchester, UK
- Stefan Lutz, now with Porsche in Germany
- Trevor Turner, previously with ICI and now retired
- Veronica Martinez, now senior research fellow in Cambridge, UK

Third, all the companies that collaborated in my research, without whom the practical insights, experiences and anecdotes would not have been possible. There is no way I can list all the companies that I have worked with, but below I list a few organisations with whom I developed long-term relationships and which have been instrumental in helping me develop at least some of the insights contained in this book. I hope I have done justice to these experiences and many thanks for the opportunities, support and friendship over the years. It certainly would have been impossible without your engagement in my work.

- Akyuz Plastic, Turkey
- Arcelik/Beko, Turkey
- Blackpoint, Poland
- Clyde Blowers Capital, UK
- Creasi, Italy
- DAKS Simpson, UK
- Diageo, formally IDV, UK
- Friterm, Turkey
- GE Caledonian, UK
- Highland Spring Group Ltd, UK
- Houston Bottling and Co-Pack, UK
- ICI Explosives, UK
- Linn Products Limited, UK
- Nimbus, Italy
- Scottish Manufacturing Advisory Service, UK
- Weir Group, UK

Fourth, the following friends and colleagues who read and gave me feedback throughout the writing of this book. They were all instrumental in helping me shape the content on the key messages contained in the book. A great many thanks.

- Jim Mather, Chairman of Gael Ltd and previous Scottish Minister for Energy, Enterprise and Tourism
- Gilad Tiefenbrun, Managing Director, Linn Products, UK

- Ian Laird, Managing Director, Moorebrook Textiles, UK
- Willie Cahill, project manager and supply chain consultant in Ireland
- Helen McKenzie, Six Sigma Champion, DuPont Teijin Films, UK

And finally, a big thank you to everyone I failed to acknowledge above. I am truly grateful.

About the Author

U mit is Professor of Business Performance at Heriot Watt University, Edinburgh, Scotland. Previously he was the Director of Strathclyde Institute for Operations Management and Professor of Technology and Enterprise Management at the University of Strathclyde, Glasgow, Scotland. He is also a member of the Scottish Manufacturing Advisory Board. In the past he served as Chairman of IFIP's[1] Working Group on Advanced Production Management[2] and as Vice Chair of the Institute of Operations Management. He has a unique blend of practical hands-on, industrial, consulting and academic experience.

Umit was born in 1960 in Ankara, Turkey and attended a variety of schools in Germany and Turkey before moving to Scotland, where he gained his Higher National Diploma in Engineering and a Master's Degree in Manufacturing Management, both with Distinction. Throughout his higher education he was engaged in a number of entrepreneurial activities, partly to fund his lifestyle and partly for fun. These included restoring old rusty cars, handcrafting windsurfing boards and a motorcycle dispatch business. His passion for practical hands-on activity continued throughout his career, with various projects that included restoring and building boats and the restoration of a 200-year-old farmhouse, which was the family home he shared with his wife, Maggie, and daughters, Yasmin and Melissa, before they moved to Edinburgh. From a young age Umit was enthusiastic about anything to do with the sea and boats. He is an accomplished water skier and windsurfer. More recently he has been spending his leisure time on a sailing yacht, which he keeps in the Mediterranean Sea.

After graduation, Umit's career started in a manufacturing business designing supermarket equipment (e.g., shelving, shopping baskets and trolleys), as well as the manufacturing systems that would produce these products. Following his Master's Degree he worked as an engineering consultant, developing advanced

---

[1] International Federation for Information Processing – www.ifip.org.
[2] www.ifipwg57.org.

manufacturing systems, before moving on to management consulting and then an academic career (although he still continues his management consulting activities).

A significant portion of his 30+ year career has been dedicated to understanding how companies manage their performance. Throughout this journey he has worked intimately with some companies over extended periods, others he has observed from a distance. Simultaneously, he has held several research grants from the UK Research Council or the European Commission, all focused around developing a better understanding of how organisations manage their performance, what works and what does not, and how some businesses consistently perform better than others.

To date, his total research portfolio is around £20m and he has published about 200 papers in international journals and conferences. He regularly appears at international conferences and workshops as a guest/keynote speaker. Over this period he has accumulated an international portfolio of companies and public-sector organisations, assisting them to improve their performance. His more recent clients and research partners include Highland Spring, Linn Products and Clyde Blowers Capital.

Highland Spring Group is the UK's number-one bottled water producer. When Umit first started working with Highland Spring back in 1995 they were a small operation turning over approximately £15m, employing 100 people and producing mainly own-label products for major supermarket chains. Today, Highland Spring is a large group that manages a portfolio of brands including Highland Spring, Gleneagles Water, Speyside Glenlivet and Hydr8, as well as a number of private labels. Umit has been in the fortunate position to follow, and to a certain extent influence, the company's journey over the past 20 years.

Linn Products is a small company with a global presence designing and producing world-leading premium hi-fi equipment that is often used as a benchmark in the industry. Through his relationship with the company's founder, Umit has had the opportunity to follow Linn's journey since its beginnings in 1973 – but rather more intimately since 2004, when they collaborated on a number of projects.

Over recent years Umit has been working with Clyde Blowers Capital (CBC), a mid-sized capital investment company specialising in buying, growing and selling mid-sized engineering business, where he has been assisting with the development of a framework for managing the performance of CBC's portfolio of companies.

Over his 30+ years of experience, Umit has worked with numerous other organisations from several countries representing large and small organisations from a variety of sectors including financial and banking, manufacturing, engineering and health sciences as well as the public sector. It is these practical experiences and observations, together with his curiosity to better understand how organisations manage their performance, facilitated by research and development grants, which has led to the accumulation of his insight and knowledge into the *science* and the *art* of managing business performance.

PART
ONE

Introduction

*Where there is balance and
harmony there is performance*

Prologue

This book is about managing the performance of organisations. It is primarily focused on managing the performance of commercial organisations (i.e., businesses), but it also includes lessons from public-sector organisations. It blends the theory and practice of managing business performance, drawing on academic works as well as lessons and observations from many large and small organisations. Its contents are based on:

- the results of a series of funded research programmes involving numerous companies from different countries with a total research value exceeding c. £20m;
- the practical experiences of designing and implementing performance improvement programmes in a wide range of companies operating in diverse sectors.

Its contents balance the theory and practice of performance management. It also focuses on providing real practical advice, methods, tools and techniques to the practitioner responsible for the performance of their organisation. Indeed, a key message is that everyone is responsible for the performance of their organisation.

Furthermore, the book recognises that 'one-size-fits-all' answers rarely apply. The world changes over time and a successful company needs to adapt its performance management approach, style and process to match the needs of that time. Selection, positioning and management of the right people for the right positions at the right time become critical to sustainable success.

1.1 BACKGROUND TO THIS BOOK

In the modern world we live in today, be it at work or at home, we cannot seem to get away from performance measures. What is intriguing, however, is the effect these measures have on organisations' performance. During my early consulting career I could not help noticing how some people worked to measures even though they knew it was the wrong thing to do and that doing so made them miserable. The quote "... *they tell us that the customer is the king, but this is rubbish... in this place the measure is the king*" reflects many such feelings of individuals from different levels of an organisation, ranging from shop-floor operator to senior management.

The purpose of my first research grant (1989–1992) was to understand the barriers to manufacturing systems' integration. Here we were concerned with manufacturing businesses as a whole and wanted to understand the barriers that prevented different parts of the organisation from working together effectively and efficiently towards a common purpose. We were three academic groups from three different UK universities working in collaboration with 11 large manufacturing organisations over a three-year period. The manufacturing organisations represented a cross-section of the industry including electronics, heavy engineering, defence equipment, construction materials and chemicals. Without exception, across all our cases, the root cause of failure to integrate was performance measures. We can probably cite several examples here, but the following adequately reflect many other cases.

An electronics manufacturing company purchased metal chassis for its products from the Far East at a cost of $14 per unit as opposed to from a local supplier for $18 per unit. But the $14 per unit was ex-works and did not include the shipping costs, which added another $6 to the cost of each unit. Because the shipping costs were charged to a different budget, buying from the Far East with longer lead times and larger batch sizes made the purchasing key performance indicator (KPI) look better. It was ironic that this practice continued for several years, even though everyone knew that it was not the right thing to do, as reflected in the purchasing manager's comment: *"... I know if we bought locally it would be cheaper in total cost terms, but that is not my KPI and the KPIs are set by the US head office – we can't just go and change them."*

A whisky producer ranked a very close number 2 in their target market. The strategy was to become number 1 by halving the supply lead times whilst maintaining 100% reliability. This would allow the distributor in the market to reduce its stock levels, thus making the brand a more attractive proposition. The strategy was rolled out, communicating clearly and concisely with everyone. Over the next few months we started to see a pattern developing where the service levels (delivery lead times) would be within three weeks of order for a couple of months but would deteriorate significantly in month 3. This pattern repeated over the next three months. When investigated, it appeared that the production manager was paid a quarterly productivity bonus based on the number of litres of product bottled on his bottling lines. This meant that for the first two months he would produce and ship what was ordered but in the third month he would run the fastest-running products, usually a mixture of 2lt and 5lt bottles, to make up his shortfall. As a result, he would get a big fat bonus, the company would have the wrong stock and the distributor would be out of stock. When we discovered this and questioned him, his response was *"… this is my family's holiday money, I cannot afford to lose this income"*. Fortunately, in this case, the KPIs and bonus structure were quickly adjusted to bring the operations into alignment with the company's objectives.

From the results of this research it became clear that lack of an integrated and systematic approach to performance measurement was a key constraint to organisational integration, effectiveness and performance. This line of thinking led to my second research grant (1995–1998). Here, working with the same consortium of academics and industry partners, our objective was to develop a reference model for integrated performance measurement systems. This was about the time that performance measurement was popularised by books and articles such as *Relevance Lost: The Rise and Fall of Management Accounting* (Johnson and Kaplan, 1991) and 'Total quality: Time to take off the rose-tinted spectacles' (Kearney, 1991), and many organisations were introducing performance measures to enable them to better manage the performance of their business. Throughout this research it became evident that although measures were important, what organisations did with these measures was even more important.

In one manufacturing company they had a six-page weekly plant report containing 312 performance measures. When we enquired what they did with all of these measures, we were often faced with blank looks. We managed to convince the team responsible for issuing this report to stop issuing it as an experiment to see what would happen. It was five weeks before the IT Manager called to ask what had happened to the plant report. When asked what he wanted it for, his response was *"… I just wondered, because the corner of my desk where it usually sits has been empty for a few weeks"*.

Simultaneously, we also noticed that when performance measures were focused on managing functions/departments and individuals, we observed them to be less effective. In contrast, when they were focused on flow of work through the organisation (i.e., the process), measures appeared to be more effective. With this it started to become clear that performance measures should be concerned with workflows within the business – that is, the key processes that make the organisation viable (more on this later).

Subsequently (1997–2002) I was involved in a multidisciplinary European consortium entitled Advanced Performance Systems, with a view to sharing knowledge and practice on the subject of performance measurement. As we all know, the practice of performance measurement has emerged from a number of disciplines that include management accounting, operations management, strategic management and human resource management, where the term *performance management* appeared to be exclusively reserved for managing the performance of individuals, also known as the annual performance review, personal development review, etc. In fact, in a performance measurement workshop where I defined *performance management as the process in which we use performance measures to manage the performance of the organisation*, I was criticised for misrepresenting the term.

Maybe because I am an engineer or perhaps because of my upbringing, I am a systems thinker. That is, I see everything as an interconnected part of the whole. As a result, I was wholly unsatisfied with the view that represented performance measurement and performance management as two exclusive concepts and indeed practices. I am a great believer that organisations at the most basic level are about people and that in organisations (public, private, commercial, industrial, charitable and so on) people do things (with computers, machines, materials, information, paper, suppliers, customers, other people and so on) that leads to good or bad performance results. I summarise this simply as ***people operate processes that deliver performance***, as illustrated in Figure 1.1.

Of course there is more to managing business performance than just a simple conceptual framework, we will come back to this later in the book. What is significant here is that in an organisation there can only be one performance measurement and management system, and this system needs to integrate strategic, financial, operational and human resource views into a single efficient and effective system. After all, we are all trying to maximise the performance of the same organisation. Using different management tools to manage the performance of different parts of the organisation, without effectively joining them together, can only serve to sub-optimise overall performance. The literature contains several examples of the disconnect between company priorities, performance measures and improvement activities, even though they were using various tools

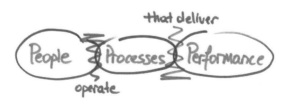

FIGURE 1.1   The universal structure that underpins performance in all organisations

for strategic planning, management by objectives, people development, appraisal and review.

Throughout these, largely research-based, experiences we were also working with a number of organisations in helping them improve their performance measurement systems. At one point we were using the approach and tools that emerged from the Integrated Performance Measurement Systems research project to implement performance measurement systems in a number of organisations. Some worked well, some worked better than others and some were outright failures... Why? We were using the same approach, the same training, the same tools and the same workshops in all cases. We were working with the management teams to help them identify measures, decide how to measure and report them, and so on. Why were some of the projects so much more successful than others?

Motivated by this question, we put together a research team to try to understand this phenomenon. What we found was that differences in organisational culture, management style and management attention led to different behaviours, resulting in different managerial and organisational practices. It was these variables that led to the development, sustained use and refinement of performance measurement systems in some organisations and not in others.

This line of thinking then led me to another research grant (2005–2009), with a view to understanding what makes successful organisations different. Here we were particularly interested in understanding the *practices* of organisations that continually outperform their competitors, irrespective of economic conditions. As part of this research we embedded ourselves into manufacturing organisations across Europe with a view to understanding their culture, management style and practices. We were particularly interested in understanding how they were managing the performance of their organisation.

What we found was astounding. All of the companies (high and low performers) measured roughly the same things and they all reported and reviewed performance in roughly the same way. However, where the low performers were primarily concerned with the mechanistic and 'processy'[1] aspects of performance measurement, in contrast, the high performers were exclusively focused on social factors, such as culture, communication, well-being and so on. This does not mean that the high performers did not measure, report and review performance. In all cases they did. But how they did this made the difference. There will be more examples of this later in the book, but here I give an example that illustrates how two different organisations can do the same thing, but differently.

---

[1] I realise that this is not a word in the common dictionary, but I hear it quite a lot in everyday management speak. It reflects activities and practices that could be codified as a process.

Both organisations reported the number of overdue orders at weekly management review meetings. In the low-performing organisation, when there were more than 10 overdue orders (an arbitrary target) there was usually a shouting match with the managing director trying to establish whose fault it was and what appropriate disciplinary action should be taken. Needless to say, the overdue orders report rarely exceeded 10 items. In one particular instance, where there were actually 22 overdue orders, only seven were reported in the overdue report.

In contrast, in the high-performing organisation, overdue orders were a rare occasion, but this was not always the case. It appears that the company had successfully reduced their overdue orders over the past three years. When an overdue was reported, it did attract management attention. However, the kind of attention was different; it was not a witch hunt as in the previous case. In this case the management was concerned with understanding the root cause and developing a permanent fix to prevent the problem from arising again. It was a much more collegiate, balanced and fear-free environment to work in.

Going back to what we said above, organisations, whether private or public, industrial or commercial, are about networks of people. In fact, the dictionaries commonly define an organisation as an organised body of people with a particular purpose. In short, organisations are social systems.

If that is the case, why do most of the performance measurement and management practices we see in organisations today treat organisations like rational machines? Only recently have we, as a society, started to wake up to the fact that if we treat organisations, and by default people, like machines then they will behave like machines. They will be disengaged from their workplace. They will be demotivated. They will practice their ingenuity and innovative capacity elsewhere, outside the workplace. All this undermining the performance of the organisations we all try so very hard to maximise.

Over the past 30+ years my research, experiences and observations have pointed towards the need for a more balanced and harmonious approach to managing organisational performance, where achieving a balance between technical controls and social controls appropriate to the context of the organisation is key to long-term sustainable performance. Thus, I have adopted the phrase *where there is balance and harmony there is performance* as the key underlying message of this book. Also, Figure 1.2 will emerge throughout the book to illustrate the dynamics between technical and social controls that serve to deliver this balance.

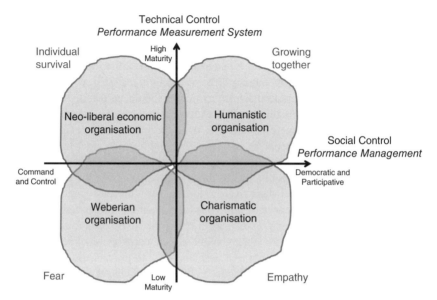

FIGURE 1.2   Organisational controls – where there is balance and harmony there is performance

1.2   MOTIVATION AND PRINCIPLES

My motivation in writing this book is the belief that the performance measurement and management approaches we use today are no longer suitable for the 21st-century economic and social environment we live in. Although not universal, as demonstrated through examples later in the book, the current approaches to how we measure and manage organisational performance serve to create resilient self-reinforcing systems that are resistant to change and encourage practices and behaviours that jeopardise sustainable performance.

The world is changing rapidly, both socially and economically. Consequently, in the 21st century we have to deal with increasingly complex and demanding global challenges that include the environment, an ageing population, energy, food scarcity and so on, as well as those challenges that we cannot yet imagine. In the meanwhile, continuing developments in almost all areas of science and technology are opening up new opportunities and providing us with the means for dealing with these challenges.

In response to these challenges and opportunities, we are trying to develop high value-adding economies that will be based on leading-edge research, techno-logical development and innovation built upon knowledge-based sectors, under-pinned by a workforce and a society that encourage experimentation, change, risk-taking and learning. However, we are now discovering that the management theories we have developed previously, and are currently using, are no longer suitable and appropriate for the emerging social and economic conditions (Ghoshal, 2005). The way we measure and manage the performance of organisations and people is at the heart of this management challenge (Hamel, 2009). Arguably some of the major social and economic problems we are facing today are, at least partially, attributable to the broken performance measurement and management practices we use, where good performance is not rewarded and poor performance is not dealt with.

Indeed, there is evidence that there are alternatives to the existing approaches to performance measurement and management, where organisations have rejected the norms and developed alternative approaches. In fact, as a result, many of these organisations have flourished and grown despite the economic challenges of the last few years. In this book I have tried to provide you, the reader, with some insights into the practices that appear to work. However, sometimes we can learn more from understanding what not to do. So, wherever possible, I have also included examples of what not to do.

Although as a child I was always a dreamer, my academic and consulting career have served to develop a discipline of objectivity and rigour to ensure that everything I say can be backed up, demonstrated and justified. This is the key principle that underpins everything I present in this book. In developing the book I have tried to ensure that everything contained here can be traced back to my experiences, my observations and my research findings, and any exceptions are clearly identified as such.

1.3   WHO IS THIS BOOK FOR?

Primarily the book is aimed at executives responsible for managing the performance of their organisations. However, if you are a practicing manager or a student of management you should also read this book… Why?

A manager's ultimate responsibility is to manage the performance of his/her organisation. If you are a chief executive of a multinational you are responsible for the performance of that organisation. Similarly, if you are an owner-manager of a small family firm you are also responsible for the performance of that organisation. If you are a sales manager or a production manager or a finance manager, you are still responsible for the performance of your part of the organisation and how it contributes towards the performance of the overall organisation. In management education we too often focus on the disciplines of management, such as strategic management, financial management, human resource management, operations management and so on, and leave the individual to work out for themselves how to knit these bits together and manage the performance of their organisation.

I believe that what is in this book will help you, the reader, to knit some of these bits together towards forming a better understanding of how to manage the performance of your organisation.

1.4 STRUCTURE OF THE BOOK

I have organised this book into four parts. Part One is the introductory section, which includes this chapter and the following chapter – providing a short history of how the performance measurement theories and practices have developed, current trends and potential future directions.

Part Two focuses on the science of performance measurement and management. Here we answer questions such as *What are we managing? What to measure? How best to communicate measures? How best to review performance?* Essentially, in this part we focus on the mechanistic 'processy' aspects of performance measurement and management, that is the *science*. However, it is quite difficult to keep the science and the art apart, because usually it is the art of performance management that makes the science bit work, as outlined in Section 1.1. As a result, the science part inevitably hints at some of the factors that we cover later in Part Three, and vice versa.

Part Three focuses on the *art* of performance management and essentially covers the behavioural and social factors that underpin the success or failure of organisational performance. Here we provide short performance measurement stories to illustrate some of the behavioural and social factors that differentiate between success and failure. Here we answer questions such as *What are the drivers of short-, medium- and long-term performance? How do organisational capabilities underpin performance? How to balance organisational controls? What happens when the balance goes wrong?*

Finally, in Part Four on effective interventions, we answer the question *How do we design and deliver performance improvement interventions that deliver short-term results, whilst contributing to growth in key organisational capabilities towards sustainable performance?*

Whilst the reader can get value from dipping in and reading various chapters of the book, it has been designed to be read from start to end as the arguments, principles and messages build up throughout. However, readers who are interested in getting into practical matters sooner rather than later can skip Chapter 2 where I provide an historical account of how the theory and practice of performance measurement and management have developed. They can always come back to that chapter later at their leisure.

At the end of the book, in Chapter 15, I have also provided an executive summary: the book in a nutshell. This provides a quick overview of everything covered in the book but without the case studies, the anecdotes and the detailed arguments that lead to the key messages. Some readers may find it a useful reminder of the book's content and logic.

I hope you enjoy this book; please do not hesitate to get back to me with any comments and feedback that you may have. For me it is all part of the learning journey. You never know, you may even find your story appearing in a future edition.

REFERENCES

Ghoshal, S. (2005) Bad management theories are destroying good management practices, *Academy of Management Learning & Education*, 4(1), 75–91.

Hamel, G. (2009) Moon shots for management, *Harvard Business Review*, 87(2), 91–98.

Johnson, H.T. and Kaplan, R.S. (1991) *Relevance Lost: The Rise and Fall of Management Accounting*, Revised reprint, Harvard Business School Press: Boston, MA.

Kearney, A.T. (1991) Total quality: Time to take off the rose-tinted spectacles, *TQM Magazine*, March, 65–72.

2

A Short History of Performance Measurement and Management

Performance measurement and performance management practices are commonplace across all sectors, industrial, commercial and public.

E ver since Johnson and Kaplan (1987) first published their seminal book entitled *Relevance Lost: The Rise and Fall of Management Accounting*, performance measurement has gained increasing popularity both in practice and in research. In fact, Neely (1999), having identified that between 1994 and 1996 over 3600 articles were published on performance measurement, coined the phrase *the performance measurement revolution*.

Today, performance measurement and performance management practices are commonplace in all sectors of industry and commerce, including the public sector. But how did the theory and practice of performance measurement and management develop? Where is it today? And more importantly, with the views presented at the end of the last chapter where we said that the performance measurement and management approaches we use today are no longer suitable for the 21st-century economic and social environment we live in, where is it going? These are just some of the questions we will try to answer in this chapter.

Similar to most management disciplines, the theory of performance measurement and management largely follows its practice. Through time, as economic and social conditions change and certain trends develop, managers adopt their practices to exploit the opportunities and mitigate the threats associated with these trends. Researchers observe and analyse what organisations and managers do, what works and what does not, why and in what context. Eventually they use the emerging data and insights to theorise about management. These models and frameworks are used by different organisations in different contexts, and further analysis leads to more insights, new understanding, refined models, frameworks and theories... and the cycle continues.

2.1 BEGINNINGS

Over the years there have been several articles and papers describing the evolution of the performance measurement and management field. According to most authors, the origins of performance measurement lie in the double-entry book-keeping that emerged in the late 13th century and remained unchanged until the Industrial Revolution in the 19th century. Starting with the Industrial Revolution, the performance measurement field has evolved through a number of phases converging with other related fields, whilst spawning subfields of interest of its own.

The Industrial Age was typified by the emergence of mass-manufacturing models, as exemplified by Ford's mass-manufacturing system, which promoted the specialisation of labour. During this period we saw a transition from piece-work payment to the wage system, and it became necessary to manage productivity. As these industrial systems grew, we saw the emergence of large organisations with multiple plants and functions, with increasing organisational and managerial complexity, resulting in power and control being delegated. This led to the emergence of divisional budgets and controls, whilst maintaining the emphasis on productivity.

During this period we also witnessed the emergence and growing influence of unions offering collective bargaining and wage system protection against the growing power base of employers. In fact, to date, some unions do not like performance measurement as it can create a focus around the individual rather than the collective.

The early stages of globalisation during the 1950s led to the development of more sophisticated approaches to productivity management, such as quality control, time-and-motion studies, variety reduction, etc. Here, productivity improvements were often gained at the expense of customer/employee/stakeholder satisfaction, with much emphasis on financial indicators. Between the 1960s and the 1980s, with the economic engine of supply and demand moving from supply side to demand side, the focus of performance measurement shifted towards new dimensions of performance that focused on the customer, such as quality, time, flexibility and customer satisfaction. It was at this juncture that we started to recognise that performance was more than just a function of productivity. It was emerging as a multidimensional construct encompassing the needs and wants of shareholders, customers and potentially all other stakeholders. It was this recognition that was popularised by Johnson and Kaplan's book *Relevance Lost*, which led to the development of the integrated and balanced approaches to performance measurement that we recognise today. It was through these works that the first formal definitions in the field started to emerge.

- *Performance* is the efficiency and/or effectiveness of an action.
- *A performance measure/indicator/metric* is the qualitative or quantitative assessment of the efficiency and/or the effectiveness of an action.
- *Effectiveness* is the extent to which the result of an action meets our expectations/requirements/specifications.
- *Efficiency* is the amount of resources the action consumes to deliver the result/output.
- *Performance measurement* is the process of collecting, analysing and reporting information regarding the performance of an action.
- *A performance measurement system* is the process (or processes) of setting goals, developing a set of performance measures, collecting, analysing, reporting, interpreting, reviewing and acting on performance data.

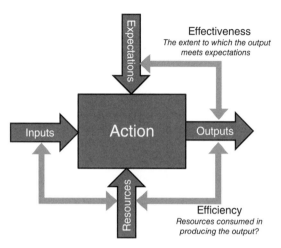

FIGURE 2.1 Performance: the efficiency and effectiveness of an action

From these definitions it is obvious that the theoretical foundations of performance measurement lie in cybernetics and systems control theories. Figure 2.1 provides a simple illustration of this control system, where an action receives *inputs* (information, materials, customers, etc.); *controls* set expectations; the action processes the inputs, consuming *resources* (time, money, equipment, space, etc.); and as a result, *outputs* are produced. Here, if the action meets all the expectations and consumes a minimum amount of resources, it can be said to be performing well. Some argue that excellent performance is associated with exceeding expectations.

It was around this period that the performance measurement literature started to converge with earlier works on strategic controls. Attention was placed on the development of short-term performance indicators as strategic controls explicitly linked to the achievement of long-term strategic goals. As a result, much emphasis was placed on *what to measure* and *how to achieve strategic alignment through these measures* to ensure that the whole organisation works towards a common objective. It was at this point that both the academic and the practitioner communities started to realise that performance measurement and strategy management were two different sides of the same coin.

On the one hand, performance measures were seen as a way of establishing strategic closed-loop control systems by deploying high-level, long-term organisational goals and objectives in various business units, functions, processes, teams and individuals. This also included feeding back information on whether strategy was being implemented as planned and whether the outcomes were those intended. In classic control theory this is known as *feedback control*.

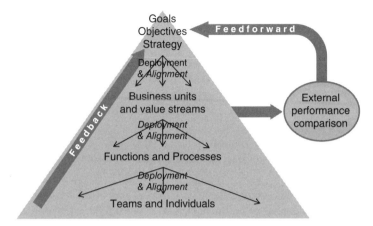

FIGURE 2.2 Feedback and feedforward – the dual-control role of performance measurement

On the other hand, performance measures were seen as a critical resource to inform goal setting and strategy development at the highest level. Particularly when we use performance measures to understand our competitive position, it enables the organisation to make some informed decisions about its goals, objectives and strategy. This is *feedforward control*. Figure 2.2 illustrates the *feedback* and *feedforward control* role of performance measurement with respect to organisational goals, objectives and strategy. In short, *feedback control* is concerned with goal attainment (i.e., are the goals and objectives being achieved?) and *feedforward control* is concerned with goal setting (i.e., are the goals and objectives appropriate?).

2.2 PERFORMANCE MEASUREMENT REVOLUTION

Throughout the late 1980s and the 1990s we witnessed the emergence of various performance measurement models and frameworks. These largely developed in response to the recognition of increasing complexity inside and outside the organisation, together with the management need for better organisational controls. The more often cited models and frameworks, roughly in chronological order, include:

- The Du Pont Model, ROI and RONA Ratios (1984).
- The Performance Measurement Matrix (1989).
- The Performance Measurement Questionnaire (1990).
- The Results and Determinants Framework (1991).

- The Strategic Measurement Analysis and Reporting Technique (SMART) – a.k.a. the Performance Pyramid (1992).
- The Balanced Scorecard (1992 onwards).
- The Cambridge Performance Measurement Design Process (1996).
- The Pyramid of Organisational Development (1995).
- The Integrated Performance Measurement System Reference Model (1997).
- The Business Excellence Model of the European Foundation for Quality Management (1999).
- The Performance Prism (2000).
- The Integral Framework for Performance Measurement (2003).

However, from the practitioner's perspective, out of all these models and frameworks, the Balanced Scorecard emerged as the single most popular framework. In fact, outside the academic community, one would be hard pushed to find anyone who has heard of, yet alone implemented, one of the other models. Perhaps one exception to this rule is the Performance Prism, which gained some traction in practice, but it is still fairly rare to find practitioners who know about it. In my view, the main reason the Balanced Scorecard gained popularity over other models and frameworks is due to its ability to capture the complexity of business in a simple and easily understandable framework. Furthermore, since its initial conception in 1992 as a simple framework for performance measurement, it has been developed into a strategic management tool.

In this section I have refrained from providing an overview of each one of these models and frameworks, which can be found in Appendix 1. However, as it is central to the key messages contained in this book, I have included an inset that summarises the Balanced Scorecard.

THE BALANCED SCORECARD

The Balanced Scorecard defines, around strategy, four perspectives of performance: Financial; Customer; Process; Learning and Growth. It suggests that any organisation should balance its performance measurement and management around these perspectives. In Figure 2.3 I have included my own illustration of the Balanced Scorecard model and an explanation of the dynamics between various perspectives.

In the Balanced Scorecard the four perspectives of performance are organised around strategy, which is the central theme. The measures contained within each perspective are aligned with both the short- and long-term strategic goals of the organisation, as well as informing the evolution of

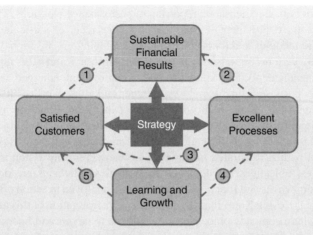

FIGURE 2.3 The Balanced Scorecard

these strategic goals. Essentially, long-term sustainable financial results are a function of: satisfied customers that keep coming back and referring new customers (1) and internal processes that are so *efficient* that they generate above-average returns (2). In turn, satisfied customers are a function of *effective* processes that deliver repeatable products and services to all customers reliably (3). Here, I simply define process excellence as processes that are highly efficient whilst being highly effective.[1]

The learning and growth perspective is all about what we invest in now that will develop our capabilities for the future. For example, investing in education, technology and improvement projects today will make our processes more efficient and/or effective in the future (4). Similarly, investing in new technology and product development initiatives today will serve to make our products and services more attractive to customers in the future (5).

---

[1] In Chapter 4 we define performance as a function of efficiency and effectiveness.

Almost all the performance measurement models and frameworks outlined above were concerned with *what to measure and how to organise and report these measures*. This includes: creating a set of measures to reflect the purpose and strategy of the organisation; creating a balanced set of measures (e.g., internal vs. customer, financial vs. operational, leading vs. lagging); deployment of measures throughout the organisation to ensure goal alignment; understanding the causal relationships between measures; reporting of performance measures. Throughout these works, the deployment of goals and objectives received particular attention, with specific methods and tools emerging for deploying organisational goals and strategies to various organisational functions. Hoshin Kanri (the Japanese for direction management), also known as policy deployment, emerged as a popular tool for this purpose (Hutchins, 2008; Witcher and Butterworth, 2001). Hoshin Kanri emerged out of the quality management literature, based on a technique known as quality function deployment (QFD),[2] where high-level objectives are propagated to lower levels through a series of matrices. A typical Hoshin Kanri deployment path is illustrated in Figure 2.4, where company vision is deployed to objectives, objectives are deployed to strategies, strategies are deployed to functional objectives and functional objectives are deployed to actions. The extract from a typical Hoshin Kanri matrix illustrates an interpretation of this deployment structure, where company objectives are deployed to targets and finance function objectives. The finance objectives are then deployed to finance function targets.

In fact, my own work on Integrated Performance Measurement Systems followed a similar path, suggesting a more specific deployment path from business objectives to business units (or value streams) to business processes. The significance of this will be discussed later in Chapter 3. In a similar fashion, as the Balanced Scorecard developed from a performance measurement framework into a strategic management approach, we have seen the emergence of strategy maps that link financial, customer, process and learning and growth objectives towards attainment of the financial results of the organisation. A simple strategy map is illustrated in Figure 2.5.

Coming back to the evolution of the performance measurement and management field, the 1990s and early 2000s saw a wide variety of organisations implementing various performance measurement models and frameworks. The common purpose behind many of these initiatives was to improve the organisational performance by implementing an integrated and balanced set of performance measures and using these to manage the performance of the company. In these initiatives success was judged by three simple criteria:

- Was a performance measurement system designed and implemented?
- Was the system being used as intended to manage the performance of the organisation?
- As a consequence, did the performance of the organisation improve?

Analysis of these initiatives delivered a diverse range of results, some with astounding success and others with failure. Consequently, our focus changed from

---

[2]QFD is commonly used in product development and quality management to deploy the top-level characteristics of a product/system to its component parts through a multi-level approach.

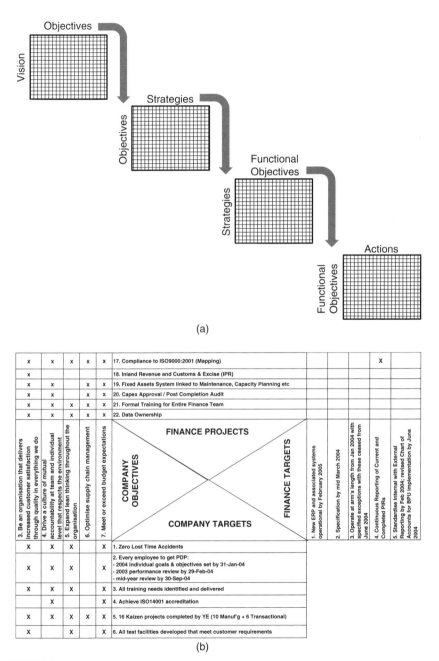

FIGURE 2.4 (a) Typical Hoshin Kanri deployment path; (b) extract from a typical Hoshin Kanri matrix

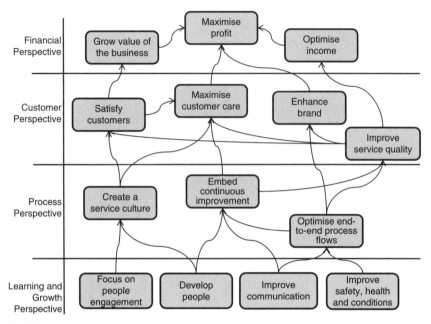

FIGURE 2.5   A simple strategy map

what to measure and how to report these measures to *the factors that drive success and failure of performance measurement systems and how to use the performance measurement systems to manage the performance of the organisation.* In this way, the notion of performance measurement extended to include performance management.

However, before going into a discussion on performance management, the following section provides an overview of how the performance measurement field developed from different contextual perspectives.

2.3 PERFORMANCE MEASUREMENT FROM DIFFERENT PERSPECTIVES

In parallel with the performance measurement field, the HRM field developed largely independently, focusing on how best to manage human resources. In this field the term *performance management* was used exclusively to describe the appraisal, development and review practices of modern-day HRM. Use of the same terminology (i.e., performance management) by two closely related fields can often be a source of confusion, even today. The recognition of the need to align

HR-based performance management practices with organisational performance measurement systems led to new perspectives on performance measurement. The fact that business processes comprised individuals from different functions and disciplines working along the process as a team led to the introduction of concepts such as *teaming* and *teaming environment measures*. These measures focused on understanding team cohesion and assessing whether the right environment for the team was being created.

From a quality management and business process management perspective, we have seen Total Quality Management, Lean Enterprise and Six-Sigma approaches making extensive use of performance measurement to manage and improve the performance of processes and organisations. From a research, development and innovation perspective, questions such as *how to measure and manage the performance of R&D and innovation activities* were also being explored.

Today, environmental and social considerations also influence the design and use of performance measurement systems from strategic, operational and supply chain perspectives. A number of authors have proposed the integration of environmental management, green supply chain and corporate social responsibility practices throughout an organisation's performance measurement systems.

Research into performance measurement in small and medium enterprises (SMEs) has concluded that the majority of the work on performance measurement, although theoretically valid, does not take into consideration the fundamental differences between SMEs and larger organisations, thus resulting in poor take-up of performance measurement practices in SMEs.

Another area spawned from the mainstream performance measurement literature is concerned with performance measurement in supply chains and collaborative enterprises. Those works, exploring performance measurement in supply chains, consider operational and informational aspects that go on to propose process-based approaches to measuring the performance of supply chains. The work exploring performance measurement in collaborative organisations recognises the additional complexity that is brought about by the potential conflicts between performance measurement considerations of the individual organisations and of the collaborative organisation. These include strategic, operational, commercial and cultural conflicts.

Performance measurement and management in the public sector is yet another area that seems to have developed from the mainstream performance measurement literature, with a range of works covering all aspects of public-sector management. As the performance measurement body of knowledge is focused mainly on the private and public sectors, some researchers are also investigating if, and how, this knowledge could be used to inform the design of performance measurement systems in non-profit organisations. In this way we have seen the development of additional performance measurement models and frameworks specifically aimed at public-sector and third-sector organisations.

2.4 PERFORMANCE MANAGEMENT

Performance management is concerned with how to use performance measurement systems to manage the performance of an organisation. Early works in performance management identified a number of factors that influenced the success and failure of performance measurement and improvement initiatives, as listed below. Throughout this book we will cover several of these factors in greater detail.

- Availability and use of appropriate information and communications systems.
- Simplicity and user-friendliness of the performance measurement systems.
- Management commitment.
- External influences, such as parent company, regulators, powerful customers.
- Organisational structure, distribution of accountabilities and responsibilities.
- Size and complexity of the organisation.
- Maturity of the organisation in learning to work with the performance measurement system.
- Organisational culture and management style. Particularly the need for transparency, consistency, openness and trust.
- Clarity of purpose.
- Design of the performance measurement system causing unintended side-effects.

However, as we progressed further into the 2000s we started to see a body of opinion emerging that questioned the need for performance measures. *Relevance Lost* by Johnson and Kaplan (1987) is cited as a cornerstone in virtually all scholarly papers on performance measurement. Kaplan's work evolved into the concept of the Balanced Scorecard (Kaplan and Norton, 1992, 1996, 2001), which in turn influenced much of the work on performance measurement and management that followed. In contrast, Johnson's work took a different direction. In his book entitled *Profit Beyond Measure* (Johnson and Broms, 2000), the message is that it is possible to run a well-performing organisation without measuring performance. In effect, the earlier opinions that suggested performance measurement and management leads to higher performance was being challenged by new opinions that suggested performance measurement, at least in certain contexts, is counterproductive to long-term sustainable performance and that we may be better off without measures. In fact, *do we need measures to manage* was the theme of a special session at the 2012 conference of the Performance Measurement Association (PMA).[3]

In essence, until the emergence of this opposing view, the field was developing under the assumption that organisations need performance measurement and that we have to make them more effective and efficient to enable improving

---

[3] http://www.performanceportal.org/

an organisation's performance. We were treating organisations as machines and had forgotten the fact that organisations are essentially social systems made up of networks of people doing things. Reflecting this view, Davenport (Davenport and Harris, 2007; Davenport *et al.*, 2010) suggests that the ultimate goal of performance measurement should be learning rather than control. In his book entitled *Systems Thinking in the Public Sector: The Failure of the Reform Regime and a Manifesto for a Better Way*, Seddon (2008) suggests that, from a systems thinking perspective, performance measures and targets create a command and control culture that often generates hidden costs and demoralises people by sub-optimising various parts of the system. He goes on to argue that performance measures and targets without a clear purpose lead to unintended and sometimes unethical side-effects, such as people cheating, lying, misinforming and misbehaving. His view is that all organisations need a purpose and the measures and methods should follow this purpose.

2.5 BALANCING THE *SCIENCE* WITH THE *ART*

It seems that both pro- and anti-measurement views agree that increased control does not lead anywhere by itself and that organisations need to learn to perform, with or without measures. My own view is that we cannot get away from performance measures. They are an integral part of our everyday life, as I will demonstrate later in this book. I believe the root cause of our dissatisfaction with measures lies *not* with the fact that we have them, but with the way that we use them. Perversely, we seem to have the ability to take some sensible and logical ideas (such as Lean Enterprise, Six Sigma, Balanced Scorecard, etc.) and pervert them into toxic weapons that destroy the very organisation we are trying to improve.

This line of thinking opens up the debate around organisational controls. I would suggest that, to date, the performance measurement literature and practices have taken a rational approach to organisational control by concentrating on the structural mechanisms to secure effective co-ordination and control in organisational interaction. This implies that control systems can be designed and operated for any circumstances in any organisation. However, the organisational control literature states that the purpose of control should be to ensure the achievement of the organisational purpose, plans and targets. Organisational control, therefore, encompasses any process in which a person (or group of persons) intentionally affects what another person, group or organisation will do. Two approaches to organisational control are suggested.

- *Technical controls.* The more rational, bureaucratic or 'processy' approach, focusing on structural elements of the organisation.
- *Social controls.* The cultural and behavioural control achieved through personal interactions between people.

Even though the performance measurement literature clearly recognises the relationship between performance measurement and organisational behaviour, existing performance measurement and management practices are largely built upon Demming's (1986) misinterpreted axiom that *"what gets measured gets managed"*. Actually, Demming's point was that many important things that must be managed cannot be measured. He was, in fact, reflecting on Albert Einstein's famous quote: *"Not everything that can be counted counts... and not everything that counts can be counted."*

In short, until recently the theory and practice of performance measurement focused on technical controls treating organisations like machines, largely ignoring social factors. It is only now that we are waking up to the fact that, if we are to succeed in creating effective organisations, we need to balance the technical controls with the social controls, hence the *science* and the *art*.

Figure 2.6 illustrates a framework that maps the maturity of the performance measurement systems (i.e., the technical controls or the *science*) against performance management (i.e., the social controls or the *art*). The organisational descriptions that correspond to each quadrant of the framework are from the organisational studies literature and will be discussed in greater detail later in the book (Chapter 10).

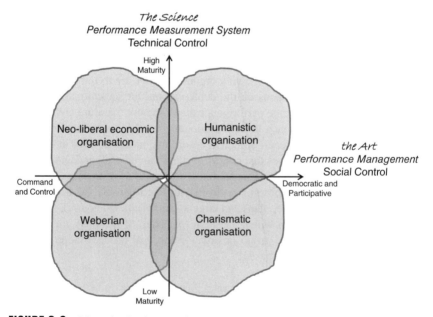

FIGURE 2.6   Managing business performance: balancing the technical and social controls

In this context we define…

- **The performance measurement system** as the process (or processes) of setting goals, developing a set of performance measures, collecting, analysing, reporting, interpreting, reviewing and acting on performance data (this is the same definition offered earlier in this section).
- **Performance management** as the cultural and behavioural routines that define how we use the performance measurement system to manage the performance of an organisation.

2.6 FUTURE CHALLENGES

Based on the brief history of performance measurement presented here, it is clear that the performance measurement field has developed in parallel with, and indeed in response to, the global trends. During the early 1900s, with increasing industrialisation, the purpose of performance measurement was productivity management. With the emergence of more complex multi-plant organisations, we have seen the purpose of performance measurement shift towards budgetary control, whilst maintaining a focus on productivity management. Then, with the emergence of global competition and the sophistication of markets, we have seen the purpose of performance measurement shift towards integrated performance measurement, and subsequently on to performance management. Effectively, in following the emerging industrial, business and social trends, the purpose, theory and practices of performance measurement broadened by compounding multiple purposes and organisational types (industrial, commercial, public sector, collaborative, SMEs and so on).

Today, as I write this book, the pace of change continues to accelerate globally. We see the global economic power base shifting towards emerging economies. Certain trends that were embryonic just a few years ago seem to be accelerating. We are witnessing emergence organisations that collaborate across global multicultural networks. We are seeing greater degrees of transparency and openness, with information, be it a new innovation or a bad customer service story, being shared openly across global social networks. It is becoming more difficult and indeed counterproductive to protect/hide our successes and failures.

We are seeing an increasing take-up of the service culture (servitisation), with examples such as the Aerospace giant Rolls Royce no longer selling jet engines but selling power-by-the-hour instead. Related to this, over the past 20 years we

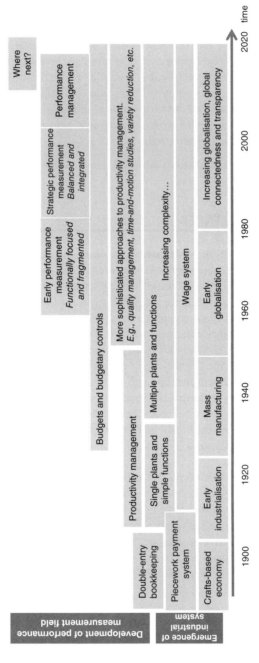

FIGURE 2.7 Global trends, emergence of industrial systems and development of the performance measurement field

Global social and economic trends / Period of development[4]	Familiar period	Extrapolable period	Familiar discontinuity period	Novel discontinuity period
Management systems	Procedures and control	Management by objectives and long-range planning	Periodic strategic planning	Dealing with unpredictable surprises
Rate and scale of change	Slow and incremental	Fast, predictable and incremental	Turbulent and discontinuous	Disruptive and transformational
Dominant means of production	Infrastructure owned by the organisation	Infrastructure and IP owned by the organisation	IP owned by the organisation supported by the knowledge worker	Knowledge and network connections owned by the networkers
Competitive forces	Unclear mix of all factors dominated by costs	Focus and differentiation	Value propositions	Being unique in different ways
Nature of work	Manual work	Manual work supported by knowledge work	Knowledge work supported by manual work	Network supported by knowledge and manual work
Organising principle	Autocracy	Bureaucracy	Adhocracy	Netocracy
Organisational power	Few powerful individuals	Organisational structure	Processes, process owners and process teams	Individuals/small groups in multiple networks
People	Labourforce seen as necessary evil	Human resources seen as assets	Team assets and investment	Individuals and autopoietic teams as innovators and heuristics
Regulatory system	Contracts, laws and regulations	Contracts, laws, regulations and industry standards	Contracts, laws, regulations, industry standards and accepted best practices	Trust, relationships and network standards
Organisational relationships	Inter-organisational and adversarial	Inter-organisational and co-operative	Inter/trans-organisational and collaborative	Trans-organisational, communities of practice
Market dominance	Producer	Cost-conscious customer	Value-conscious, loyal customer	Disloyal, picky, curious, impulse customer

FIGURE 2.7 (*Continued*)

[4]Periods of development and corresponding management systems are based on Ansoff (1984).

have witnessed a huge shift from manual work towards knowledge work. Today we have more graduates working in jobs that require intellectual and cognitive skills, providing services, diagnosing and solving problems, and innovating. We have fewer people working in factories, doing repetitive manual work, even though our manufacturing output has increased. In effect, where feasible, we are using people at higher levels as problem solvers and innovators and replacing manual work with automation.

We are seeing more and more ground-breaking innovations emerging from small technology-based companies, universities and even from individuals working in their garage, rather than from large multinationals with big R&D budgets. Individuals and small organisations are collaborating, sharing ideas, co-developing and co-innovating using global social and professional networks. In other words, world power is shifting from large multinational organisations to self-managing and self-organising networks of individuals. Just look at how Linux competes with Microsoft, powering one out of four corporate servers in Fortune 500 companies, and how Apache has become the underpinning technology for almost all Internet search engines.

And finally, we are seeing the growing importance of environmental and social responsibility. It is no longer sufficient to meet the minimum standards. Market and consumer expectations are that corporations, particularly large ones, actively contribute to sustainability, be it environmental, social or economic. In particular, manufacturing in the West is increasingly subject to safety legislation which removes people from direct interaction with equipment, raising ethical questions over moving production to cheaper economies that do not have the same controls.

Potentially all these trends have far-reaching implications in the way we measure and manage the performance of organisations, networks and individuals. Although in this book I provide an insight into how to effectively manage the performance of an organisation by integrating the *science* of performance measurement with the *art* of performance management, all the knowledge contained within is based on my own research findings, experiences and observations over the past 25 years. I will tell you what works, in what context and why. Most of it will be valid for today and the near future. However, the world is changing fast and there is still a lot we do not know about how to manage the performance of new and emerging organisational forms. We have a lot of exploration, experimentation and learning to look forward to!

Figure 2.7 illustrates an overview of global trends mapped against the development of, and potential future challenges for, the performance measurement field. For an academic article that outlines the future research challenges for performance measurement, please refer to Bititci *et al.* (2012).

REFERENCES

Ansoff, I.H. (1984) *Implanting Strategic Management*, Prentice Hall: Englewood Cliffs, NJ.

Bititci, U.S., Garengo, P., Dörfler, V. and Nudurupati, S. (2012) Performance measurement: Challenges for tomorrow, *International Journal of Management Reviews*, 14, 305–327.

Davenport, T.H. and Harris, J.G. (2007) *Competing on Analytics: The New Science of Winning*, Harvard Business School Press: Boston, MA.

Davenport, T.H., Harris, J.G. and Morrison, R. (2010) *Analytics at Work: Smarter Decisions, Better Results*, Harvard Business School Press: Boston, MA.

Demming, W.E. (1986) *Out of the Crisis*, MIT Press: Boston, MA.

Hutchins, D. (2008) *Hoshin Kanri – The Strategic Approach to Continuous Improvement*, Gower Publishing: Farnham.

Johnson, H.T. and Broms, A. (2000) *Profit beyond Measure: Extraordinary Results through Attention to Work and People*, Prentice Hall: Englewood Cliffs, NJ.

Johnson, H.T. and Kaplan, R.S. (1987) *Relevance Lost: The Rise and Fall of Management Accounting*, Harvard Business School Press: Boston, MA.

Kaplan, R.S. and Norton, D.P. (1992) The balanced scorecard: Measures that drive performance, *Harvard Business Review*, 70, 71–79.

Kaplan, R.S. and Norton, D.P. (1996) *Translating Strategy into Action: The Balanced Scorecard*, Harvard Business School Press: Boston, MA.

Kaplan, R.S. and Norton, D.P. (2001) *The Strategy-Focused Organization: How Balanced Scorecard Companies Thrive in the New Business Environment*, Harvard Business School Press: Boston, MA.

Neely, A. (1999) The performance measurement revolution: Why now and what next? *International Journal of Operations and Production Management*, 19, 205–228.

Seddon, J. (2008) *Systems Thinking in the Public Sector: The Failure of the Reform Regime and a Manifesto for a Better Way*, Triarchy Press: Axminster.

Witcher, B.J. and Butterworth, R. (2001) Hoshin Kanri: Policy management in Japanese-owned UK subsidiaries, *Journal of Management Studies*, 38(5), 651–674.

But are today's practices fit for the contemporary organisations and societies of the 21st century...

... there is still a lot we do not know and we have a lot to learn!

PART
TWO

The Science

3

What Are We Managing?

*Complexity is the killer
of performance…*

*… different people from the
same organisation perceive the
organisation differently.*

Despite many people believing that their organisation is different, I have come to the conclusion that fundamentally all organisations are the same. At the most basic level, just like human beings, all organisations (private, public and third sector) comprise the same vital systems that enable the organisation to function efficiently and effectively. I call this the *anatomy of an organisation.* It provides us with the *universal competitive structure* that we need to understand if we are to manage the performance of our organisations effectively.

In my experience, many organisations fail to understand and effectively manage the competitive structure of their business. There are many reasons why this is the case, however the most common cause is the complexity of the organisation coupled with different people's perspectives on *what is important… what needs to be managed… and how.*

In this chapter I will first demonstrate how different people from the same organisation may perceive that organisation differently. I often find that complexity is the killer of performance and it is also the main reason why different people's perceptions of the same organisation may be different.

What my research and experience has concluded is that those companies which consistently outperform their counterparts have a clear, concise, simple and shared understanding of how their organisations compete and the underlying structure that needs to be managed. What is really significant is that their models are remarkably similar. They start with a fundamental understanding of how their organisation competes, and culminate in a profound awareness of the competitive structure that underpins the success of the organisation.

3.1   EVERYONE HAS A DIFFERENT VIEW

One of my favourite questions is, *Why do customers come to you?* Sometimes you get a very clear answer, such as *"because we are the cheapest"* or *"because we have the best technology"* or *"because we are the most flexible".* But in many cases the answer is convoluted and requires lengthy explanation as to why their business is different, how complex their products and customers are. Occasionally you get an arrogant answer, such as *"because we are the best"*, at which point you might want to ask *"best at what… everything?"* Sometimes it is easier just to walk away.

Another point is that when you ask this question of different people from the same organisation, you are quite likely to get different answers. You do sometimes get the same answer using different words, but quite often it is completely different answers. For example, the managing director of an SME I worked with during a European project said *"because we have a great relationship with the customers and we take hassle away from them"*, whereas on the same day in a separate conversation, the operations director said *"because we are efficient"*. Now both may be true, and it is indeed important to capture the different voices of the customer. But do we really understand how the customer is making his/her buying decision? In this example, different people seem to have different ideas as to how this organisation works.

One of the exercises I often do with management teams is to ask them to sketch a picture/image of their business. You always get a different picture from each individual. What is surprising, however, is that they rarely convey the same message. In fact, they often convey quite different messages. For instance, Figures 3.1–3.3 convey three similar but different messages from three different people in the same organisation.

In Figure 3.1, the person clearly sees the individual functions as kingdoms with people/managers running between them. The suppliers keep on coming with innovative ideas and the customers keep on wanting better products and services faster and cheaper. The parent company keeps on firing demands at the organisation.

In Figure 3.2 we see a slightly different perspective. The functions are still there, but in this case the functions are represented as turrets of the same castle,

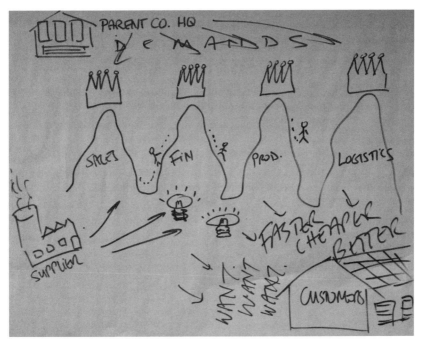

FIGURE 3.1 Example 1

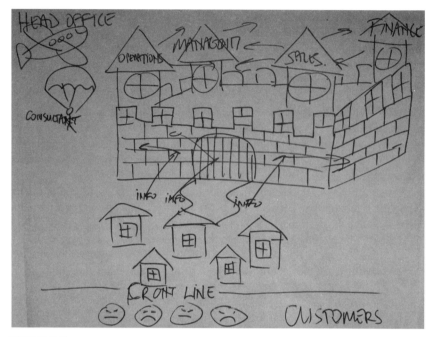

FIGURE 3.2 Example 2

firing arrows at each other (in-fighting). The frontline staff is outside the castle walls, trying to serve a bunch of angry and unhappy customers. Their feedback keeps bouncing off the walls of the castle and head office is parachuting a consultant in to help them.

In Figure 3.3 we see yet another perspective. Here, the business is trying to serve a market which values quality, safety, compliance and innovation. There are various systems (CRM, CAD, CAM, ERP) to enable efficient and effective delivery of customer orders from sales and marketing through production to installation in the field. There is also an issue with attracting and retaining good-quality people with the right attitudes and skills. But what the parent company is doing is undermining the business.

Try it! The whole exercise takes about 30 minutes, it is fun and it gets people talking to each other about their perception of the business. The exercise goes as follows:

- Get your colleagues in a room and ask them to take five minutes to sketch an image/picture that depicts your business from their perspective... how do they see it?

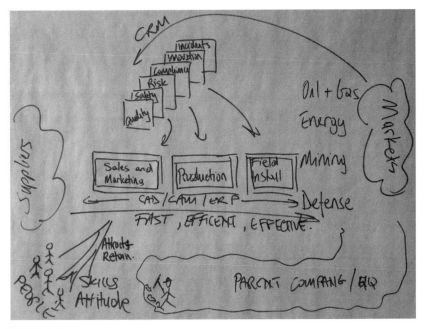

FIGURE 3.3 Example 3

- Show them a couple of examples, such as those in Figures 3.1–3.3, and then ask them to take five minutes to sketch the first image that comes into their head.
- Then ask them to share their images/drawings with each other. If it is a small group, everybody can take a couple of minutes to talk through their picture. If it is a large group, ask them to get into groups of two or three to share and talk about their sketches.
- To sum up, ask them what they have learned from the exercise.

At the outset it is always good practice to say that you will not be collecting the sketches, so people can take them away if they want to. Sometimes people leave theirs behind and sometimes they take it with them. This also tells us something about the culture of that organisation, but we will talk more about that in Part Three of this book.

The key message is as follows: everyone in the business may have a different view of what the organisation is about, and they are often valid views. But when we all manage different things from different perspectives and do not understand and respect each other's view, we compromise organisational effectiveness and ultimately performance.

> My analogy here is that you are in your car with some friends and you have
> run out of fuel, with the petrol station only 50 metres away. You want your
> friends to get out and push the car towards the petrol station. You do not want
> one of them standing alongside the car trying to push it sideways and another
> one standing in front trying to push it backwards. This would not be helpful.

When different people have different perspectives they could be managing
different things or the same things differently. If we do not understand what we
are managing then the above scenario, although unlikely in a car, is highly likely
in a complex organisation.

3.2   HOW DO COMPANIES COMPETE?

What is a business for? When you ask this question, sometimes you get a very
straight answer and at other times people think it is a trick question and give
you complex answers such as: to contribute to the economy, to solve customers'
problems, to create employment. Indeed, these are all valid views and a business
should seek to do all of these. But it will not be able to contribute anything towards
these objectives if it does not generate wealth for its owners or shareholders. So,
at the most fundamental level, a business is about creating wealth for its owners
and shareholders.

How does a business create wealth? Again, when you ask this question you
get a different range of answers, including: it buys and sells goods, it supplies
demand, it provides services – all of which are partially correct. But again, at the
most fundamental level a business creates wealth by fulfilling a market need whilst
creating positive returns, sustainably. In other words, it has to be competitive in
the markets in which it operates.

In its most basic form, competition is the rivalry among providers of products
or services trying to secure the business of a third party by making their offering
more attractive. Typically, companies make their products or services more attractive to their customers/markets by manipulating the following competitive factors:

- Price/cost
- Quality
- Functional performance
- Delivery speed
- Delivery reliability
- Product support
- Styling/design
- Image/brand identity
- Customer support
- Flexibility and responsiveness
- Innovation
- Relationship and empathy

Studies conducted by various industry, academic and government bodies over the past 20 years confirm that the competitive factors listed above have not changed much in this time. In other words, they are equally valid now as they were 20 or even 30 years ago. What has changed, however, is the customers' behaviours in combining these factors in making buying decisions.

> For example, if you are in the market for a family car you may make a list of requirements you wish your new car to fulfil. These requirements may include factors such as maximum price, functional features (e.g., reliability, fuel consumption, performance, comfort, etc.), image, styling and availability of a local service network. Using these criteria you will make a shortlist of potential family cars and then go to various car showrooms, talk to sales people, take test drives, talk to other owners, etc., until you come to a decision on which family car to purchase.

If we analyse this process, the initial criteria you used to create a shortlist of potential cars to buy is known as the *order qualifying criteria*. In other words, those alternatives that fulfil this criteria make it onto your shortlist. What follows is a complex process of analysis and the compromises you typically make to come to a final decision. Perhaps in this case you have put fuel consumption, price and reliability ahead of price and image in making your final decision. Others may have different priorities. This is known as the *order winning criteria*.

Many companies, when you ask *"why do customers come to you instead of going to your competitors?"* do not really know the answer. Many of them say *"because we are better"*, but better at what! Similarly, when faced with the question *"why do some customers go to your competitors instead of coming to you?"* even more companies struggle to provide a coherent response. This is usually because their business is complex and there is more than one answer. Another typical answer is *"it depends which customer"*. This usually suggests that they do not understand the competitive structure of their business, which we will discuss further in this chapter.

Figure 3.4 illustrates the relationship between competitive criteria and growth. For example, if our quality levels are well below market average (position 1), we will need to make significant improvements before we can see any significant benefits arising from the improvements. Similarly, if our quality levels are significantly ahead of our competitors (position 5), any further improvements will generate little growth. In contrast, however, if our quality levels are on or around market average, any improvements we make are likely to result in significant benefits.

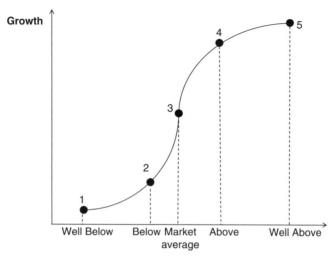

FIGURE 3.4   Behaviour of competitive criteria vs. growth

Working with companies, I found the following a useful exercise to highlight some of the complexities.

Step 1.   Try to list the order qualifying and order winning criteria. If this becomes complex, just take one product (or product group) and/or one customer (or customer group).

Step 2.   Plot where you are for each criterion against the five-point scale that corresponds to the five-point scale in Figure 3.4. An example of how this can be done is shown in Figure 3.5. The circle shows the current position and the head of the arrow points to the desired position. The absence of an arrow suggests that there is no improvement required from the current position.

In this example, which is based on a medium-sized company manufacturing critical components for wind turbines, price, product quality and customer satisfaction are seen as order qualifiers. The price is positioned as more expensive than that of the competitors but offering a better product quality. The order winning criteria include: on-time delivery, responsiveness (turnaround time) and ability to increase order volumes at short notice (upside flexibility). The company is content that their upside flexibility is ahead of their competitors' and does not require further improvement, but enhancement of on-time delivery and turnaround times is required to further differentiate competitive advantage.

Although over the years the competitive factors have not changed, with more sophisticated and demanding customers our maturity in how we combine and

Performance Indicator		Order criterion	Comparative Performance				
			Well below average	Below average	Average	Above average	Well above average
Customer Facing Indicators	Price Competitiveness	Qualifier	O				
	Product Quality	Qualifier				O	
	Customer Complaints	Qualifier			O		
	On-Time Delivery	Winner			O ———→		
	Turnaround Time	Winner				O ——→	
	Upside Flexibility	Winner				O	

FIGURE 3.5 Matrix analysing the competitive position of order qualifying and order winning criteria

manipulate these factors to gain competitive advantage has changed significantly. During the 1980s we tried to be good at everything only to discover, during the 1990s, that only those companies who focused and differentiated themselves from the others were growing and performing better. Then Treacy and Wiersema (1996), in their book entitled *The Discipline of Market Leaders*, introduced the concept of value propositions, that is the explicit promise a company makes to its customers. They identified three fundamental value propositions:

- Operational Excellence – providing the best total cost.
- Product Leadership – providing the best products.
- Customer Intimacy – providing the best total solution.

In their book they intimated that market leaders focus on excelling only in one of these areas, whilst maintaining an average performance in the other two. This line of thinking suggests that the competitive criteria (discussed above) are configured and bundled together into an attractive proposition. For example, the Product Leadership value proposition could be made up of bundling competitive factors such as functional performance, quality, styling and image. Meanwhile, the Operational Excellence value proposition may comprise a different bundle, such as price, quality, delivery reliability and speed. This line of thinking led to the development of the six pillars (Finkelstein *et al.*, 2006) that underpin the value propositions – illustrated in Figure 3.6 by a competitive profile of a product leader from the UK's food and drink sector.

In short, even though we have got a lot more sophisticated in the way we bundle competitive factors into various value propositions, at the most fundamental level it all boils down to the same fairly deterministic set of competitive factors. The real test is that, if you can answer the following questions concisely and clearly, you know how your business competes and probably understand the underlying competitive structure. But if your answers begin with "*it depends…*", or if you have a lot of "*ifs…*" and "*buts…*", then it is highly likely that the complexity of the

PRICE	FEATURES	QUALITY	SERVICE & SUPPORT	AVAILABILITY	REPUTATION
1. Premium	1. Original	1. Excellent	1. Comprehensive	1. Restricted	1. Prestigious
2. Premium/ Competitive	2. Original/ Customised	2. Excellent/ Average	2. Comprehensive/ Standard	2. Restricted/ Selective	2. Prestigious/ Respected
3. Competitive	3. Customised	3. Average	3. Standard	3. Selective	3. Respected
4. Competitive/ Leader	4. Customised Basic	4. Average/ Acceptable	4. Standard/ Minimal	4. Selective/ Universal	4. Respected/ Functional
5. Leader	5. Basic	5. Acceptable	5. Minimal	5. Universal	5. Functional

FIGURE 3.6   The six pillars of value propositions: an example from a UK food and drink company

business is getting in the way and clouding the fundamental performance drivers you need to deal with.

TIME FOR REFLECTION

- Why do customers come to you instead of your competitors?
- Why do some customers go to your competitors instead of coming to you?
- How do your customers make buying decisions? What are their order qualifying and order winning criteria?
- How do customers measure your performance? How would they rate your performance against that of your competitors?
- What is your customer value proposition? What bundle of competitive criteria underpins this value proposition?

3.3   VALUE STREAMS – FOCUSED BUSINESS UNITS THAT CREATE VALUE

In many cases it would be relatively simple to answer the above set of questions if the business had just one coherent group of customers buying a single product or service. But many businesses, even small ones, have several products and customers with differences in:

- the structure of their products or product groups;
- how different customers or customer groups make buying decisions.

In effect, this is best described as different small businesses within each business. These small businesses are often called *business units* or *value streams.*[1] In this context a value stream is defined as a purposeful and coherent set of business processes that are aligned with delivering value to a customer or specific group of customers, whilst creating value for the business. Therefore, unless we understand how each value stream competes in the marketplace and what its critical success factors are, we cannot effectively manage the business performance as a whole. Let me illustrate what I mean…

What is the difference between a £12 bottle of whisky and a £300 bottle of whisky? If you say the answer is £288, you would be technically correct but that is not the answer I am looking for.

One is a value brand selling at a low price on the bottom supermarket shelf. Once customers consume what is inside the bottle, they throw the bottle away. They are rarely concerned if the bottle is scratched and the label is slightly squint. The product sells in high volumes and the competition is highly price sensitive. Manufacturers produce these in highly automated, fast production lines in long, if not continuous, runs in order to keep costs down.

In contrast, the £300 product is a premium brand that is often bought as a gift for a good friend or an important client. Apart from its taste, it needs to look good on the shelf and in the drinks cabinet. If bottles are scratched or have crooked labels they will stay on the shelf. Would you give a scruffy-looking gift to your friend? They are usually sold in lower volumes, generally around festive periods when gifts are given. Customers are interested in what is inside the bottle as well as the bottle itself. Essentially, it behaves like a fashion item, or an ornament! The bottles are usually coated to make them glossier and more scratch resistant. They also use higher-quality embossed labels. Sometimes they come in cardboard, metal or wooden boxes with additional items such as crystal glasses and decanters. Manufacturers produce these on slower-running, semi-automated lines to avoid damaging the bottles or the labels. Usually, manual lines are used for packaging them into boxes with crystal glasses, etc.

In the above example, although both products comprise a liquid, in a bottle, with a label, one is more complex and uncertain in comparison with the other. So, in this whisky business there are two distinctly different value streams. One competes as a commodity with a high level of price sensitivity and the other competes on its image and is branded as a fashion item. The customers of each value stream make a buying decision using different criteria. The manufacturers structure their operations differently in order to deliver a product that customers value whilst creating value for the business.

---

[1] In the remainder of the book I will refer to these business units as value streams.

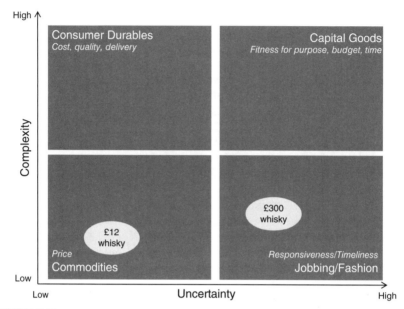

FIGURE 3.7   Complexity–uncertainty matrix illustrating the whisky example

Over the years I have found the complexity–uncertainty matrix a very useful tool to help identify value streams. This is best done by creating a discussion around products and product groups by placing them relative to one another on the complexity–uncertainty matrix. Figure 3.7 illustrates the use of the complexity–uncertainty matrix for our whisky example. Here the £12 product, which is highly price sensitive and competes as a commodity, is positioned in the low-complexity, low-uncertainty corner. In contrast, we see the £300 whisky positioned as a fashion product, in a slightly more complex but significantly more uncertain position.

THE COMPLEXITY–UNCERTAINTY MATRIX

The complexity–uncertainty matrix was developed to characterise and classify the competitive forces and the underlying characteristics of the manufacturing businesses serving in different sectors. It is a product of a European Commission-funded project entitled Factory of the Future,[2] which was

---

[2] Department of Trade and Industry, 'Factory for the Future', Eureka Project: Factory EU 1005, DTI, London, 1995.

completed in 1995. The main premise of the model is that it characterises manufacturing organisations according to the level of complexity and uncertainty they have to deal with. In this model complexity is defined as the complexity of the product or the market (including the supply chain) that we have to manage. Uncertainty relates to the predictability of the market conditions and demand for that product in the foreseeable future.

- In the low-complexity, low-uncertainty quadrant we have **commodities** that compete mainly on price, where the organisation needs to work efficiently (like well-oiled clockwork) to ensure that the unit cost and thus price can be kept to a minimum. Examples include light bulbs, clothes pegs, etc. as well as tradable commodities.
- In the high-complexity, high-uncertainty quadrant we have **capital goods** where fitness for purpose is of utmost importance. Here the organisation needs to ensure that it works effectively to deliver a product that is fit for purpose, on budget and on time. Examples include oil platform construction and military aircraft.
- In the low-complexity, high-uncertainty quadrant we have **jobbing and fashion products** where responsiveness and timeliness are key competitive factors. Here the organisation needs to be agile and responsive to meet customers' and markets' specific requirements and timescales.
- At the low-complexity and high-uncertainty quadrant we have **jobbing and fashion products** where responsiveness and timeliness are key competitive factors. Here the organisation needs to be agile and responsive to meet customers and markets specific requirements and timescales.

The two examples that follow illustrate further the use of the complexity–uncertainty matrix for surfacing the value streams in complex manufacturing and service operations.

VALUE STREAMS: PUMP MANUFACTURING EXAMPLE

A large engineering company is engaged in the design, manufacture and installation of pumps for their customers in the mining, oil and gas sectors.

The standard pump, with relatively low levels of uncertainty and complexity, is positioned as a commodity competing on price. In this business these standard pumps are made to stock based on a forecast. Customers expect short delivery lead times and make buying decisions based on price.

The configured pump is more complicated because it has a number of customer-selected configuration options and it is slightly more uncertain because it is difficult to predict which options customers will select. So, the major subassemblies of these pumps are produced to stock and when the customer order arrives specifying the selected options, subassemblies are pulled from stock and the pump is configured (or assembled) to the customer's order. Here the specific functionality of the product, with relatively quick delivery time, is the main order winning criterion.

The custom engineered pump is effectively a unique pumping solution that has been engineered and manufactured as a one-off to meet customer-specific requirements. It is highly unlikely that two pumping solutions will be the same. The main order winning criterion is the organisation's capability to design, develop, manufacture, deliver and install a pumping solution fit for purpose, to budget and to timescale. Thus, these products are significantly more complex and uncertain compared with the configured or standard products.

Clearly, we have three different value streams (Figure 3.8) with three different competitive factors that require the underlying processes to be organised differently to deliver value to the customer and to the business.

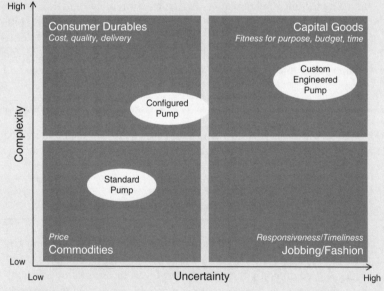

FIGURE 3.8 Complexity-uncertainty matrix for a pump manufacturer

VALUE STREAMS: SERVICE SECTOR EXAMPLE

A company provides a range of landscaping and construction services to a wide variety of clients including private households, small and large companies, municipalities and other large public-sector concerns. At a workshop held with the management team they were asked to create a list of jobs to characterise the entire portfolio of jobs they deliver across the business. Then they were asked to position each job on the complexity–uncertainty matrix with respect to one another (Figure 3.9). Discussion ensued; jobs were positioned and repositioned on the matrix. Finally, three different value streams were identified.

Simple repetitive jobs were jobs such as cutting the grass on the playing fields of Smiths High School every Monday morning. This is a job with low complexity and high levels of certainty. The low skills base suggests that anyone with a lawnmower can do the job, thus it is highly price sensitive (i.e., a typical commodity).

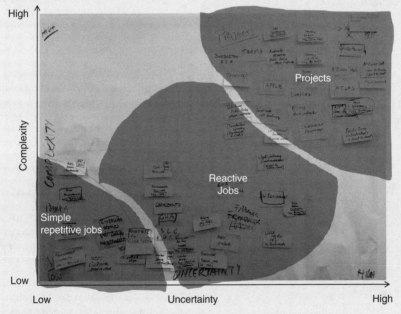

FIGURE 3.9   Complexity-uncertainty matrix for a service provider

In contrast, projects are major construction projects such as the stone cladding of a new government building or the refurbishment of the interior marble work in the HQ of an international bank. They know that jobs such as these will come, but their work content, skills and equipment requirements will be unknown. They will require higher skills levels and high levels of project management. The quality of the job, followed by timely completion within budget, are the key factors that the clients will consider when making a purchasing decision.

Reactive jobs are those where there is a contract with a client to maintain their infrastructure with a 48-hour service level. What makes them highly uncertain is that the exact work content is unknown until the client calls and explains the problem, which may be a broken manhole cover this week, a damaged overhead gantry next week. The company can be certain that the client will call, but it will not know the nature of the job or the resource requirements until the call is received and the job is assessed. Here, the client values a quick response and flexibility. The underlying process needs to be able to access jobs and deploy slack resources very quickly. Agility, flexibility and responsiveness are the key competitive factors.

By now it should be becoming clear that if we are to manage the performance of our organisations effectively, we need to understand what different value streams we have in our organisations and how they compete individually in their respective markets (Figure 3.10).

TIME FOR REFLECTION

- Do you sometimes find that your customers' requirements conflict with each other? Do you find that when you optimise your processes for one product/service it conflicts with other products/services? Do you feel that your business lacks purpose at times?
- Are you sure you have identified your value streams accurately?
- Try having a go at using the complexity–uncertainty matrix by mapping your products on to it. Is there a pattern emerging that suggests you have more than one value stream?

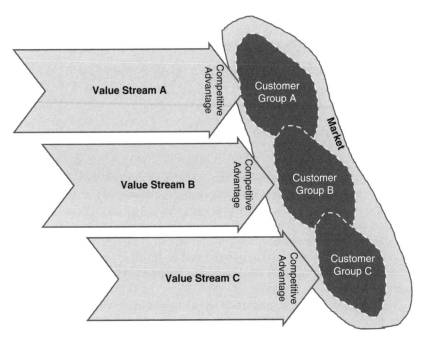

FIGURE 3.10   Value streams that deliver competitive advantage

---

CAUTION

If you are identifying more than four value streams then you may be analysing too much and not grouping your products and/or your customers' buying patterns adequately. I cannot recall seeing a business with more than four value streams.

Remember, the more value streams you have, the more complicated your business becomes to manage – so there is a balance to be had. What you are trying to do is define well-focused units of business that can be managed coherently.

3.4   BUSINESS PROCESSES – THE UNIVERSAL BUILDING BLOCKS

To be competitive, what does the value stream need to be good at? The usual response to this question includes answers such as *"it must have good products"*, *"it must satisfy customers"*, *"it must be efficient or productive"*, *"it must be good at*

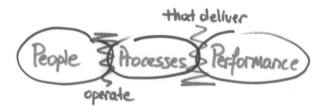

FIGURE 3.11   The universal structure that underpins performance in all organisations

marketing" and so on. Once again, all these point are valid. However, if we go back to basics, in all businesses people do things using resources that lead to good or bad results. If we string what people do end to end, what we get are business processes. In short, in organisations (public, private, commercial, industrial, charitable and so on) people do things (with computers, machines, materials, information, suppliers, customers and so on) that lead to good or bad performance results. I summarise this simply as **people operate processes that deliver performance** (Figure 1.1; repeated here as Figure 3.11).

So going back to our question, to be competitive what does the value stream need to be good at? The question we should really be asking is this: *To remain competitive, what are the fundamental processes that we need to be good at?*

At this point most people look for complex answers, with a big long list of processes. In fact, there are a number of models and frameworks that list numerous business processes. Don't get me wrong, I am not saying they are incorrect, but complexity is usually the main source of confusion. In fact, I find the answer to be astoundingly simple. We need to be good at only four processes, as follows:

- Developing the products and services that our customers want – Develop Product.
- Generating demand for our products and services – Get Order.
- Fulfilling demand; satisfying, if not delighting, our customers – Fulfil Order.
- Providing aftersales service and care to our customers – Support Product.

In short, if each one of our value streams is to be competitive (i.e., deliver its intended competitive profile), we need to be better than our competitors across all four of these processes. So at the most fundamental level, in each one of our value streams, we need to be managing the four processes illustrated in Figure 3.12.

The reaction I sometimes get when I present this to people is *"this is fine for manufacturing businesses, but what about banks and other service organisations?"* My argument is that this is universal and applies to all organisations. Let me demonstrate...

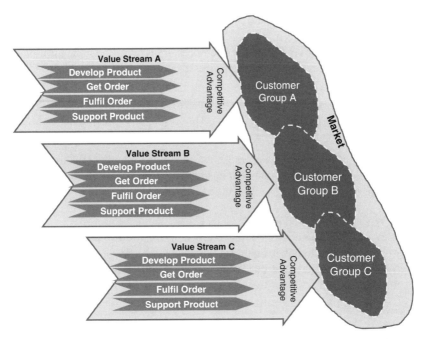

FIGURE 3.12   Value streams and the key processes that underpin competitive advantage

A bank has different products, ranging from current and savings accounts to credit cards, mortgages, loans, insurance products and so on. They have processes that review, refine and develop these products. They have processes that market these products with a view to generating demand for their existing or newly launched products. We quite often see adverts for these products on our television screens. They even call you at home to see if they can sell you a loan or an insurance policy. Once you have signed up for one of these products they have processes that fulfil the order. In a bank, the order-fulfilment process is likely to take a number of years (I have held my current account with the same bank for over 30 years), and the product may develop throughout the order-fulfilment process. They have processes that deal with enquiries after you leave the bank or move your account/mortgage to another bank.

Universities also have products. Just look at the web pages of a university and you are quite likely to find new degree programmes or courses coming online on an ongoing basis. They have processes for marketing these programmes and recruiting students onto the programmes. When I am teaching this particular part of the syllabus, I always ask my students in the class *What are we doing now?* The answer is *"we are in the middle of fulfilling their order"*. They are our customers, they have given us an order to educate them and from the time they start their first year until they graduate at the end of their studies, which could be as long as four or five years later, we are in the process of fulfilling their order. After students graduate they contact us regularly for references, transcripts and more information on a particular subject. Thus we have processes that support our products.

TIME FOR REFLECTION

I can give several other examples to reinforce this point, but if you are not convinced try to think through your business in these terms yourself. *It does, and will, make sense!*

- What are your products?
- What are the activities that make up your *Develop Product* process?
- What are the activities that make up your *Get Order* process?
- What are the activities that make up your *Fulfil Order* process?
- What are the activities that make up your *Support Product* process?

CAUTION

This is an appropriate point for a word of caution for service organisations. I have seen many management teams looking at product development and deciding it is not relevant to them as they do not have physical products. You need to be looking at this as *anything you are selling to the customer is a product*. Below I have provided two examples to emphasise this point.

A financial consultant provides services to her clients by advising them where best to invest their savings. Essentially, her product is advice. By attending training courses and undertaking market research on the investment products available she will be enhancing her capability to provide a better service (i.e., she will be developing her product).

A jobbing shop provides a range of services, including welding, cutting, milling and turning. If a customer wants a customised trailer for his boat, all of these products may need to be used to fabricate the trailer. When the company invests in more accurate and faster welding equipment and training of its welders, then they are developing their 'welding' product.

3.5 MANAGERIAL PROCESSES – THINKING ABOUT THE FUTURE

Going back to the four business processes that underpin the competitive advantage of each value stream, if these four processes are better than those of our competitors then we will have competitive advantage here and now! But what about the future?

Although we may not readily recognise these as business processes, in organisations we have routines that are concerned with the future. The fact that you are reading this book should be making you think about *what you can do today that will improve your ability to be better in the future.* Whether consciously or subconsciously, all management teams think and plan for future performance. I call these business processes *managerial processes*, and they typically include:

- *Setting a purposeful direction for the organisation*, that is, as meaningful internally to people at all levels as it is to customers and the wider group of stakeholders.
- *Scanning the operating environment* for opportunities and threats. These opportunities and threats may be coming from the wider operating environment and may be political, social, technological, environmental or legal (PESTL) in nature. Or, they may be coming from our immediate operating environment, such as customers, suppliers, competitors, new entrants and potential substitutes (Porter's five forces).
- *Assessing the significance of these opportunities and threats.* It is rare that new technology or competitors appear from the left field to catch us by surprise. In many cases we know they exist but we choose to ignore them because we think they are insignificant. The problem is that by the time they become significant, it might just be too late for us to be able to do anything about it.
- *Creating innovative strategies and responses* that exploit the opportunities and mitigate the threats.
- *Responding and changing* efficiently and effectively with minimum disruption.
- *Managing the performance of the organisation*, the subject of this book, by measuring and monitoring progress against objectives and plans. Informing decision makers of potential and impending trends (opportunities and threats) whilst ensuring strategies and responses achieve their intended outcomes.

In my experience, all organisations have these processes. Those organisations that do them well and treat them as one interconnected set appear to perform better than others. They go through the above cycle of *scanning–sensing–responding* faster than their competitors. Effectively, it is these managerial processes that are collectively responsible for sustaining and driving an organisation's performance in the future. They achieve this by configuring and re-configuring the value streams and developing the capabilities of the value-creating operational processes. We will discuss this in more detail in Chapter 8.

TIME FOR REFLECTION

- Is your organisation any good at these managerial processes?
- What do you do well?
- What can you do better?

Don't worry if you do not have all the answers at this stage, we will cover at least some of these in later chapters.

3.6 SUPPORT PROCESSES – SERVING TO CREATE VALUE

There are many other business processes within an organisation. Most, if not all, of these serve to make the operational value-adding processes and the managerial processes work more efficiently and effectively. These include processes such as:

- support technology
- support human resource management
- support financial management
- support communications
- support facilities.

These processes are akin to the support functions we have in organisations, such as the HR function, the finance function and so on. The fundamental difference is in the thinking: they do not exist in their own right, they exist only to serve the value-creating operational processes or value-sustaining and value-growing managerial processes. As such, it is important to manage them by recognising this internal customer–supplier relationship. Let me illustrate through an example…

In an electronics manufacturing organisation, one of the value streams needs to operate to a 24-hour service level with its key customers, who manufacture low-volume, high-variety electronics products. To achieve the necessary levels of responsiveness, the Order Fulfilment process needs to be agile and responsive and if any of the manufacturing equipment breaks down, it needs to be fixed and made available with urgency. As a customer of the HR function, the order fulfilment process requires a multi-skilled, flexible workforce that can be made available at short notice (2 to 4 hours) and as a customer of the engineering function, it requires a 3-hour service level to resolve production line equipment failure.

In this company, the HR and engineering budgets were set according to the service level they were providing and any planned improvements. The HR function had engaged with housewives in the local area. They had trained them and contracted them to stay at home ready for a call. The engineering function was focused on the average time between failure and repair (average downtime) and was striving to get it below 2 hours by optimising and justifying its resources (engineers, equipment, spare parts, shift patterns, etc.) accordingly.

3.7 ANATOMY OF AN ORGANISATION – THE UNIVERSAL COMPETITIVE STRUCTURE

You have probably guessed by now that in this chapter we have justified and explained the anatomy of a business. This is the universal structure that makes an organisation, irrespective of the specific peculiarities associated with its customers, products, services and people. We will get to them later.

This is similar to the anatomy of people. A concert pianist, a ballerina, an Olympic athlete, a Nobel laureate – although different, they all have approximately the same anatomy. They all have a nervous system, a digestive system, a cardiovascular system, a skeletal system, a muscular system and so on that makes them work as a human being, even though they are all good at different things. Understanding this universal structure as a set of interconnected systems helps us to better manage the performance of our organisations.

In short, the universal structure of an organisation comprises:

- One or more value streams with unique products/services and competitive characteristics.
- Each value stream having four operational processes that create value for that value stream here and now:
  - Get Order
  - Develop Product
  - Fulfil Order
  - Support Product.

- Managerial processes that are responsible for scanning, sensing and responding, to ensure the future prosperity of the value streams individually and the organisation as a whole.
- Support processes that exist to serve operational and managerial processes, making them more effective and efficient.

This universal competitive structure is illustrated in Figure 3.13. In short, what we are managing is a series of value streams and processes.

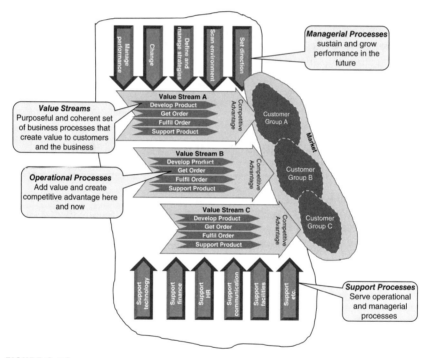

FIGURE 3.13   The universal competitive structure of organisations

3.8   SUMMARY

We started this chapter with a look at how companies compete, from which we went on to develop the universal competitive structure of organisations. In short, in managing business performance we have to manage value streams and processes. But remember, these are not just things. Value streams and processes are all about people doing things in the organisations. Although we need to understand and manage the competitive structure of our organisation, we cannot forget about the social factors. More on this in Part Three.

TIME FOR REFLECTION

- Do you know what value streams exist in your business?
- Do you know the critical competitive factors for each value stream?
- What does each operational process need to be really good at to give your value streams the competitive advantage they require?
- Can you explain your managerial processes as an end-to-end process, with starting and finishing points? Even better, can you show me your managerial processes?
- Are your support processes subordinated to operational or managerial processes in a customer–supplier relationship? Or is the power base the other way around, as it is in many cases?

ORGANISATIONAL NOTE

I am compelled to include this organisational note here as on several occasions I have been confronted with a question on how to organise a business around its value streams. My usual answer is as follows.

These value streams exist because of how your products and services interact with customers and markets. Ignoring them is not going to make them go away. We have to accept them and then think about the best way we can organise ourselves to manage them. There are three options:

1. We recognise them, and design and manage the underlying business processes to optimise their performance without formally organising ourselves around them. Essentially, if you were a one-man business and had to deal with different value streams, you would mentally switch from managing one value stream to another as long as you were clear on which value stream an order/job belongs to.
2. We organise each value stream as a profit centre. This creates a very distinct organisation around the value stream but in some cases it can be problematic as many resources can be shared between different value streams, making their allocation difficult. Another potential problem

with this approach is that it can set up competition between value streams, which may artificially allocate marginal jobs to their own value stream to boost their revenues. Having clear guidelines that define how jobs/contracts should be allocated to each value stream does help moderate this problem.

3. We organise each value stream as a cost centre. This approach, whilst eliminating some of the issues associated with the profit centre approach, ensures that a distinct organisational structure can be defined around the value streams. It also allows for various resources to be shared between different value streams without creating potential competition between the value streams.

There is no magic answer here. Once the value streams are identified and validated, it is up to the management team to identify how best to structure the business to optimise the performance of each value stream.

Another question I am regularly asked is what happens to customers who do business with more than one value stream. Here the answer is the creation of an account management structure as the interface between the customer and the business. The account management structure will liaise with the customer and bring the job/contract to the business whilst keeping the customer one step removed from the intricacies of how the business operates internally. The important point here is that the customer gets a seamless and consistent experience/service through a single point of contact, even if they are dealing with a number of value streams within the business.

REFERENCES

Finkelstein, S., Harvey, C. and Lawton, T. (2006) *Breakout Strategy: Meeting the Challenge of Double-Digit Growth*, McGraw-Hill Professional: New York.

Treacy, M. and Wiersema, F. (1996) *The Discipline of Market Leaders*, Harper Collins: New York.

... many organisations do not understand the value streams and business processes that underpin their competitive structure!

4

Understanding and Managing Business Processes

*The most important things about a process
are purpose and flow.
The purpose of a process needs to be aligned
with the competitive priorities of the
value stream it serves.*

We concluded Chapter 3 by suggesting that if we are to effectively manage the performance of our organisation, we should be managing its value streams and business processes. We explained the anatomy of an organisation and suggested that we need to understand how each one of our value streams competes in its markets. We also said that we need to configure the business processes within each value stream to optimise the performance of that value stream. In short, to effectively manage the performance of our organisations, we need to manage the performance of our business processes in the context of the value streams they serve. Furthermore, if we are to manage the performance of our business processes we need to better understand their anatomy and behaviour.

In this chapter, we will examine the business processes to better understand their anatomy and behaviour.

4.1   PURPOSE AND FLOW

At the outset, we defined performance as the efficiency and effectiveness of an action. In Chapter 3, we introduced business processes as the fundamental building blocks of an organisation. We also suggested that if we are to manage the performance of our organisations effectively, we need to manage the performance of our business processes in the context of the value streams they serve. Consequently, if we are to manage the performance of our organisation effectively, we need to understand the composition and behaviour of our business processes.

Earlier, we explained business processes as follows: *in organisations people do things using various resources (machines, computers, pen, paper and so on). If we string what people do end to end we get business processes.* We then went on to conceptualise the relationship between people, processes and performance by stating that *in organisations, people operate processes that lead to results.* We also illustrated this conceptualisation in Figure 1.1 (repeated here as Figure 4.1).

A more formal definition of a business process is as a series of continuous or intermittent cross-functional activities that are naturally connected together with work flowing through these activities for a particular outcome/purpose (Bititci *et al.*, 2011). This definition contains two pertinent points: purpose and workflow.

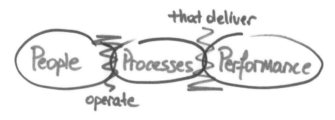

FIGURE 4.1   The universal structure that underpins performance in all organisations

Concerning purpose, from our earlier discussions on the anatomy of a business we identified a number of operational, managerial and support processes. The purpose of each process is clearly evident in the name of the process. For example, the purpose of the Develop Product process is to develop products that the market wants; the purpose of the Scan Environment process is to identify potential opportunities and threats. But of course, the purpose would need to be aligned more specifically with the competitive priorities of the value stream a business process serves. For example, to develop the best-performing product or to develop the most economical product or to develop the most flexible product. In short, the competitive priorities of the value stream define the specific purpose of the process.

In a process, work flows through various activities to deliver the purpose of that process. One of my favourite interview questions, particularly when recruiting a process improvement engineer/analyst, is *What is the most important thing about a process?* Almost always the responses include waste, value, people, resources, costs and so on, but rarely do candidates mention flow. In fact, after its purpose, **flow** is the most important concept when managing the performance of processes. But do not confuse flow with speed. The flow of a process needs to be synchronised with the demand upon that process.

UNDERSTANDING FLOW

Let's look at two different types of restaurant. In a fast-food restaurant you want the customers to come and order without waiting too long, you want them to be served quickly and you want them to vacate the table after a reasonable time so that you can use your capacity effectively to maximise your revenues. The customers are OK with this because they know that it is a fast-food restaurant.

In contrast, in an upmarket restaurant where people 'dine out' we see a different dynamic. Customers book a table for the evening, arrive around 8 pm and may stay until midnight. It is about ambience, relaxation and immersion in the experience. Here the flow rate is completely different from that in the fast-food restaurant. It is much slower, as this is what the customer expects.

The point I am trying to make is that *purpose and flow are the two most important things about a process*. The purpose of a process should align with the competitive priorities of the value stream and the flow of the process should harmonise with the purpose of the process.

4.2   WHAT FLOWS THROUGH THE PROCESS?

So far we have talked about business processes and workflow in general terms. But there are fundamental differences between processes and what flows through these processes. In general, three things flow through a process: information, materials and customers. In a manufacturing process it is primarily information and materials that flow through the processes. The customers experience the output of the process (e.g., the quality and on-time delivery of their product). In a service process, however, it is information and/or customers that flow through the process. For example, in a process that reviews and approves or rejects mortgage applications, the customer submits her mortgage application at one end of the process, information is processed through various stages and the customer experiences the decision at the other end of the process. In the case of the restaurant example, the customer is part of the process and experiences the process directly. This is the same in tourism or health care, where the customer and information flow through the process.

SERVICE VS. MANUFACTURING

A consultancy retained to assist with the implementation of lean management in a public-sector service organisation proceeded to train employees using examples and training materials that were originated and designed for manufacturing processes. The lean teams worked under the guidance of the consultants, analysing processes, removing non-value-adding activities and streamlining processes. Although the first impression was that significant cost savings would be achieved, customer service suffered, complaints went up, failure demand increased and in the end productivity suffered.

In contrast, in a nearly identical organisation a very similar lean management project yielded more positive results. Here the team focused on the experiences of the customers flowing through the process; they applied the same lean management approach, removed non-value-adding activities, introduced new value-adding activities and streamlined the process. The results were astoundingly different. Customer satisfaction went up, failure demand reduced and productivity improved.

In the latter case the difference can be entirely attributed to the team's focus on the customer experience throughout the process, which was lacking in the former case.

The point here is that *service and manufacturing-like processes can exist in any organisation*. A manufacturing firm will have several service processes through which information and customers flow. Similarly, a service business will have manufacturing-like processes where the customer experiences the output of the process (e.g., the mortgage application process example above). What is critical is that *we need to understand how customers interact with processes.*

4.3   ANATOMY OF A PROCESS

Before we attempt to manage the performance of a process, we need to understand its anatomy. As illustrated in Figure 4.2, each process has:

- *Inputs* and *outputs* – the information, materials and customers that flow through the process.
- *Controls* – the expectations, requirements, purpose, objectives and targets, as well as policies, rules and constraints, within which the process needs to operate.

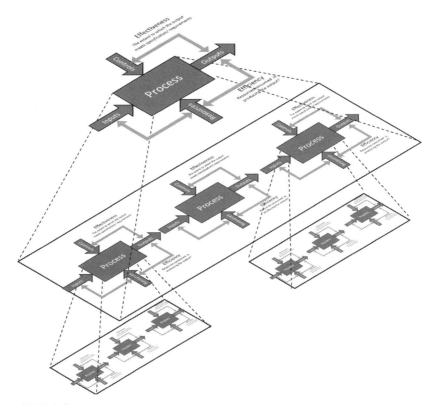

FIGURE 4.2   Anatomy of a process

■ *Resources* – that are consumed in processing inputs into outputs. This may include human resources, machines, consumables, energy, information technologies and so on.

■ *Subprocesses* – these are activities that make up the process and essentially work flows through these activities. Each process and subprocess can be broken down to reveal a further level of detail.

At a higher level of abstraction a process may look quite simple and straightforward to understand. When we look into the details, a process comprises several subprocesses (activities), which in turn could be further broken down into sub-subprocesses (tasks). The problem is that this recursion (process, subprocesses, activities and tasks) can continue to form several layers of complexity. Usually the analysts amongst us prefer to analyse the process at the lowest level of detail. Others prefer working at higher levels of abstraction.

My experience here is that there is no single correct answer. How we break it down and conceptualise it all depends on the complexity of the process and what we are trying to do with it. But, as a guide, my own preferred approach is that we take a process at the highest level (e.g., Fulfil Order) and break it down into its key components to create a reasonable representation of the process, without making it overcomplicated. I will demonstrate this later in Section 4.5. I would advise against breaking a process into subprocesses and analysing and attempting to measure and manage the performance of a subprocess (activity or task) in isolation. This will only result in sub-optimisation of the process and will undermine overall process performance.

4.4   UNDERSTANDING WHAT AFFECTS FLOW

So far we have established that, in a process, work flows through a series of activities to deliver the purpose of the process. When flow gets interrupted, we get waste. So, in managing the performance of processes, what we are really managing is the flow of work through various activities of the process. But flow of work through activities is rarely consistent. That is, the flow rate of work through each activity varies. This variation can significantly impact the overall performance of the process.

For example, take a perfectly designed and balanced process comprising five activities (Figure 4.3), with each activity taking an average of 10 pieces of work per hour. This could be a manufacturing process in a factory, a tax-returns handling process or a student registration process in a school. What would the average output of the entire process be?

The first logical answer that comes to mind is that the overall process output will be 10 pieces per hour. But in reality it would be very unlikely that this output could be achieved, because an average of 10 pieces per hour means that sometimes an activity will produce 7 and sometimes 13 pieces per hour. This will result in inventory building up between some activities and shortages in other cases. That is, when an activity is ready to work there will not be any pieces available because of the variation in the preceding activity. This variation over time would result in an output profile averaging less than 10 pieces per minute for the whole process, with significant variation in the output. The exercise outlined below effectively demonstrates this phenomenon.

EXERCISE: THE IMPACT OF VARIATION ON PROCESS PERFORMANCE

- Set up a production line with five work centres, as illustrated in Figure 4.3.
- Use coins as work pieces.
- Give each workstation a pair of dice.
- Start with six work pieces in each stock location, with the first work centre having an unlimited supply of coins.
- Appoint a customer who calls for product at regular intervals (say 15 or 20 seconds).
- On the call of the customer, each work centre:
  - throws a pair of dice;
  - picks up the number of work pieces indicated by the dice (between 2 and 12) from the left-hand-side stock location and passes them on to the right-hand-side stock location.
- Let the game run for about 20 calls.
- During the game the customer records the number of work pieces received from work centre number 5 for each call.
- Each work centre should record the dice value and the actual number of pieces processed at each call.

What does the overall output profile look like? If you ensure that for each call the output coins are piled, you will see the output as a histogram.

Activity #1 — Average output 10 pieces/hour
Activity #2 — Average output 10 pieces/hour
Activity #3 — Average output 10 pieces/hour
Activity #4 — Average output 10 pieces/hour
Activity #5 — Average output 10 pieces/hour
Customer

FIGURE 4.3 A balanced process of five activities

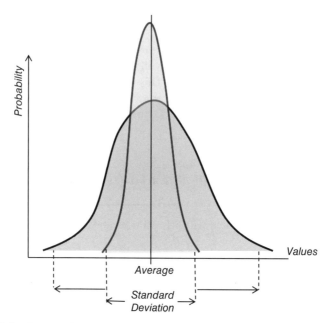

FIGURE 4.4   Impact of variation of process performance

In statistical process control, standard deviation is used to measure the amount of variation or dispersion from the average. The two normal distribution curves shown in Figure 4.4 illustrate the two processes with wider and tighter standard deviations, whilst having the same average values. A smaller variation suggests a tighter dispersion with outputs closer to the average value. The widely popularised Six-Sigma process improvement approach focuses on understanding and reducing the variation in a process.

Contrary to general belief that it is only useful for repetitive manufacturing processes, this line of thinking can also be applied in the wide range of business processes discussed earlier. Think about some of your business processes. What are their key sources of variation? Why do you not get consistent and repeatable results every time? The following example may help.

THINKING ABOUT VARIATION

Think about how you get from home to work every morning. Make a list of activities and think about their variation. Which one of the activities suffers from the largest variation? What can you do to minimise the variation?

In my own case the activity with the largest variation is the drive from home to my office, sometimes it can take 45 minutes and sometimes 2 hours. *So what do I do to manage the variation?* I have learned that it is futile to try to get to my office for 9 am. If I am lucky it takes me about 1 hour and if I am unlucky, which is quite often, it can take me 2 hours with an average time of about 1 hour 40 minutes. If I plan to be at work just before 10 am, however, it can take me as short as 45 minutes and usually the maximum time I am driving is 1 hour 30 minutes with an average of around 1 hour. So I have modified my working hours to start at 10 am. I also check the traffic report before I leave home for any potential holdups and modify my route if required. As a result, I spend less time commuting and my journey time is more reliable.

In short, by understanding and managing the variation within a process we are managing the ability of that process to reliably perform to expectations. This is also known as process capability, which is underpinned by the interaction and variation of a complex set of factors (Figure 4.5) that may include: leadership and management style; people skills, knowledge and behaviours; policies and procedures; resources and partners. The reality is that a variation in any of these factors will impact on the overall performance of the process. We will talk more about capabilities later in Chapter 7. For the time being, suffice to say that business processes are the key building blocks of our organisations; in managing the performance of our organisations we need to be managing the performance of the key processes; the purpose of the process needs to be aligned with the value stream it serves; we need to be sensitive to what flows through the processes (i.e., materials, information and customers); investing in developing the underlying capabilities of the process will reduce the variation and enhance the inherent reliability of the process; and finally, the performance measures we use to manage

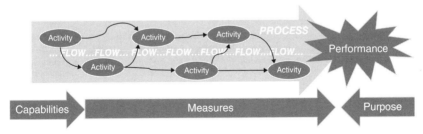

FIGURE 4.5　Interaction of purpose, flow, measures and capabilities

the performance of the process need to reflect the purpose and workflow through the process.

4.5 MEASURING PROCESS PERFORMANCE

We have already defined performance as the efficiency and effectiveness of an action. Based on the discussion so far in the context of business processes, *performance is the efficiency and effectiveness of a process*. In other words:

- Does the process fulfil its intended purpose (effectiveness)?
- How much resources have been consumed to fulfil the purpose (efficiency)?

As a process comprises a series of interconnected activities through which work flows, we can have several measurement points along the process. In the example shown in Figure 4.6, the purpose of the process is to maximise customer satisfaction by delivering all orders on time, as promised.

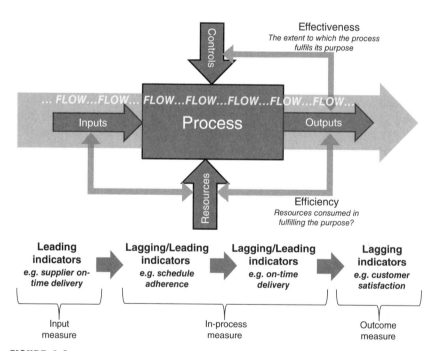

FIGURE 4.6 Leading and lagging indicators along the process

Along the process we can also measure schedule adherence and suppliers' delivery performance. In this example, if we look along the process from right to left, each one of these measures becomes a leading indicator for the preceding measure. That is:

- *Customer satisfaction* is a lagging indicator as there is nothing we can do to prevent the outcome if we know that we had 50 customer complaints last week. It is too late; they have complained already.
- *On-time delivery* is a leading indicator of customer satisfaction, as late deliveries today will probably mean that customers will complain tomorrow. But, as before, knowing that 25% of our orders were delivered late will not help us to prevent the problem in the first place.
- Similarly, *suppliers' delivery performance* and *schedule adherence* are leading indicators for *on-time delivery*. If our suppliers have delivered late then our ability to work to our original plan/schedule is compromised, which in turn will have an adverse effect on our on-time delivery performance and customer satisfaction outcome.

- *Lagging indicator* – A performance indicator that communicates the performance outcome of a past action. In practice, all performance measures are lagging indicators with respect to the action they report.
- *Leading indicator* – A performance indicator that could be used to predict the future performance outcome of a process. In practice, leading indicators tend to be in-process or input measures to the process.

In practice I have observed several good examples of businesses gaining control of their processes using this line of thinking. For example, in a whisky manufacturing operation the company can gain market share by delivering reliably on time to significantly reduced lead times. This means that the customer has to hold less stock, thus making the product more attractive in comparison with competitors' products. This is particularly an issue for their Make-to-Order value stream, where products are produced on receipt of the customer's order. Figure 4.7 illustrates the end-to-end process.

In this particular case the company used cause-and-effect-analysis (also known as fishbone or Ishikawa diagrams) to analyse the process and identify potential causes that may lead to on-time delivery failures. The cause-and-effect analysis is illustrated in Figure 4.8. Note how the boxes at the bottom and top of the cause-and-effect analysis reflect the activities in the process map above. Each box has two sections, the activity name and the performance criterion, which

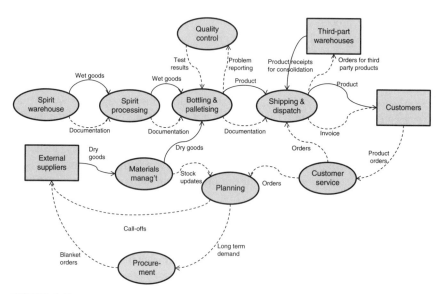

FIGURE 4.7   Fulfil Order process for make-to-order products

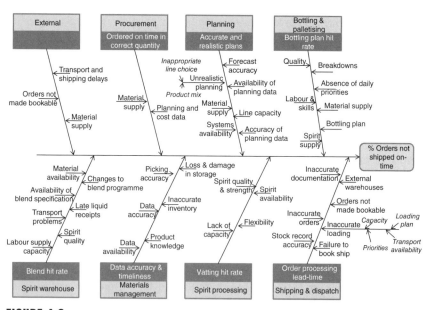

FIGURE 4.8   Process cause-and-effect analysis of the Fulfil Order process for percentage of orders not shipped on time

TABLE 4.1 FMEA on factors that impact the bottling plan hit rate

Failure mode	Likelihood of occurrence	Severity of impact	Detectability	RPN
Breakdowns	6	9	7	378
Absence of daily priorities	5	6	6	180
Quality	3	4	5	60
Material supply	2	7	4	56
Bottling plan	3	7	4	84
Spirit supply	2	7	4	56
Labour supply and skills	1	3	3	9
Total				823

explains how each activity impacts on the overall performance criterion we are trying to improve – in this case, *on-time delivery*.

Table 4.1 illustrates a failure-mode-and-effect analysis (FMEA) conducted on the bottling and palletising activity to analyse the impact of various factors on the bottling plan hit rate and, consequently, on the on-time delivery performance.

An FMEA rates each failure mode according to three criteria:

- **Likelihood of occurrence** is rated between 1 and 10, with 1 being the least likely and 10 being the most likely.
- **Severity of impact** is rated between 1 and 10, with 1 being the least severe and 10 being the most severe.
- **Detectability** refers to the ability to detect and intervene in order to eliminate or minimise the impact. It is rated between 1 and 10, with 1 being the most detectable and 10 being the least detectable.

The risk priority number (RPN) is then calculated by multiplying the three scores: RPN = Occurrence × Severity × Detectability. In this case the total RPN of 823 is an indication of the inherent unreliability of the bottling and palletising activity. Although the total RPN is meaningless as an absolute measure, when it is used as a relative measure to improve the inherent reliability of the process it becomes more meaningful. In this case the team conducting the analysis set a target to reduce the total RPN by 50% within three months.

Table 4.2 illustrates the same FMEA updated after three months, where the total RPN has been reduced from 823 to 427 by:

- Introducing simple condition-monitoring procedures into critical parts of the bottling line, improving the detectability of potential breakdowns.
- Issuing daily priorities for each job, so that high-priority jobs can be scheduled first, thus reducing the impact of any stoppages on delivery performance.

TABLE 4.2   FMEA updated after three months

Failure mode	Likelihood of occurrence	Severity of impact	Detectability	RPN
Breakdowns	6	9	③	162
Absence of daily priorities	⓪	6	6	0
Quality	3	4	5	60
Material supply	2	7	4	56
Bottling plan	3	7	4	84
Spirit supply	2	7	4	56
Labour supply and skills	1	3	3	9
Total				427

In this example, this line of thinking together with the systematic use of these continuous improvement tools at operational levels of the organisation resulted in significant improvement in the overall performance of the organisation.

4.6   SUMMARY

The purpose of this chapter was to help you think through and understand the anatomy and behaviours of business processes in universal terms. What we have discussed here applies to all kinds of processes, whether they are managerial processes, support processes or operational processes. In short: all processes should have a purpose that is aligned with the value stream they serve; work (materials, information and/or customers) flows through a process; all processes comprise activities (subprocesses) with their own inputs, outputs, controls and resources; all processes have customers that interact with the process in different ways; all processes suffer from variation and investing in the underlying capabilities of the process will reduce the sources of variation and enhance the process reliability.

TIME FOR REFLECTION

- Do we recognise and understand all our key processes?
- Are our processes aligned with the value streams they serve?
- Are the purposes of the processes explicit?
- Do we understand what flows through our processes?
- Are we sensitive to how the customers interact with our processes?
- Do we understand the sources of variation in our processes?

- Are the performance measures aligned with the purposes of the processes?
- Do the performance measures enable us to manage the flow of work through our processes?
- Are we consciously investing in developing the underlying capabilities of our processes?

CAUTION: ARE YOU FOCUSING ON THE RIGHT PROCESS?

We must remember to manage processes in the context of the value streams they serve. Quite often I find a disconnect between how the company competes and the processes that are being managed. It is sometimes quite easy to lose sight of what is more and what is less important. Here is an example.

We were working on a European-wide project involving a number of SMEs. Early in the project our purpose was to conduct high-level business reviews with each SME to better understand their business and the issues they were facing. This example is from one of these companies, providing contract packaging services to the food industry. Their response to the question *Why do customers come to you instead of going to your competitors?* was a categorical *"because we have a really good relationship with our customers"*.

Later, when we asked them about their improvement initiatives and business processes, their response was *"... we are into lean manufacturing in a big way. We have a really good team that is continuously improving our manufacturing operations..."* So we asked about their customer relation management process, we said *"you told us earlier that the main reason customers come to you and don't go to your competitors is because you have a really good relationship with your customers. If that is the case, what are you doing about understanding and continuously improving your customer relationship management process?"* At first we got blank stares, then the response *"we never thought about it in that way"*. At this point it became clear that the only process that was conceptualised as a process was the order fulfilment process, with emphasis on the production operations. They did not conceptualise the customer relationship management (in other words Get Order) as a process they could map, study and continuously improve.

To finish the story, we ended up helping them to map and understand customer relationship management as a process. The lessons and insights developed through this intervention helped them to better understand their customers and their customers' business, resulting in significant increases in high-value orders.

Here the caution is that sometimes, because we are doing continuous improvement, lean or some form of process improvement, we too readily jump to the conclusion that we are focusing on the right processes. Too often I have seen organisations focusing on the wrong process. In short, *are you improving the right processes?*

REFERENCE

Bititci, U.S., Ackermann, F., Ates, A., Davies, J.D., Gibb, S., MacBryde, J., Mackay, D., Maguire, C., van der Meer, R. and Shafti, F. (2011) Managerial processes: An operations management perspective towards dynamic capabilities, *Production Planning & Control*, 22(2), 157–173.

The flow of work through the process needs to be harmonised with its purpose...

... performance measures need to reflect the purpose of the process and the workflow through the process.

5

Measuring Performance

*We use performance measures and comparisons
all the time in our everyday lives...
... there is no getting away from them.*

5.1 DO WE NEED MEASURES?

This chapter is primarily concerned with how to create effective performance measurement systems that are valued and used every day by the people in the organisation. However, before we go on to describing the intricacies of creating effective performance measurement systems, I would like to deal with the question *"Do we really need measures to manage performance?"*

In the modern world we live in measures seem to be everywhere, we cannot seem to get away from them. Some recent thinking appears to be critical of the way we use measures to run our businesses, schools, hospitals, even to a certain extent our societies and lives. There is a growing feeling that in the modern, knowledge-economy-based world, where the majority of people are self-motivated and engaged, there is little room for performance measurement and management.

Indeed, it may be wholly possible to manage the performance of an organisation without measuring it, but as yet I have not seen this. All organisations use and rely on performance measures to manage their performance. The only difference is that some are more formalised, more explicit and more developed. In contrast, others are less well developed, more informal and more implicit. When businesses issue quarterly reports to their shareholders they are reporting their performance against formalised explicit measures. Similarly, university league tables rank institutions against predefined criteria that are formalised and explicit. Every day on our television screens we see advertisements that claim greater performance or lower costs for the products and services that are being advertised. Again, some of these are more established, formalised and explicit, such as fuel consumption figures of a car, others less so as they target more subjective features that could be affected by personal preferences and taste, such as the styling of a car.

If you think about it, even at home you instinctively feel/assess the happiness of your family (a subjective measurement system) using some arbitrary signals (indicators) and consciously or subconsciously make an effort to improve the mood. Similarly, in social situations, when we say *"Joe is a good guy"* we are making an assessment often using some subjective implicit criterion.

Implicitly or explicitly we use performance measures every day. Wherever we look, we are confronted by performance measures and comparisons. Like it or not, we cannot get away from them. We need them to manage our everyday lives.

The same applies to our businesses and organisations. We need measures to manage them. However, as some measures are more important than others we need to know which measures to use and which ones to ignore, and how best to use these measures to create an effective performance measurement system. The last thing we want is for the performance measurement system to become a bureaucratic overhead that no one uses, as in the manufacturing company example I gave in Chapter 1 (included again below).

In one manufacturing company they had a six-page weekly plant report containing 312 performance measures. When we enquired what they did with all these measures, we were often faced with blank looks. We managed to convince the team responsible for issuing this report to stop issuing it as an experiment to see what would happen. It was five weeks before the IT Manager called to ask what had happened to the plant report. When asked what he wanted it for his response was "... *I just wondered, because the corner of my desk where it usually sits has been empty for a few weeks*".

Indeed, I am very sympathetic to the argument that *we do not need performance measures to manage the performance of modern organisations* because I understand where this is coming from. If we look at the performance measurement systems we have in many of our organisations, and if you study how they are used, you will see the devastating effect they have on the motivation and engagement of people. They are a far cry from being balanced and harmonious workplaces. In some of these cases they are right, the organisation would probably perform better without any measures. The evidence from my research, experience and observations over the years suggests that this is a symptom of two interrelated factors. *First*, a badly designed performance measurement system that is not fit for purpose. *Second*, inappropriate management practices where measures are used in a command-and-control style to create internal competition and fear. At a recent seminar one of the participants blamed performance measures for suppressing innovation. He was probably right, but for the wrong reasons. Let me explain through this analogy.

You probably drive your car most days and find it quite useful to have a speedometer, rev counter, fuel gauge, engine temperature gauge and so on to tell you what you or your is car doing. As yet I have not come across anyone complaining that their instruments get in the way of their driving. However, it is a different story when your partner, parent or child sits in the passenger seat and tells you to watch your speed, not rev the engine so much, check your fuel level and so on. Although this is annoying, we don't often complain about or blame the instruments. The braver ones amongst us may just tell our partners, parents or children to shut up. Others may avoid driving when they are in the car, preferring to let them drive (sounds familiar?). In reality, the issue is rarely about performance measures as long as they have been designed appropriately. Most issues with performance measurement are attributable to the way we use them.

In this chapter we will deal with the design of performance measurement systems, that is the design of technical controls. In Part Three of this book we will deal with the issues relating to management practices and organisational culture, that is the way we use measures.

5.2 DEVELOPING A PERFORMANCE MEASUREMENT SYSTEM

In Chapter 2 we defined a performance measurement system as the process (or processes) of setting goals, developing a set of performance measures, collecting, analysing, reporting, interpreting, reviewing and acting on performance data. That is a closed-loop control system comprising both feedback and feedforward control loops (see Chapter 2 for further information).

We concluded Chapter 3 by suggesting that if we are to effectively manage the performance of our organisation, we should be managing its value streams and business processes. We explained the anatomy of an organisation and suggested that we need to understand how each of our value streams competes in its market, going on to configure the underlying business processes to optimise the performance of each value stream. In Chapter 4 we examined the anatomy and behaviour of a business process and concluded that performance measures need to reflect the purpose of the process, as well as the flow of work through the process.

In the remainder of this chapter we will examine how to design effective performance measurement systems that engage people in a conversation about the performance of the organisation.

5.3 COMMUNICATING WITH MEASURES

In this section I will cover how to design effective performance measurement reports that engage people in a conversation around performance. I can safely say that there are as many performance reports as there are organisations that use performance measures. However, at the most fundamental level they use a mixture of:

- Data, in the form of tables.
- Colour coding, such as the traffic light system, to draw attention to specific areas of opportunity or problem.
- Time series reports, to show trends as they develop over time.

In its most basic form, a colour-coded table or a time-series graph is sufficient to tell us what is happening to performance in relation to the target. Figures 5.1 and 5.2 depict the same performance information in two alternative forms, tabular and graphical.

	Target	Sept	Oct	Nov	Dec	Jan	Feb
On-time Delivery	95%	98%	97%	94%	87%	96%	98%

FIGURE 5.1 Colour-coded table showing performance against target

The choice of which format to adopt is entirely up to the preferences of the organisation. However, I would strongly recommend that a single format for reporting and displaying performance information should be used throughout the company. This is akin to using the same language to communicate throughout the organisation. When different parts of the organisation adopt their own language to communicate performance information, miscommunications can arise. Figures 5.3–5.5 show examples of different performance reports using the same reporting format. This is a company operating in the process sector and on the shop floor the use of statistical process control (SPC) is widespread. Consequently, they have adopted an SPC-like approach to displaying all of their performance information, including technical measures, such as the thickness of the laminate coming from the production lines, the number of customer complaints, delivery performance and health and safety incidents.

Figures 5.3 and 5.5 contain annotations, as identified by the circle. These annotations explain the causes behind the process behaviour. In Figure 5.3 the main reason for the process being out of the upper control limit is attributed to cutting and dips. Similarly, in Figure 5.5 the problems with the delivery performance have been attributed to raw material supply problems. Such annotations are immensely powerful for helping us to understand the underlying problems and adopt a more proactive management of processes and overall organisational performance.

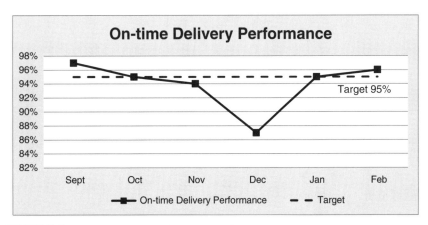

FIGURE 5.2 Graph showing performance against target

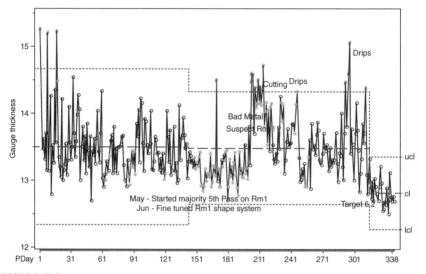

FIGURE 5.3   Laminate gauge

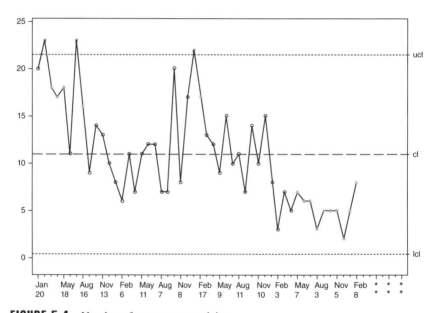

FIGURE 5.4   Number of customer complaints

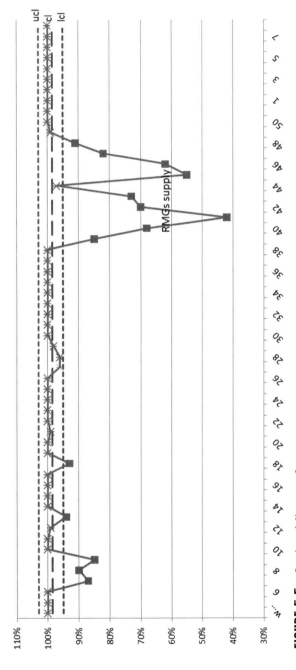

FIGURE 5.5 On-time delivery performance

In statistical process control, upper and lower control limits are used extensively to monitor whether a process remains under statistical control. In effect, they provide a measure of the natural variation in the process that cannot be attributed to an external cause. In Figure 5.3 it can be observed that the process has been improved at two points. The first improvement, at day 135, results in a tightening of the upper and control limits of the process, indicating that some sources of variation have been removed and the process now has a tighter standard deviation, whilst the process average remains approximately the same. The second improvement, at day 318, results in further improvements in the standard deviation of the process whilst also delivering a reduction in the process average. In the customer complaints and on-time delivery performance charts one can observe the use of similar control limits.

The point to note here is that it is not always necessary to use statistical control limits. But, where possible, using such limits allows better management and interpretation of process behaviour and its performance. Some organisations go even further and compute separate control limits for different periods of their performance data, as illustrated in Figure 5.6. This is certainly not the usual practice, but where there may be a lot of seasonality in the process it does provide greater levels of control.

Moreover, using time-series analysis in the form of graphs and control charts also provides a degree of predictability as to the future performance of the process. In Figure 5.6, whatever intervention has been made, it appears that the overall trend is reducing. The dotted part of the graph predicts how this trend may continue whilst accounting for seasonality.

There are other more sophisticated graphs and charts one can use, but the general rule should be to keep things as simple as possible. In the above examples we have focused on reporting performance against an internally set target (i.e., feedback control). Sometimes this is not enough, as exemplified below.

Your performance data shows that your current performance is as follows:
- On-time delivery – 70%
- Quality – 99%

If you had to make an investment to improve one or the other area, which one would you invest in?

A. On-time delivery.
B. Quality.

Go to page 88 once you have answered this question.

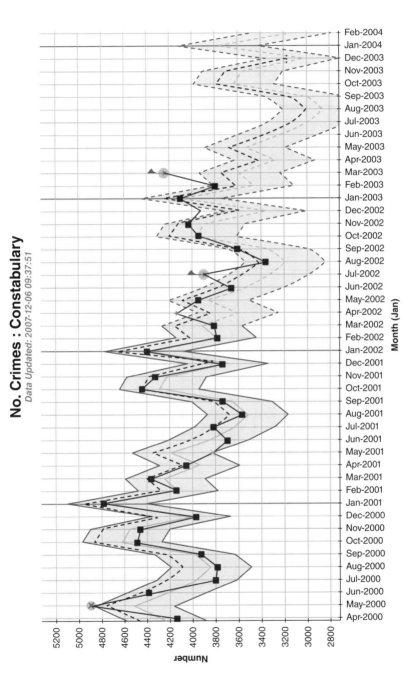

FIGURE 5.6 Number of crimes in a constabulary with varying control limits (courtesy of Lightfoot Solutions)

If you now have additional information from the market that, on average, your key competitor's performance is as follows:

- On-time delivery – 64%
- Quality – 99.9%

Where would you invest now?

In this exercise many people's initial response is that they would invest in improving on-time delivery, which in isolation makes sense as the numbers suggest that your quality performance, at 99%, is OK. However, the picture changes when we introduce the additional information that reveals how the market or competitors are performing.

Let's put it this way, would you ever attempt to drive your car with its windows blanked out and just relying on the internal indicators such as engine revs, speedometer, fuel level, engine temperature gauge, etc. When you are driving you need to know what other cars are doing around you and you adjust your driving accordingly.

This is the same when we are using performance measures. We need to understand how our organisation's performance compares with what is happening in the market, or at least to our competitors. Where there is sufficient data available, more sophisticated techniques, such as box charts, can provide valuable information on how your own organisation's performance compares with what is happening in the broader market. In Figure 5.7 the box chart positions the customer

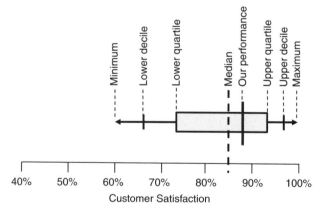

FIGURE 5.7   Box chart for customer satisfaction

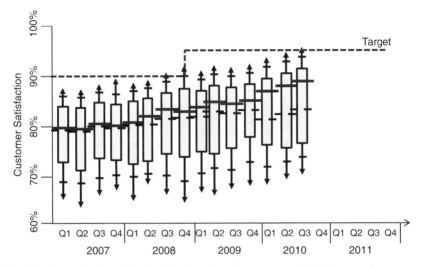

FIGURE 5.8 Box chart showing the dynamics of customer satisfaction over time

satisfaction performance of an organisation against broader data available from the market.

Similar to previous charts, such box charts can also be organised in a time series to illustrate the dynamics of performance over time, as illustrated in Figure 5.8.

However, in most cases simpler and less sophisticated approaches work as well. Figure 5.9 illustrates how one engineering company evaluates and communicates their competitive position with respect to the indicators they feel pertinent. They use the five-point scale on the competitiveness curve introduced earlier in the book (see Section 3.2 in Chapter 3) to position their performance against that of their competitors. They focus on assessing customer-facing and internal-facing indicators. The customer-facing indicators represent how their customers assess their performance and make their buying decisions (i.e., effectiveness). The internal indicators are concerned with the efficiency of their processes. The current performance, in comparison with that of competitors, has been marked with an X and an arrow is used when there is a need to improve a particular performance area, with the head of the arrow indicating the desired future position. Traffic lights (red, amber and green) have been used to prioritise each performance area, with red indicating areas where immediate action is required and amber indicating areas to keep a close eye on.

Essentially, externally focused performance comparisons, such as those described above, provide a good mechanism for communicating performance gaps and improvement priorities. In other words, they provide the feedforward mechanism that could help to shape the organisation's strategic, tactical and operational plans and priorities.

When we discuss such charts, people often ask "*... but where do we get the data?*" or sometimes you get a comment such as "*... that would be OK if we were making widgets but there is no way we can do this, we do not have the data?*".

These questions and concerns are partially valid because to create box charts, such as those described previously, you need reliable data. However, competitive position maps, as illustrated in Figure 5.9, can be created quite simply without a

	Performance Indicator	Comparative Performance					Priority
		Well below average	Below average	Average	Above average	Well above average	
Customer Facing Indicators	Product availability			X——→			Red
	Product reliability				X		Green
	Price competitiveness			X			Amber
	Customer service			X——→			Red
	Delivery performance				X		Green
	Product range			X———→		→	Red
Internally Facing Indicators	Health and safety					X	Green
	Compliance				X		Green
	Warranty costs			X——→			Red
	Value-added productivity			X			Amber
	Cash-to-cash cycle time				X		Green
	Cost of goods sold			X			Green

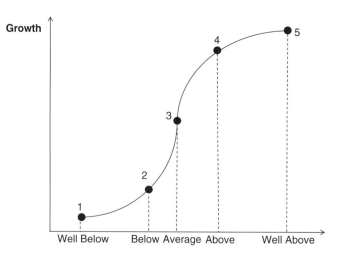

FIGURE 5.9 Externally focused performance comparison helping to communicate performance gaps and improvement priorities

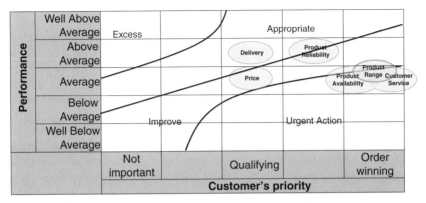

FIGURE 5.10 Mapping performance against customers' priority

lot of data, even though they would be better with objective data. The management team, the marketing function or the sales team should have an idea where they are in comparison with their competitors. If your company cannot do this then I suggest there is a need for urgent action!

Another option is to ask the customers. Some companies even commission independent surveys of their customers, often using students from local universities or colleges. Such surveys produce an opportunity to develop a more intimate understanding of customers' thinking processes. Figure 5.10 maps customers' assessment of a company's performance against how the customers prioritise or value each performance dimension.

Remember, all of this is about communicating performance information. It is not about being clever with complex and sophisticated charts and diagrams. My general recommendation is to keep things simple. The objective here is to have control over the performance of our organisation but also engage as many people as we can in the conversation about performance. Remember, when it comes to performance measurement, less is more. Focus on a few indicators, where possible use graphs and charts to illustrate trends. Use colours in a meaningful way to draw attention to key areas. Annotate graphs and charts to enable constructive conversation about performance. Also, in your performance reports don't forget to position your organisation's performance against its competitors or the market.

5.4 SCORECARDS, COCKPITS, DASHBOARDS AND WAR-ROOMS

So far we have explored how performance could be reported using different, more or less visual, methods. It is common practice to collect key performance information into a single performance report. Although this practice has been commonplace for several decades, the way we report and use this information has evolved significantly over the years. Whereas during the 1990s a report containing all performance information in a single document was not uncommon, today we see increasing use of scorecards, cockpits, dashboards and war-rooms,[1] all with the purpose of creating an environment where we can engage people to have a conversation about the performance of the organisation.

The key purpose here is to make all the pertinent information available in a single place so that it can be seen, shared, communicated, reviewed and acted upon. Again there are no hard-and-fast rules on how to create the right environment to enable these conversations. In this section I will try to impart some of the practices that seem to work well and others that do not.

Although there are no formal definitions for these expressions, scorecards are the most basic performance reports, where we collect all the pertinent performance information, ideally on a single piece of paper. The example below illustrates one of the scorecards used by an engineering company in their engineer-to-order value stream.

A company engineers, manufactures and installs complex engineering solutions. Each product is designed and manufactured as a one-off solution to do a specific job for the customer. Large multi-million-dollar orders are won as a result of a tendering process. Once the orders are confirmed, the company then works with its customers to develop, manufacture and install the engineering solution. On installation, the project is handed over to the customer, at which point the profitability and the customer satisfaction of each project is assessed. However, often the ensuing warranty period would create additional costs as well as revenue opportunities. During the warranty period the customer's satisfaction could also change significantly.

In order to gain better control of this process, the company developed the scorecard shown in Figure 5.11. The three columns represent End-of-Contract, End-of-Warranty and Overall Performance. The report is issued at the end of each month.

In the first (i.e., leftmost) column, the profitability and customer satisfaction results of each completed contract are reported. In the 2×2 matrix at the top of the scorecard, the horizontal axis reports the input vs. output

---

[1] I hate the term 'war-room' as it has a negative connotation, nobody likes being in a war. But it is the accepted term today and I am using it here with some reservations until we can collectively think of a better name.

margin (i.e., the margin planned at the start versus the actual margin realised at the end of the contract). The vertical line in the middle represents the planned margin. Jobs in the right-hand quadrants have been more profitable and jobs in the left-hand quadrants have been less profitable than planned. The vertical axis represents customer satisfaction. At the end of each contract the project manager completes a project handover with the customer, during which he conducts a customer satisfaction review against five points that include: ease of relationship, communications and responsiveness, timeliness of hardware, timeliness of software and innovation. The overall customer satisfaction performance is a function of these five diminutions. The horizontal line on the 2×2 matrix represents the minimum acceptable overall customer satisfaction level. Any jobs that fall below this level (i.e., in the lower quadrants) fail to meet this minimum threshold and jobs above this line (i.e., in the upper quadrants) have exceeded the customer satisfaction threshold. In short, we want to see more jobs in the top-right quadrant and no jobs in the bottom-left quadrant.

The 2×2 matrix at the top of the middle column represents the same performance indicators for contracts that are at the end of their warranty period. In this matrix the dynamic of each job is illustrated by mapping its position at the end of the contract (circle) and at the end of the warranty period (square). The line graphs below the 2×2 matrix provide month-by-month time-series data for the average input–output margin variance and customer satisfaction performance. The third column provides line charts for delivery and financials of the value stream.

It is also worth noting the use of traffic lights on the right-hand side of each line chart to draw attention to the current performance. Also, to make comprehension easier, an arrow is included beside each line chart to indicate the desired direction of travel. That is, in some charts an upwards-pointing line represents a good trend and in others a downwards-pointing trend may be preferred.

Whilst such scorecards work well, enabling conversations between managers in meetings, they tend to be produced just in time for a meeting rather than being available in real time. Whilst it is possible to produce large versions of these scorecards and display them in public areas or meeting rooms, they become dormant and meaningless if they are not updated and used regularly.

Visual war-rooms, cockpits or dashboards that integrate end-to-end performance information along the value stream provide a more constructive environment where performance information can be displayed, discussed and acted

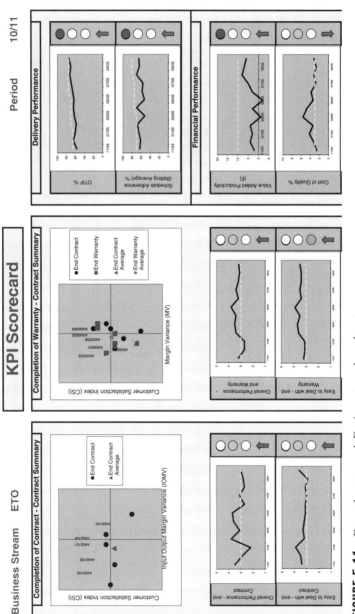

FIGURE 5.11 Example scorecard: Engineer-to-order value stream

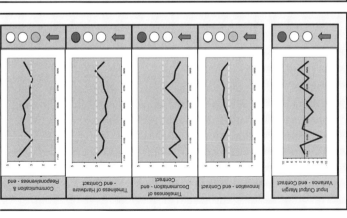

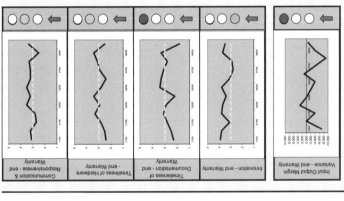

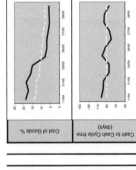

FIGURE 5.11 (Continued)

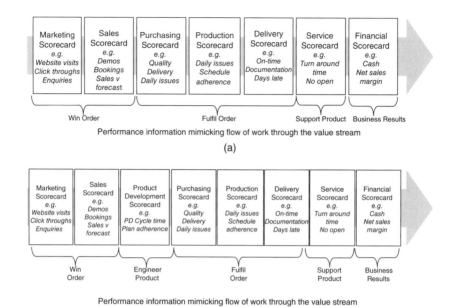

FIGURE 5.12   Structure of a good cockpit, dashboard or war-room for (a) a make-to-order value stream and (b) an engineer-to-order value stream

upon. Some of the best examples I have observed focus on a single value stream and display performance data from winning orders at one end through engineering, order fulfilment and customer support to financial performance. Figure 5.12 illustrates how an engineering company manufacturing high-value precision-engineered products for the consumer market has organised their performance information to mimic the flow of work through their business. The example illustrates two different performance information structures, for *make-to-order* and *engineer-to-order* value streams, respectively.

Other examples include electronic dashboards, where all key performance information is summarised and represented as percentages in the form of traffic lights and supporting information. The high-level dashboard of Figure 5.13 represents a good example of this for a facilities services company. Colour coding is used extensively to represent poor (red), borderline (amber), good (green) and excellent (purple) performance.

Although this particular dashboard provides a snapshot of current performance, the richer information embedded in the dashboard provides further insight. For example, the Technical Services (Reactive) indicator at 11.20% is currently highlighted red (i.e., poor performance). However, the green box with an upward

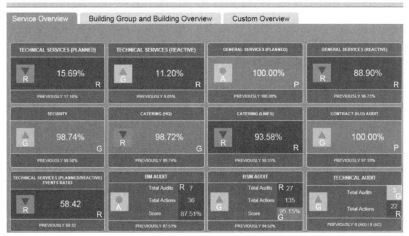

Note: R = Red (poor); A = Amber (borderline); G = Green (good) and P = Purple (excellent).

FIGURE 5.13   A high-level electronic dashboard (courtesy of G2 Business Services)

arrow is showing an improving trend over the past six periods, with the previous period's performance being 9.05%. Such electronic dashboards can also be used to drill down for more detailed information revealing further dashboards or time-series analysis as appropriate.

In my experience there is a distinct trade-off between electronic and manual dashboards. The main advantage of electronic dashboards is that they can integrate with other business systems – data loggers and programmable production line controllers, enterprise and accounting systems, customer and supplier portals – providing automatic real-time updating and replication capability across multiple sites and locations. However, they present two significant disadvantages. *First*, unless they are supported with large electronic displays that are replicated at key locations across the business, they get buried, hidden in computers and are only looked at when required. *Second*, even if they are made accessible and visible through large electronic displays positioned at key locations across the business, the information flow tends to be one way (i.e., not interactive). Even though modern, interactive electronic boards are available today, they are expensive and impersonal. The simple act of printing out a performance report from an electronic system and hanging it up on a manual visual display board engages the person with the information on the performance report. For this very reason, even multinationals with many global locations, who manage their performance information through integrated electronic systems, prefer creating manual paper- or whiteboard-based performance measurement displays in key locations at their facilities.

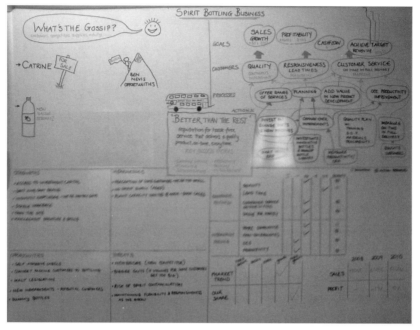

FIGURE 5.14   A simple strategy wall

One of the most effective ways of communicating performance information and engaging people in a conversation about the performance of the organisation is through the use of war-rooms or strategy/performance walls. Conceptually, these are large rooms or walls upon which company strategy and performance information is displayed, reviewed and continuously updated. A simple strategy wall example is illustrated in Figure 5.14.

The strategy wall illustrated has five zones:

- Guiding Vision/Purpose (centre). A short statement of what the company is about and the top priorities acting as a constant reminder and assisting in day-to-day decision making. In this case *"Better than the rest – reputation for hassle free service that delivers quality product on-time every time"*.
- Horizon Scanning (top left). An area where people at all levels are encouraged to highlight any information they feel pertinent. This information is reviewed during regular management meetings held in front of the wall. In this case the company is aiming to capture all the gossip. A competitor is up for sale and there are new business opportunities at Ben Nevis.
- SWOT (bottom left). An area where the strengths, weaknesses, opportunities and threats are captured and regularly updated.

■ Current Performance (bottom right). An area where the company's performance is compared against that of its key competitors relative to customer-facing and internal-facing measures. Market dynamics in the form of market growth and market share (rapid decline, decline, stable, growth, rapid growth) are captured, together with the company's revenue and profitability results over the past three years.

■ Strategy/Action Map (top right). A simple strategy action map links key actions to companies' growth goals using a Balanced Scorecard-like structure that includes key measures and targets, as appropriate.

In this company the weekly management meetings are held in front of this wall. Meetings start by reviewing the gossip and updating the SWOT area, if required. The updated performance information (bottom right) is then reviewed in the context of the strategy map and SWOT information, before moving on to another part of the wall (the progress wall, illustrated in Figure 5.15), which reviews the progress of each action identified on the strategy map. At the end of all meetings the strategy map is updated and a photograph taken of the two walls for the records. Here, strategy making is embedded in the regular management routine of the organisation.

The progress board relates directly to the current performance and strategy map areas of the strategy wall. It has three zones. The guiding vision area once

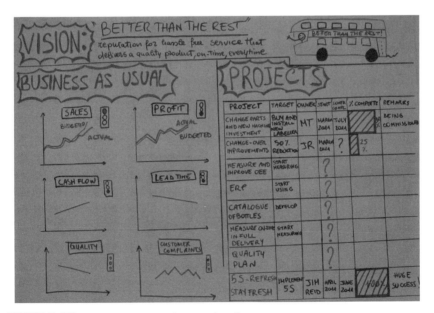

FIGURE 5.15 Progress or strategic control wall

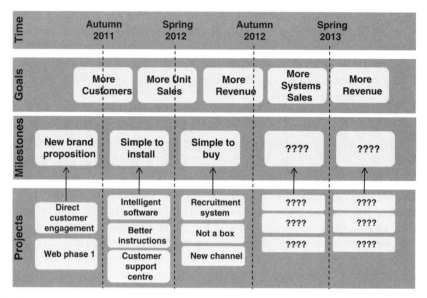

FIGURE 5.16   Strategy map incorporating milestones

again reminds everyone about the purpose of the business. The projects area provides a status update on the progress of each project identified in the strategy wall. The business as usual area includes performance charts for each KPI that is expected to be impacted by the projects. In this case, weekly reviews enable the management team to create a conversation around the prioritised actions/projects and their expected impacts. It also provides a platform for reviewing the impacts of each project against expectations and taking remedial action, if necessary.

In another company a similar structure was employed but with a slightly different layout, using six-monthly milestones to underpin the company's strategic progress (Figure 5.16). Here the strategy map has been replaced by six-monthly milestones. Effectively, this approach provides the company with a strategic development takt-time[2] of six months. In other words, every six months the company delivers a major development that gets the company one major step closer to its strategic goal. In the example illustrated, the company had planned only 18 months ahead and had not yet decided on the nature of the milestones for the fourth and

---

[2]Takt-time is a term used in manufacturing to represent the average time needed to produce one unit of output. For example, if the customer wants to buy 10 units per week and we have a 40-hour week the average time to build a unit must be 4 hours (or less), i.e. a unit needs to be produced every 4 hours.

fifth periods ahead. Each milestone is associated with a number of projects, where everyone in the company is engaged in delivering these projects and ultimately the milestone. In short, everyone is working towards the same goal.

5.5 CREATING EFFECTIVE VISUAL PERFORMANCE MEASUREMENT AND MANAGEMENT SYSTEMS

Many organisations make use of visual management approaches but rarely are they integrated. They are most commonly found in operational areas of organisations, particularly if they have been using lean management tools and techniques. As part of the lean management toolkit the 5S[3] approach, in particular, encourages visual management techniques to create awareness and engage people in issues around operational performance. However, the adoption of visual management approaches for strategic management is less common. Although there are a number of strategic management approaches that lend themselves to visualisation, such as strategy maps and Hoshin Kanri planning (see Chapter 2), they are rarely used in practice for visual management. Strategy maps are often used by senior management teams in workshops and boardrooms, but they are rarely used for communicating strategy and priorities. Their content and logic are usually buried in strategy documents which, even if widely circulated, are not widely read and understood. Hoshin Kanri planning usually uses complex spreadsheets to deploy strategic objectives and priorities for processes, functions and teams. Although they make sense at the time they are being constructed, after a few months the conversations that led to their construction fade from memory and they become harder to explain and follow.

Figure 5.17 illustrates a Hoshin Kanri map that was compiled to deploy the company objectives for the manufacturing function. The company had seven such maps for each one of its functions. Every year the strategy review and deployment process would start with an off-site meeting of the senior managers, where strategic objectives were decided. It would then take approximately three months to deploy these objectives to seven functions using complex matrices, as illustrated. This sort of approach, although robust and effective for the purpose of policy deployment, in the context of creating visual performance management systems has two problems, as illustrated through the following example:

- slow response times;
- ineffective communication.

---

[3]5S is the name of a workplace organisation method based around five Japanese words that are loosely translated into English as sort (seiri), set (seiton), shine (seiso), standardise (seiketsu) and sustain (shitsuke). For further reading see Hirano (1995).

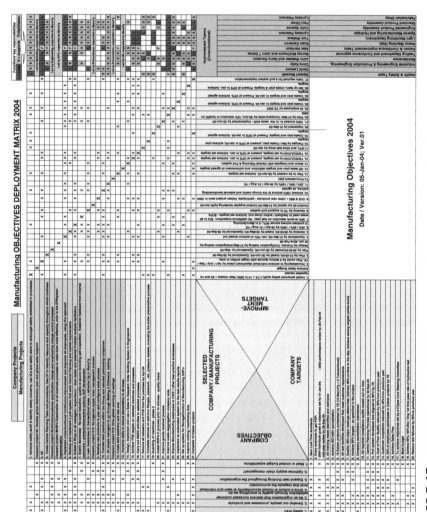

FIGURE 5.17 Hoshin Kanri map deploying company objectives for manufacturing

PROBLEMS WITH STRATEGY DEPLOYMENT

As part of a research project, we were studying how companies deployed their strategy. We were particularly interested in strategy deployment and performance management in times of uncertainty and turbulent change. In working with a company in Turkey, manufacturing critical components for air-conditioning systems, we discovered that after some research the company had developed and implemented a Hoshin Kanri-based approach using matrices similar to the one illustrated in Figure 5.17. When we asked how long it took them to review and deploy strategy, their response was "... *about three months, but with a push we can probably do it in two months*". Our next question was: *So that means, if required, you should be able to review and deploy strategy four times a year?* To this, the company's response was "... *no we can't! Doing it once a year is enough... the process is too time consuming... we wouldn't want to do it more than once a year*".

During the same research project, but with a different company (where the Hoshin Kanri example of Figure 5.17 came from), we queried a particular relationship between company objectives and manufacturing projects to try to understand how the *Guarding of Machines* project was going to contribute towards the *meeting budget* objective and why there was no contribution to the *safety first* objective. The response we received from the manufacturing director was "... *the problem is I really cannot remember the conversation at the workshop where these matrices were produced, but I see no reason why it should not contribute to our safety objective*".

Although approaches such as Hoshin Kanri and strategy maps are effective in deploying strategy, they need to be simplified and made more usable if they are to provide us with effective approaches to visual management. In my experience, strategy maps, compared with Hoshin Kanri, lend themselves better to visual management. The example in Figure 5.18 illustrates a strategy map that was created to replace the seven complex spreadsheets used by the company mentioned above. Although this strategy map did not contain as much detail as the seven Hoshin Kanri maps, it was considered more effective as a continuous reminder of the strategic initiatives the company had to pursue.

The best examples of visual performance measurement systems that I have seen have a number of components in common. In fact, these components emerged from a European-wide research project, *FutureSME*. The purpose of the project

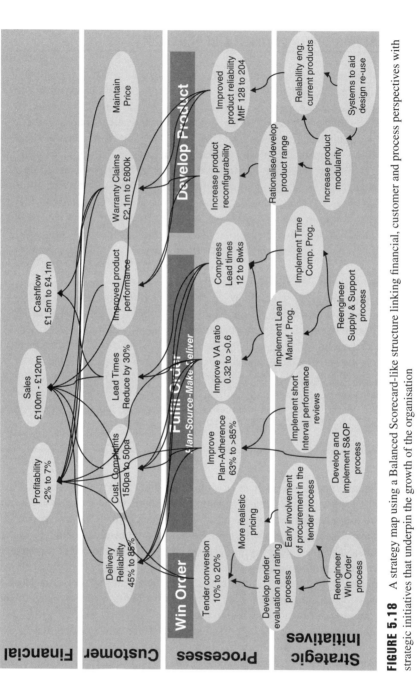

FIGURE 5.18 A strategy map using a Balanced Scorecard-like structure linking financial, customer and process perspectives with strategic initiatives that underpin the growth of the organisation

was to develop the competitive capabilities of European manufacturing SMEs. This involved developing their strategic management processes by embedding capabilities for: *scanning* the environment for changes, opportunities and threats; *analysing* the significance of these threats and opportunities; *developing innovative responses* to exploit or mitigate the opportunities and threats as appropriate; *changing* to implement these responses. The proposition is that companies which can cycle through this *scanning–analysing–innovating–changing* cycle faster than their competitors would be more dynamic and adaptive, and thus better equipped to survive in a rapidly changing, uncertain and turbulent environment. The emerging visual management tools and techniques have since been adopted and used by a wide variety of organisations, reaching well beyond the manufacturing and SME sectors.

An effective visual management system integrating the strategic and operational aspects of business performance comprises three main components:

1. A visual strategy board/wall that
   - provides a constant reminder of the purpose of the organisation
   - engages people in and enables horizon scanning
   - captures and communicates key strengths, weaknesses, opportunities and threats (SWOT)
   - analyses current performance with respect to competitors and the market
   - provides a strategy map linking strategic company initiatives to company objectives.
2. A performance measurement system that visually maps the key performance measures of the organisation and mimics the flow of work through its value streams.
3. A progress board that enables the organisation to track the progress of each strategic project and monitor its impact on business performance.

This structure, which can be replicated in different parts of the organisation at different levels, is illustrated in Figure 5.19.

It is possible to find visual management systems such as those described above. However, more often than not they tend to be fragmented and not so well connected. A key to success is how we design and deploy them. In many organisations such systems are often used for a short time and then fall into a state of disuse and disrepair. In others they become a useful part of the organisation's management system and culture. The key is in the way we design and deploy them. The box below summarises some of the design guidelines. In the coming chapters we will talk more about how we deploy and use such systems more effectively.

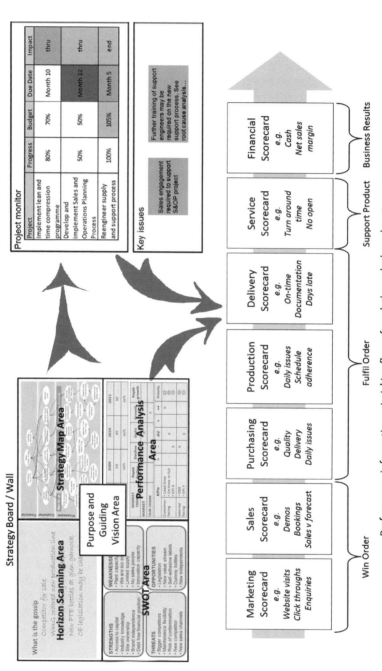

FIGURE 5.19 Structure of a visual management system integrating strategic and operational controls

GUIDELINES FOR DESIGNING VISUAL MANAGEMENT SYSTEMS

- Remember that the whole purpose is to engage people in a conversation about the performance of the business.
- Keep them simple.
- Focus on the few critical indicators.
- Use graphs and charts to illustrate trends.
- Use colours in a meaningful way to draw attention to key areas.
- Ensure that from a distance (5 metres) they communicate some high-level information.
- Close up (from 1 metre) the displays should communicate more detailed information.
- Annotate graphs and charts to enable constructive conversations about performance.
- Where possible, position performance against the market/competitors.
- Manual systems appear to be more engaging than electronic automated systems.
- Handwritten whiteboards seem to be more engaging than computer-generated alternatives.
- Think about where you are going to position them.
- Make them visible and accessible at all times.
- Make them interactive – the more people interact with them the better.
- Position them close to where people work.
- Experiment and learn what works for you and evolve systems to suit.

However, one critical point is that I have not seen a single company which got the design and deployment of such systems right the first time. In the more successful applications what usually happens is: the basic idea of the visual management system is adopted; a system is designed and implemented; the system is used; the company takes its time to experiment and learn what works for them and what does not; the learning is used to evolve and refine the design and use of the system over a period of time. In other organisations where the use of such systems has fallen by the wayside, what usually happens is: a consultant, senior manager or even the parent company recommends such a visual system; a structure is recommended and agreed; the company uses the system, which inevitably does not work; the company just gives up and goes back to its old ways of working; in some cases the new systems are maintained just to keep the senior manager or the parent company happy with no real value to the company, creating additional overheads.

The trick here is to create a system that people value and want to use, and the only way to do that is through involving people, experimenting and learning.

5.6 REVIEWING PERFORMANCE

In the above sections we have already intimated that the performance information that is displayed in the dashboard, cockpit, or war-room-type visual management system should be used on a regular basis to conduct performance reviews. The frequency and how these systems are used depend very much on what works for your organisation. However, over the years I have seen some very good examples where people value the system and want to use it. I have also seen some awful examples where people dread attending performance review meetings. Below I have provided examples of contrasting practices, where one creates a culture of engagement and teamwork and the other dread and trepidation.

Two companies produce sophisticated electronic products for consumer markets. They both have mature strategies and well-developed performance measurement systems. They both use similar visual management systems based on the war-room concept.

Company A

Company A has a dedicated war-room, which is covered in whiteboards, where the company performance is reviewed every Thursday at 9.30 am. A stand-up meeting structure is used that takes around 30 minutes. The performance information is organised, enabling review of the end-to-end value stream performance from marketing through sales, operations and distribution to company financials. Throughout the week, running up to the Thursday meeting, there is a nervous energy in the business. A lot of people seem to be preoccupied with finding out what has gone wrong and why. There is an obvious sense of relief when people find out that whatever went wrong, it wasn't their fault. Every Thursday morning all the senior managers are in their offices early, to update the performance information in the war-room. If anything is below target or expectation, it is marked in red. At the start of the meeting each senior manager stands in front of the board that contains performance information on their area of responsibility. The managing director comes in to start the meeting. He begins at the start of the value stream and systematically questions each senior manager about their performance. If there is anything marked in red on the board, the MD will poke the manager on the forehead and ask for an explanation. He will ask each manager what they intend to do to sort out the problem. He will either accept their solution or tell them what to do.

Company B

Company B uses one of their meeting rooms as a war-room. One wall in the room has the company's strategy wall, complete with milestones. Another wall shows, also on handwritten whiteboards, the scorecard for each critical process in the business, from winning orders, through product development and order fulfilment to business results. The performance of the company is reviewed on a daily basis at a 10 am meeting. Again, this is a stand-up meeting that rarely lasts more than 15 minutes. The focus is on exceptions. Prior to this 10 am meeting there are similar 10- to 20-minute meetings in other key areas of the business (such as sales and marketing, operations, product development and finance); these meetings are used to review the progress and performance in these key areas, and a representative from each area attends the 10 am meeting. The 10 am meeting is attended by whoever is the right person to attend, as the meeting focuses on exceptions, the person with the most knowledge about the issue attends. The managing director is rarely at these meetings. His view is that he can go and see what is happening whenever he wants and if he is needed, he will be invited to the meeting. Quite often, after the meeting is over, a few people will stay on to discuss and agree potential actions that need to be pursued to deal with the issues.

Who would like to work for Company A? Fortunately they have since changed their practices, but that was after losing many valuable people and a management buyout.

The two contrasting cases above are based on real examples, where I personally sat in on performance review meetings to observe what was being discussed. In fact, over the years, I have sat in on many such meetings and rarely are they as contrasting as the two outlined above. In some cases the information reviewed is incomplete and inaccurate, which leads to non-value-adding discussions around what the facts may be rather than dealing with the issues. In many cases companies have well-developed performance measurement and reporting systems, even though not all of them are as simple and visual as those discussed above. Although the information presented and discussed may be very similar, it is often the way these meetings are conducted that leads to success or failure. In the two examples given above, nobody in Company A, apart from the managing director, wanted to be at the meeting. It was the MD's meeting, where he asked all the questions. Nobody volunteered any information and the performance review was only as good as the questions the MD asked. The way the meeting was being run was suppressing the sharing of information and open communication. The MD was the central control point, and the success or failure of the whole system relied on that single point of control. In contrast, Company B had successfully created a system that people wanted to use. Even though the information that was being communicated on the whiteboards was largely the same, the open and inclusive environment encouraged people to engage in conversations about the company's performance. The presence of a performance measurement system, based around a network of motivated people, rather than a central point of control, was clearly evident. What is more, the room in which these meetings were held every day was regularly used for other meetings. The information on the boards was seen as critical but not confidential to people within or outwith the company.

In short, we do need well-developed performance measurement systems that are informative and appropriate to the needs of the business, but it is how we use these systems to manage the performance of the organisation that makes all the difference to the engagement of people and performance in the long term. We will discuss more of the *art* of performance management in Part Three of the book.

5.7 SUMMARY

Performance measures…! Love them or hate them, we cannot get away from them. We use performance measures in our everyday lives, but in many cases we are unclear why we are using them and why we need them. The purpose of performance measurement is to give us control over the parameters that are critical to our business. Whilst using individual measures to understand the behaviour of individual processes or activities is fine, it is the collective use of these measures as a system of performance measures that gives us real control over what is happening in our organisations. When we organise our measures in scorecards, dashboards or war-rooms we create such systems. When our scorecards, dashboards and war-rooms are organised to follow the flow of work through our business processes and value streams, we create performance measurement systems that give us control over how work flows through our value streams. In my experience the best performance measurement systems are organised around business processes and value streams that reflect the work flow through the organisation.

The purpose of performance measurement should be to engage people in a conversation about the performance of the organisation. For this reason, hiding performance measures, scorecards or dashboards on computers is not effective. We need to create visual areas where people can interact with performance measures. Whilst visual performance measurement systems are effective for one-way communication, some degree of effort and ingenuity is required to make them interactive in such a way that we engage people in a conversation about the performance of the organisation. Performance measurement systems need to: bind the organisation towards a common purpose and provide a constant reminder of its strategic objectives and priorities; link strategy to actions; use operational feedback and external intelligence to shape goals and strategies; facilitate internal and external communication to engage people and external stakeholders in conversations about the performance of the organisation; enable the whole organisation to act as one towards a common purpose, encouraging a cycle of thinking–acting–reflecting–learning together; encourage continuous improvement innovation and change, further enabling the dynamic and adaptive capabilities of the organisation to survive and indeed prosper in the face of uncertainty.

In short, we need to create performance measurement systems that people value and want to use!

TIME FOR REFLECTION

- Do we have a shared understanding of why we are measuring performance?
- Are our performance measures aligned with the processes and value streams they serve?
- Do we have too many or too few measures?
- Do our performance reports provide us with an understanding of how the process behaves over time?
- Do we have sufficient facts on the factors that cause good or bad performance? Are we often left wondering or even arguing over the causes of good or bad performance?
- Does our performance measurement system provide sufficient comparative information with respect to our competitors, our market and/or best practice?
- Do we have scorecards, dashboards and war-rooms that enable us to organise our performance information to reflect the way work flows through our value streams?
- Is our performance measurement simple, easy to understand and communicate?
  - Is it visual?
  - Does it act as a constant reminder of our purpose?

- Does it encourage people to scan the horizon and contribute ideas, information and intelligence?
- Does it link strategy to purpose and actions (improvement projects)?
- Are we using our performance measurement system to conduct regular strategic and operational reviews?
- Is our performance measurement system helping us to *think–act–reflect–learn together*?
- Is our performance measurement system evolving and improving over time as we learn how best to use it?
- Do our people, at all levels, value our performance measurement system? Do they use it regularly, both as a part of formal review cycles as well as informal conversations about performance?

REFERENCE

Hirano, H. (1995) *5 Pillars of the Visual Workplace*, Productivity Press: Cambridge, MA.

> ... the purpose of a performance measurement system should be to engage people in a conversation about the performance of the organisation...
>
> ... we need to create performance measurement systems that people value and want to use!

6

Summary: The *Science* of Managing Business Performance

I started this book with the quote *"where there is balance and harmony there is performance"* and conceptualised this as the balance between the *science* and the *art* of measuring and managing business performance. We defined the *science* bit as the rational or technical controls (i.e., the 'processy' things we do to manage the performance of organisations). In a similar vein, we defined the *art* bit as the social and cultural controls (i.e., the way we use the 'processy' bits to manage the performance of organisations).

In this part (Part Two) we explored the *science* of business performance management. In Chapter 3 we asked the question *What are we managing?* and started by understanding the anatomy of an organisation. We have developed and argued that although all organisations may be different at some level, at the most basic level they comprise the same core business processes. Here we introduced the concept of value streams as a purposeful and coherent set of business processes aligned with delivering value to a specific group of customers whilst creating value for the business. We gave examples how, in a business, the failure to recognise the complexities of value streams could result in sub-optimising the performance of the whole organisation.

We then went on to introduce business processes as the universal building blocks of our organisations. We demonstrated, through examples, the relevance of the four core processes (i.e., Get Order, Develop Product, Fulfil Order and Support Product) to any value stream, be it industrial, commercial or public sector. We developed this line of thinking further and introduced the managerial and support processes leading to the universal competitive structure of organisations.

The first key message of this part is that everyone in the organisation has a different mental model of the organisation. The danger here is that everyone tries to manage different things, thus compromising overall performance. Here, the key point is that *we should all try to manage the same thing*. Furthermore, from a systems point of view, *there is really just one thing we should all be trying to manage and that is the universal competitive structure of our organisation (i.e., the value streams and constituent business processes)*.

In Chapter 4 we went further towards understanding business processes. We surmised that *purpose* and *flow* are the two most important things about business processes. We stated that the purpose of a process should align with the competitive priorities of the value stream, and the flow of the process should harmonise with the purpose of the process. Having examined what flows through a process, we went on to explore the anatomy of processes and understand the factors that can cause variation in the process performance. We introduced the concept of measuring the performance of the process using a set of leading and lagging indicators as work flows across the process. We demonstrated, through the use of some simple tools (such as process flow diagrams, process cause-and-effect analysis and failure-mode-and-effect analysis), how this line of thinking could be used to measure, manage and improve process performance.

The second key message of this part is that *everyone in the organisation needs to understand how the key business processes behave and be focused on optimising the flow of work through these processes to maximise the performance of each value stream*. Everyone needs to understand what constrains the flow and, thus, manage that constraint.

We started Chapter 5 by asking the question *Do we need measures?* We concluded that we use performance measures every day, we cannot get away from them and we need them to manage our everyday lives. We also highlighted the importance of designing effective performance measurement systems that people value and want to use. We articulated the main purpose of a performance measurement system as communications. We said that we need performance measurement systems to engage people in a conversation about the performance of the organisation. We provided examples of different performance reports and built these up into scorecards, dashboards and war-rooms that are used to review the performance of organisations on a regular basis. We provided examples of various visual displays providing information on various aspects of business performance, operational as well as strategic. We concluded this section with the third key message, that is *simple and interactive visual management systems that mimic the flow of work through the value stream, whilst seamlessly integrating strategic and operational priorities and measures into people's everyday work, are more likely to be valued and used*.

In concluding Chapter 5 we provided examples of how a similar performance measurement system was used by two companies in two extremely different ways: one serving to disengage and drive fear into people and the other serving to engage and motivate people towards sustainable growth. Thus, our fourth and final message from this part of the book is that *we need well-developed performance measurement systems that are informative and appropriate to the needs of the business, but, it is how we use these systems to manage the performance of the organisation that makes all the difference to the performance in the long term*.

Even though in this part of the book we set out to discuss and explore the *science* of performance measurement, it has probably started to become evident that the *science* and the *art* are intrinsically linked and it is difficult to talk about one without the other. In Part Three we will explore the *art* of performance management, but in doing so we will inevitably touch on some 'sciency' bits.

TIME FOR REFLECTION

- Do we as a team know what we are managing?
- Are we managing the same thing? Or is each one of us trying to manage a different thing?

- Do we really understand the competitive structure of our business?
- Does everyone in the organisation understand how the key business processes behave?
- Is everyone focused on optimising the flow of work through the critical processes to maximise the performance of each value stream?
- Do we have an integrated, simple-to-understand, visual management system that mimics the flow of work through our business/value streams? Is it interactive? Does it engage everyone in a conversation about the performance of our organisation?
- Are we using our performance measurement systems the right way?

All organisations need performance measures but it is how we use them that makes all the difference to the performance in the long term!

PART
THREE

The Art

7

Drivers of Performance

Performance is timescale sensitive…

… What we do to improve performance
for the short-term is not necessarily what
we would do to improve performance for
the medium- and long-term.

n organisations there are a wide range of factors that drive performance. However, some are more important than others. Performance is also timescale sensitive. What we do to improve performance for the short-term is not necessarily what we would do to improve performance for the medium- and long-term. The objective of this chapter is to focus attention on the drivers of sustainable performance, but first we must understand the performance drivers we need to manage, depending on our timescale.

7.1 MEASURES OF BUSINESS PERFORMANCE

Over the years there have been many attempts to develop a single performance indicator that summarises and communicates business performance as a whole. These include:

- EBITDA – Earnings Before Interest, Taxes, Depreciation and Amortisation. A measure of how much profit a company makes with its present assets, operations and cash flow. It is effectively a measure of operating profitability.
- RoI – Return on Investment. A measure of investment gains used to evaluate the performance of an investment. In business terms it considers profits in the context of the capital invested.
- RoNA – Return on Net Assets. Similar to RoI, a measure of financial performance in relation to the value of a company's assets. It is a measure of how well a company is using its assets and working capital. It is more commonly used in asset-intensive organisations, such as the petrochemical and pharmaceutical sectors.
- EVA – Economic Value Added. A measure of a company's financial performance, based on the residual wealth calculated by deducting cost of capital from operating profit (adjusted for taxes on a cash basis).

There is a lot of debate in the literature on the appropriateness of these measures for assessing the performance of organisations. Many argue that they do not represent the full picture – the real performance of the organisation – and that they could be manipulated to make the performance of an organisation better than it is. In this chapter my objective is not to open yet another debate about the appropriateness of these measures and their relative merits and limitations. Suffice to say, at best these measures are a snapshot of a company's performance at a particular instant in time; at worst they can be manipulated to hide a myriad of issues that could jeopardise the future performance of the organisation. However, despite all these debates and criticisms,[1] EBITDA appears to be one of the most commonly used measures to value a business when selling and buying businesses.

---

[1] For an in-depth discussion on the limitations of EBITDA, see Jennings (2006).

Whichever way we look at it, all these measures are a function of revenues, costs, profitability and cashflow at a given point in time. They do not effectively consider factors such as customer satisfaction and goodwill, employee morale and engagement, operational performance factors such as on-time delivery, end-to-end turnaround times, product and service quality amongst many others. So they are all somewhat flawed. They tell us very little about the performance potential of the company (i.e., the likely performance of the business in the future).

In fact, there are some CEOs and investors I have come across who look at these measures and then use a few more operational indicators to make a judgement about the performance potential of the firm they are about to invest in. The four most common questions investors seem to ask are:

- Are people happy?
- Is the place well organised and clean?
- What is the delivery performance?
- What do the customers think?

From a different perspective, during one of our research projects we discovered that using performance measures to manage the performance of organisations makes little difference to the actual performance the organisations achieve (Bititci *et al.*, 2011). We looked at 37 manufacturing companies across Europe. In each company we studied how they measured and managed performance. We also looked at their performance over a 10-year timescale and grouped them as high, medium and low performers in the context of the sectors they were operating in. We found that, by and large, they all measured the same things and they used very similar processes to report and review their performance.

So, faced with all of this, how do we really manage the performance of our organisations? What makes the difference?

7.2 MANAGING PERFORMANCE FOR THE SHORT-TERM (UP TO 2 YEARS)

It is in fact remarkably easy to improve a business's performance in the short-term. You just strip out all the cost drivers. Simply cutting out everything that you do not need to operate the business in the short-term will deliver a remarkable reduction in costs and expenses, improving profitability and making a huge impact on EBITDA, RoI, RONA or whatever variation we use. As an exercise, take a look at your latest profit and loss account and work out your profitability (= profits/revenues). Then cut out all research and development, training and education, travel, marketing and anything else that you can think of that you do not need to run the business on a day-to-day basis. You will be surprised by just how much you can improve your profitability. And this can be done quickly, within the current financial year. The year-end results will show much improvement! If you are lucky, this type of intervention may yield positive effects for another financial year before it all starts falling apart.

Naturally, I am not suggesting that this is the right thing to do. It just strips out the capability of the organisation to perform in the longer term. However, we all know that this does not prevent unscrupulous owners of a business from stripping away its assets and capabilities in order to make the numbers look good so they can sell the business at an inflated price. The sad fact is that when people do not understand the limitations of these top-level measures they are misled by the numbers and poor advice and end up buying a whole load of trouble and stress whilst the seller is relaxing on his luxury yacht in the Caribbean!

Of course, there are ways of improving performance in the short term. Continuous improvement interventions that focus on customer service, minimise non-value-adding activities, cut out waste and improve the quality of products and services will all make a constructive contribution towards improving the performance of the business. However, there are usually two problems with continuous improvement initiatives.

The first problem is that they tend to deliver incremental operational improvements that take time to surface as either top-line or bottom-line performance improvements.

For example, an apparel manufacturer operating in Scotland, selling to major clothing chains, after feedback from a key customer, improved its delivery performance from 72% to 94%. After 18 months the customer's perception was that they still had a lousy delivery performance. This was because nobody told the customer of the improvement. Because things were working OK, customers were preoccupied with other issues in their business and had not taken note of the improvement. It took a high-level awareness-raising campaign to eventually result in increased orders from that customer. But this process took about two years from realising the improvement to seeing its impact on business performance.

Of course, although other interventions can deliver a top- or bottom-line result much quicker, the time lag between intervention and its impact on performance is always there. Sometimes in a business environment where business results are reported annually and in some cases quarterly, the window of opportunity for making investments and realising their returns is limited.

The second problem is the sustainability of the improvement. It is quite common to come across stories where a company has made a concerted effort to improve performance with some astounding results in a very short period of time. But over time, the gains made are lost and the performance ends up deteriorating to previous, and sometimes lower, levels.

For example, a UK-based engineering company was featured in the press for outstanding performance improvement after a week-long Kaizen Blitz.[2] During this week significant changes were made to the way the company was manufacturing its products. The shop floor was tidied up, its layout was redesigned, lean techniques were used to control the flow of orders and materials through the factory – all resulting in significant improvements in quality, cost and lead times. However, I was somewhat surprised when I was asked to visit the company three months later as they had lost all the gains they had achieved and the performance had reverted to previous levels. The management's view was that the company was not ready for a Kaizen Blitz.

[2] A Kaizen Blitz is a rapid improvement workshop designed to deliver results within a few days. It is a way for teams to carry out structured problem solving and process improvement, in a workshop environment, over a short timeframe. Kaizen is the Japanese word for 'good change' and is now the established term for continuous improvement used in the lean management vocabulary.

The ironic thing is that this is not a unique story; there are many such stories from both large and small organisations. Normally, there are two related factors that are at play here: the Hawthorne effect and organisational capability.

The Hawthorne effect (Adair, 1984), in this context, is essentially a symptom of management attention. Suddenly, when management places increased attention on one area of the business, the performance dimensions that are being observed improve. The original Hawthorne study demonstrates that just emphasising management attention on productivity could lead to temporary increases in workers' productivity. Usually the effect is short lived, and once management attention is diverted elsewhere the improvement deteriorates. In fact, this was exactly what happened in the above case. Initially the Kaizen Blitz was conducted with the help of an external consultant, with the attention of the management being placed on quality, service and productivity improvements. Soon after, management attention was diverted to an issue with a new product launch and the consultant who helped with the initial project was no longer on the scene. As a result, the performance deteriorated to its previous levels.

Organisational capability can be defined as the inherent ability of an organisation to do something, in this case sustain the improvements realised. Clearly, the management's view that they were not ready was correct. The company, culturally, was not ready to sustain the practices they adopted. They lacked the capabilities to sustain the improvement realised! Having a performance measurement system such as that described earlier would have helped immensely here by facilitating a continuous conversation around performance. But in itself it would not have been sufficient to instil underlying capabilities to ensure long-term sustainability.

TIME FOR REFLECTION

- Do we understand the limitations of the top-level performance measures we use to assess the performance and value of our business?
- Are we too focused on managing cost drivers for short-term performance gains?
- Are we in danger of stripping away longer-term capability?
- When we think about performance, do we take a longer-term view?
- Are our corporate reporting requirements getting in the way of how we would ideally deal with performance improvement investments and interventions?
- Have we experienced, or are we likely to experience, the Hawthorne effect?
- Do we have the necessary capabilities for sustaining performance improvements?

7.3 MANAGING PERFORMANCE FOR THE MEDIUM-TERM (2 TO 5 YEARS)

When we raise our heads slightly higher and make our performance planning horizon two to five years (medium-term), we start thinking differently and seeing different challenges. This increase in our planning horizon helps us question the things that create value in our organisations, that is the value drivers.

At the most fundamental level, there are three value drivers that underpin the performance of our organisations in the medium term:

- *Product leadership*. The ability to offer customers leading-edge products and services that consistently enhance the customer's use or application of the product and/or service, thereby making rivals' products and services obsolete.

- *Operational excellence*. The ability to provide customers with good-quality, reliable products or services at competitive prices, delivered with minimal inconvenience.
- *Customer intimacy*. The ability to segment and target markets and tailor offerings to match exactly the demands of those segments. Companies that excel in customer intimacy combine detailed customer knowledge with operational flexibility so they can respond quickly to almost any need, from customising a product to fulfilling special requests. As a consequence, these companies enjoy high levels of customer loyalty.

These three value drivers were originally identified by Treacy and Weirsema (1996) when they studied the disciplines of market leaders. Today, in our businesses, these three disciplines continue to serve as the key drivers of value creation, but in a slightly different way than Treacy and Weirsema originally suggested. When they published their book, they had observed the disciplines of market-leading companies throughout the early 1990s and come to the conclusion that these companies focused and excelled in one of these three disciplines: they either provided the *best product*, the *best price* or the *best solution*. They concluded that the organisational capabilities that underpin these three generic value propositions were Product Leadership, Operational Excellence and Customer Intimacy.

However, that was some time ago. In today's ultra-competitive and globalised economy companies are continuously exploring new ways of gaining competitive advantage. It is now quite common to see companies investing and trying to excel in all three of these value drivers.

The relationship between competitive criteria and growth, discussed in Chapter 3, is equally valid for relationships between organisational capabilities and value growth. Figure 7.1 illustrates the S-curve-type relationship between the maturity of organisational capabilities and value. Here, when an organisation's capability is in or around the *market average zone*, small improvements in capability maturity could yield significant gains. In contrast, when the capability is *well below market average*, significant improvements are required in order to realise relatively small gains. Similarly, at the opposite end of the scale, where the capability is *well above market average*, any further differentiation delivers little benefit.

In fact, Clyde Blowers Capital (CBC),[3] a mid-market equity investment company that specialises in buying, growing and selling mid-sized engineering businesses, explicitly uses these three value drivers when acquiring and managing

---

[3] At the time of writing this book, Clyde Bowes Capital had an exceptional track record of creating value in their portfolio of businesses with their first fund delivering 3.4× and funds 2 and 3 expected to deliver 2× and 3× returns on original invested capital respectively.

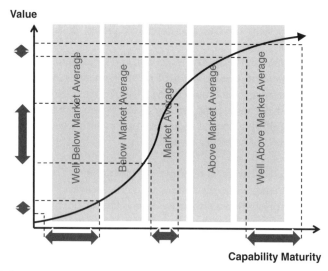

FIGURE 7.1   Maturity of organisational capabilities and value growth

the growth of their portfolio of businesses. Figures 7.2 exemplifies how they positioned two of their portfolio companies at the point of acquisition and prioritised investments for improving organisational capabilities in Product Leadership, Operational Excellence and Customer Intimacy areas.

Company A, an engineering manufacturing business, at the point of acquisition already had above-average capability in product leadership and operational excellence. The company was run by an enthusiastic group of engineers who were motivated by the excellence of their engineering capabilities and the technical features of their end products. It was this enthusiasm and the high levels of engineering excellence that underpinned their position as a product leader in the market. Their engineering excellence was also demonstrated in the pristine manufacturing facilities and the wider operations of the business, which ran like clockwork – underpinning their capabilities in operational excellence. However, when it came to customer intimacy the company was rated as being below market average. Although the company was working intimately with a small group of customers, it did not have the capability to leverage its product leadership and operational excellence to broaden its customer base and increase its sales. Thus, the development of the company's capabilities in the customer intimacy area became a priority. Investments made in this respect resulted in significant growth in a short period of time (i.e., approximately 2× growth in two years).

Company B is a different engineering manufacturing business. In contrast to Company A, its previous owners, through lack of investment, had stripped the

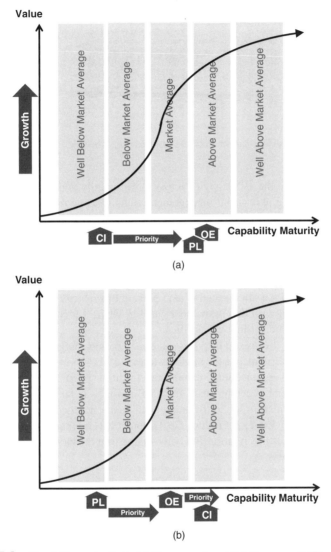

FIGURE 7.2 Capability maturity in (a) Company A and (b) Company B (PL = Product Leadership; OE = Operational Excellence; CI = Customer intimacy)

company of its engineering capabilities, thus undermining their product leadership position. The first priority for Company B was to rebuild its engineering capability and re-establish its product leadership position in the market. This was achieved by establishing a new engineering team and investing in engineering systems, which in turn led to the development of new product ranges. In parallel, investments were

FIGURE 7.3 Organisational capabilities, business processes and value streams

made to modernise the 1950s-style factory, both socially and technically. Use of lean manufacturing and visual management techniques across the operations of the business served to further improve the operational excellence capability of the organisation. The investments were set to yield 2× growth in value but over a longer, five-year, timescale.

At this point you may be thinking how to objectively assess and position a company's capabilities against the market, as illustrated in the above examples. This is a question I am often asked when I present this material in my lectures and courses. I will deal with this in the next chapter, where I focus on understanding and managing organisational capabilities.

At this point, in concluding this section I would suggest that to manage organisational performance in the medium-term (i.e., 2 to 5 years) we need to focus on developing our organisations' capabilities in three specific areas: Operational Excellence, Product Leadership and Customer Intimacy. In fact, these are the three capabilities that underpin the four fundamental business processes we introduced earlier in Chapter 3: Develop Product, Get Order, Fulfil Order and Support Product. Figure 7.3 illustrates this relationship between the four business processes and the three capability areas.

TIME FOR REFLECTION

- Do we understand what drives value in our organisation?
- Do we think in terms of the three capability areas: Operational Excellence, Product Leadership and Customer Intimacy?
- Are we focused on just one area at the expense of others?
- Can we objectively position our organisations' capabilities against our competitors/markets?
- Do we understand where the critical gaps are?

CAUTION

This is an appropriate point for a word of caution to service organisations that think product leadership does not apply to them as they do not have products. Similar to the caution given in Chapter 3, here a product is whatever a customer buys. Consequently, all organisations have products. Service organisations, in particular, need to think carefully about the nature of the service product they offer and how it compares with those of its competitors and the product leadership capabilities that underpin their service offering.

Of course, most manufacturing organisations that have a product also have a service offering that complements the product. In considering their product leadership capabilities, manufacturing organisations should not forget about their service products.

7.4 MANAGING PERFORMANCE FOR THE LONG-TERM (5+ YEARS)

When we consider a planning horizon of five years and more we are then faced with a number of other parameters that we need to manage. Whilst everything we have said so far in this chapter holds true, we also need to be able to deal with uncertainty. Some will even say that they have to deal with uncertainty in even shorter timeframes. Whatever the timeframe, sooner or later we have to deal with uncertainties and changes that take place in the dynamic environment that our organisations operate within. Organisations need to be ready to deal with the opportunities and threats that emerge in their operating environments. They need to develop the capabilities that enable them to detect, evaluate and respond to changes that represent significant opportunities and threats. In other words, they need to be dynamic and adaptive.

Indeed, organisations need to excel on two fronts if they are to perform and grow over the longer timeframe. On the one hand they need to have a focused business model that they deliver efficiently and effectively, whilst on the other hand they need to be able to anticipate and respond to change in innovative ways. Figure 7.4 illustrates a 2×2 matrix that uses these two dimensions of organisational capability and classifies organisation into four categories.

- *Star*. These companies have a focused business model with clear value propositions, profit formula and operating model that is delivered efficiently and effectively. They are also able to anticipate opportunities and threats,

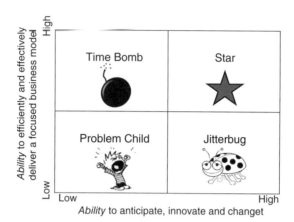

FIGURE 7.4   Organisational capabilities that underpin sustainable performance

formulate innovative responses and change faster than their competitors. Faced with opportunities and threats they can change their existing business models, or create new value streams with new focused business models with little pain or disruption. In short, they are both focused and adaptive.

- **Time bomb**. These companies also have a focused business model with clear value propositions, profit formulas and operating models that are delivered efficiently and effectively. However, they do not possess the dynamic capabilities required to deal with disruptive changes in their operating environment. They are time bombs because all it will take is a significant change in their environment and they will not be able to respond at all – or fast enough – to exploit the opportunities or mitigate the threats. In simple terms, they are very good at what they do but they are set in their ways and find it difficult to change.

- **Problem child**. These companies lack capabilities on both axes. On the one hand, their business model is unfocused and its delivery is ineffective and inefficient. On the other hand, they lack the capabilities required to deal with disruptive changes in their operating environment. Usually they struggle to grow, just about managing to survive. In adverse economic conditions they are usually the first businesses to sink.

- **Jitterbug**. Typically, these are entrepreneurial companies that demonstrate high levels of capability in networking, seeking out opportunities and innovation. They can usually react to opportunities and threats quickly with innovative responses. But because they lack a focused business model, they tend to jump from one opportunity to another and the efficiency and effectiveness of the business suffers.

In short, for long-term sustainable performance organisations need to demonstrate capabilities in two areas. *First*, they need to be able to efficiently and effectively deliver a focused business model. *Second*, they need to be able to anticipate opportunities and threats, develop innovative responses and change with minimum pain. All well and good, but what does all this mean in practice? We will explore the answer to this question in the next chapter.

TIME FOR REFLECTION

- Do we have a focused business model for each of our value streams?
- Do we deliver our business models efficiently and effectively?
- Are we able to sense and anticipate significant threats and opportunities quicker than our competitors?
- Are we able to develop innovative responses to exploit or mitigate these opportunities and threats?
- Can we implement our responses and change faster than our competitors?

7.5 SUMMARY

Clearly, performance is timescale sensitive. What we do to improve performance for the short term is not necessarily what we would do to improve performance for the medium and long term. We need to understand the limitations associated with the top-level business performance measure and balance these with more forward-looking factors that consider social factors, such as employee morale and engagement; customer service, satisfaction and opinion; as well as the organisational capabilities that underpin performance in the medium- to long-term. Also, we need to achieve a balance between having a focused business model that we deliver efficiently and effectively and our ability to anticipate, innovate and change in strategic ways. Remember, the best-performing companies worry less about performance and more about managing their organisational capabilities that underpin performance.

REFERENCES

Adair, J.G. (1984) The Hawthorne effect: A reconsideration of the methodological artefact, *Journal of Applied Psychology*, 69(2), 334.

Bititci, U.S., Ackermann, F., Ates, A., Davies, J.D., Gibb, S., MacBryde, J., Mackay, D., Maguire, C., van der Meer, R. and Shafti, F (2011) Managerial processes: Business processes that sustain performance, *International Journal of Operations & Production Management*, 31(8), 851–891.

Jennings, M. (2006) *The Seven Signs of Ethical Collapse: How to spot moral meltdowns in companies… before it's too late*, Macmillan: New York.

Treacy, M. and Wiersema, F. (1996) *The Discipline of Market Leaders*, Harper Collins: New York.

The best-performing companies worry less about performance and more about managing their organisational capabilities that underpin performance.

8

Capabilities, Culture and Performance

It is the organisational capabilities and culture that determine how people interact with processes that deliver performance.

U p to this point our discussions have been around efficient and effective delivery of a business model (i.e., the vertical axis of the 2×2 matrix introduced in the previous chapter). In Chapter 3, when we introduced the universal competitive structure for organisations, we highlighted the importance of each value stream and the need for clear understanding of the competitive priorities of the said value stream. In Chapter 4 we went further and argued the need to align the business processes to efficiently and effectively serve each value stream. At the outset of the book we conceptualised performance as *people operating processes leading to performance results*. At several points of the book we have also highlighted the importance of the underlying organisational capabilities and culture to long-term performance. In Chapter 7 we started to introduce different organisational capabilities (Product Leadership, Operational Excellence and Customer Intimacy). Furthermore, when we introduced the 2×2 matrix in the previous chapter (Figure 7.4, repeated here as Figure 8.1) we hinted at other capabilities that may be equally important for long-term sustainable performance.

Clearly, organisational capabilities and organisational culture have an important role to play in creating organisations that perform sustainably over time. Figure 8.2 reconceptualises our original *people–processes–performance* relationship by introducing Capabilities and Culture into the equation. It is the organisational capabilities and culture that determine how people interact with processes that deliver performance.

The objective of this chapter is to develop a framework to enable the reader to understand how organisational capabilities and culture drive long-term sustainable performance by governing the interaction of people with processes towards delivering sustainable performance.

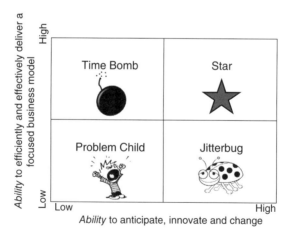

FIGURE 8.1   Organisational capabilities that underpin sustainable performance

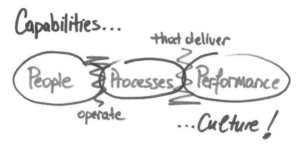

FIGURE 8.2 Organisational capabilities and culture determine how people interact with processes that deliver performance

8.1 UNDERSTANDING ORGANISATIONAL CAPABILITIES

The literature around organisational capabilities is rather confusing. There are many terms bouncing around that sound similar but are different. Others appear different but they refer to the same thing. The following terminology is often found in the literature on organisational capabilities.

- Operational capability
- Adaptive capability
- Dynamic capability
- Abortive capacity
- Learning capability
- Technical capability
- Ambidexterity
- Strategic capability
- Exploitative capability
- Explorative capability

In the following sections I will provide my definitions for these terminologies and position them in relation to the axis of the 2×2 matrix we discussed in the previous chapter.

Operational capability (also referred to as *technical* or *exploitative capability*) is the ability of an organisation to efficiently and effectively exploit its existing resource base. This capability area clearly relates to the vertical axis of the 2×2 matrix and comprises the following more specific capability areas:

- *Strategic capability*. The ability of an organisation to create a focused business model comprising a clear value proposition, profit formula and operating model.
- *Product leadership capability*. The ability of an organisation to develop and deliver superior products and services.
- *Operational excellence capability*. The ability to organise resources to deliver superior operational efficiencies whilst maximising effectiveness.

- *Customer intimacy capability.* The ability to understand markets and customers, and to tailor offerings into solutions that exactly match the markets' and customers' needs.

Dynamic capability (also referred to as *adaptive* or *explorative capability*) is the organisation's ability to explore, integrate, build and reconfigure internal and external competencies to address rapidly changing environments. In this respect they correspond to the horizontal axis of the 2×2 matrix introduced earlier. In practice, dynamic capabilities are:

- The ability to sense opportunities and threats.
- The ability to evaluate and anticipate the significance of opportunities and threats.
- The ability to develop innovative responses through enhancing, combining, protecting and, when necessary, reconfiguring the intangible and tangible assets or resources of the organisation.
- The ability to change with minimum pain and disruption.

Ambidexterity is an organisation's ability to achieve an effective balance between its operational and dynamic capabilities. In the context of our 2×2 matrix, organisations that demonstrate high levels of ambidexterity are likely to emerge as *Stars* in the top-right quadrant of the matrix.

Learning capability (also referred to as *absorptive capacity*) is the ability of an organisation to recognise the value of new knowledge, assimilate it and apply it to commercial ends. In short, it is the ability of an organisation to learn. Organisations with higher levels of learning capability demonstrate higher levels of learning through experimentation and exploration, resulting in enhancement of their dynamic and operational capabilities, as well as ambidexterity.

Figure 8.3 attempts to summarise these concepts in the context of the 2×2 matrix introduced earlier.

TIME FOR REFLECTION

- How mature are our operational capabilities? Do we have mechanisms for continuously reviewing and enhancing our operational capabilities?
- How mature are our dynamic capabilities? Do we have mechanisms for continuously reviewing and enhancing our dynamic capabilities?
- Do we have an appropriate balance between exploitation and exploration?
- Are we a learning organisation?

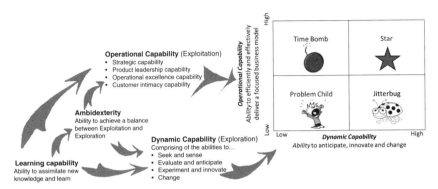

FIGURE 8.3   The relationship between absorptive capacity, ambidexterity and operational and dynamic capabilities

8.2   HOW DO ORGANISATIONAL CAPABILITIES DEVELOP?

In the previous section we argued that long-term sustainable performance is a function of an organisation's ability to efficiently and effectively deliver a focused business model (operational capability) and its ability to anticipate, innovate and change (dynamic capability). We also said that ambidexterity (i.e., the ability to achieve a balance between operational and dynamic capability) is fundamental for creating a platform for long-term sustainable performance. We also suggested that these capabilities develop as organisations learn from their experiences. In short, at this stage there are four kinds of capabilities organisations need to develop:

- Operational capability.
- Dynamic capability.
- Ambidexterity.
- Learning capability.

In this section we will look further into how these organisational capabilities develop and try to understand their prerequisites. The first thing we need to appreciate is that any type of capability comprises two dimensions: *maturity* and *capacity*.

Maturity is about how good we are at doing something. The fact that we may be good at doing something does not, however, mean that we have the time to do it (i.e., *capacity*). For example, an owner-manager of a business may have learned how to engage with his/her markets and customers effectively to develop new business (i.e., the business has a *mature* business development capability) but, because they have to deal with operational issues to ensure that the business they developed previously is satisfactorily fulfilled, they may not have the *capacity* to practise this capability, thus constraining growth. In this particular example *capacity* may be increased in one of two ways. One option would be to release the owner-manager from operational duties to enable him/her to spend more time on new business development or to bring in additional *capacity* with the right *maturity* to help with new business development.

The second thing we need to understand is that organisational capabilities are rather like the sand-cones we all used to play with on the beach when we were kids. The first layer of sand-cone supports the next layer of sand-cone and so on. That is, one type of organisational capability supports the next type of organisational capability and without the foundation layer of organisational capability, the next layer just collapses. In this respect what is important to appreciate is that the four organisational capabilities are not mutually independent, rather they are highly interdependent. Figure 8.4 illustrates this interdependency between the four organisational capabilities identified earlier. It also illustrates the maturity and the capacity dimensions of organisational capability on the vertical and horizontal axes. According to this figure, as organisations learn how to learn (learning

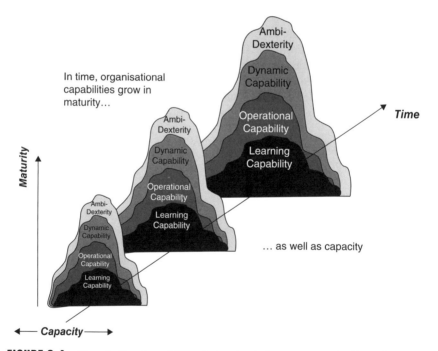

FIGURE 8.4 Organisational capabilities that underpin long-term sustainable performance and their co-evolution over time

capability) their operational capability develops and they get better at delivering a focused business model efficiently and effectively (operational capability). Then, as they have to cope with changes in their operating environment, they learn how best to deal with these changes, what works for their organisation and what does not. They get better at anticipating potential threats and opportunities to their business model. They get better at developing innovative changes and changing. They start to understand the key constraints and barriers to change. They learn how to eliminate and manage these constraints and barriers. As a result, a more innovative, flexible and dynamic organisation emerges. Throughout this journey, in time the organisation also learns how best to balance between focusing and delivering their current business model and dealing with disruption and change (ambidexterity).

In short, over time, as organisations learn, their organisational capabilities grow both in maturity and capacity. But this does not happen by accident. Organisations have to learn to learn!

8.3   LEARNING TO LEARN

Learning capability provides the foundations upon which other organisational capabilities develop. As organisations learn from their own experiences and from their networks, their organisational capabilities develop. As they practise their organisational capabilities they learn how to achieve an appropriate balance between operating their current business model effectively and efficiently and strategic change and adaptation. Clearly, learning capability drives the development of other organisational capabilities, but how do we enhance our organisation's learning capabilities?

This is a question that has been preoccupying many academics and practitioners since the inception of the Learning Organisations concept popularised by Peter Senge (Senge, 1990). Senge's main premise is that as organisations grow, and as company structures and individual thinking become rigid and embedded, organisations lose their capacity to learn. Thus, purposeful interventions are required to reverse this trend and create an organisation that learns. The literature identifies a number of organisational characteristics that serve to create a culture of learning. At the highest level, learning organisations have five main features.

First, they see the **organisation as an interconnected system**. They manage and think about the organisation as a whole rather than as a collection of mutually exclusive, independent parts. They see the organisation as a collection of interacting parts/components/actors in which the interactions result in system-level properties and behaviours not attributable to the sum of the individual parts. Management teams that think about the organisation as a whole appear to perform better than those that think about the organisation as a mutually exclusive sets of activities/departments or functions.

Second, they demonstrate **commitment to personal learning**. This is the commitment by individuals to learning. In practice, this is about learning to learn. Individual learning is rarely acquired through training and education. Most learning takes place in the workplace and it tends to be emergent. At the outset we said *people operate processes that deliver performance.* Personal mastery is about embedding behaviour so that as people operate these processes and experience the good and bad performance outcomes they reflect on what worked, what did not and why. It is this continuous pursuit of knowledge that enables personal mastery to develop.

Third, they have **flexible mental models that evolve** *as the organisation learns.* Mental models are the assumptions held by individuals and teams within organisations. Mental models usually develop as a result of people's experiences – personal or professional. They represent their unwritten beliefs about what works, when, how and why. The problem is that in many cases these mental models develop in a certain context that may or may not be appropriate to new emerging situations. So individuals and teams must be open to: challenging their own mental models; unlearning old and outdated mental models; and learning new ones through experimentation, networking and open communication.

Fourth, they have a **shared higher purpose**. Shared purpose is deemed essential for focusing, guiding and energising learning. In our experience most successful companies have built their visions upon the individual aims, objectives and values of the people in their organisation, rather than those created by the management team and imposed top-down by the organisation. Traditionally, in most organisations, the organisational purpose is centred around financial goals and succeeding over competitors. However, these types of vision or purpose statements tend to be short-lived and, in many cases, de-motivational. In contrast, having a *shared higher purpose* that projects beyond financial goals provides a more profound source of focus and energy. Good examples of higher-purpose statements include:

- To use our imaginations to bring happiness to millions (Disney).
- To improve every company, every home, every life (3M).
- To enrich people's lives through music (Linn).

Fifth, they demonstrate **collective learning**. Collective learning is about the organisation learning as a whole. As the organisation learns, the innovation and problem-solving capacity of the organisation increases disproportionately to the sum of the individuals' learning. Shared learning requires open communication, trust, honesty, openness to new ideas, time for discussion and reflection to create shared understanding. Typically organisations learn by reflecting on an action.

Given a problem, an opportunity or a threat, they first think about the appropriate courses of action, then they decide to pursue a particular course of action, then they review and reflect on the outcomes – discussing what worked, what did not and why. They discuss how the system design can be improved and change the system. In practical terms, it is this cycle that enables organisations to learn.

In fact, what I have discovered is that the very act of combining visual performance measurement systems, such as those discussed earlier in Chapter 5, with an open and participative culture creates fertile ground for learning. What happens is that they enable people to have an open conversation about the performance of the organisation. Together they decide what actions to take and how they are going to implement them. Then they go ahead and implement them. They continue to use the performance measurement system to review how the implementation is progressing and whether it is delivering the expected results. They reflect on the outcomes, discussing what worked and what did not. If the expected outcome is not achieved, they try a different approach. They keep on going through this cycle of thinking–acting–reflecting–learning together (Figure 8.5).

It is difficult to explain the phenomenon of organisational learning in simple terms. Although the organisational characteristics that enable learning are well understood, they interact in complex ways, resulting in organisations with different levels of learning capability. Although Figure 8.6 is an attempt to illustrate the interaction between various organisational characteristics, it is by no means complete or comprehensive. One could probably add more factors and many more connections between them to create a more comprehensive picture. But it will be very messy and probably will still be incomplete.

Essentially, Figure 8.6 is my attempt to summarise the antecedents of organisational learning. In the following paragraphs I have refrained from a rather long and boring description of each component and each connection. Instead, I have tried to explain the picture as a whole.

In my research and practice, working with all of these companies, across several countries, I started to see a pattern emerging that is somewhat reflected in Figure 8.6. Across all the companies that appear to perform well above market average – despite the economic conditions, social and technological challenges – the same organisational characteristics seem to be present. To start with they have an open culture where all information is openly shared inside and outside the company (open communications); they have very few restricted confidential meetings and documents; this open culture nurtures trust and respect; it encourages people to be open to other people's views and ideas (i.e., multiple views and multiple truths); it opens minds to new ideas and new ways of working; it encourages dialogue and reflection, demanding and indeed making time for reflection; this in turn seems to create a can-do culture that is calm and confident; it encourages flattening of organisational structures, decentralisation and the creation of networks, where individuals work autonomously as individuals but as part of a larger support

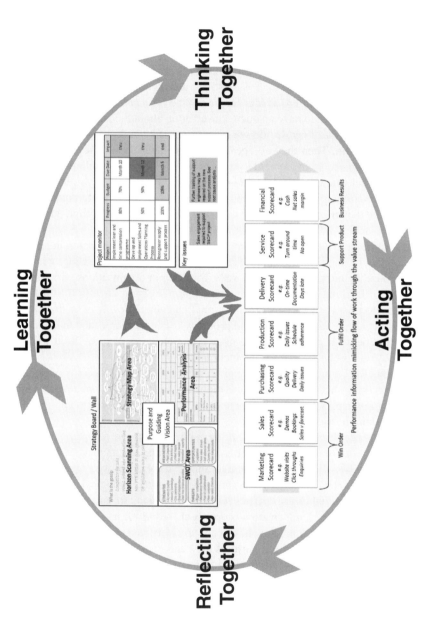

FIGURE 8.5 How organisations learn using visual performance measurement systems

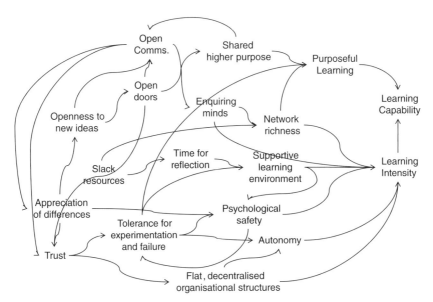

FIGURE 8.6 Interaction of organisational characteristics that drive organisational learning

network, with a sense of shared purpose binding their plans and actions together. Trust, together with autonomy, creates a sense of adventure and experimentation which, in turn, leads to new insights, knowledge and innovations; members network extensively inside and outside the organisation; the richness of the external network brings in new knowledge that enriches organisational learning through sharing and reflection. Guided by the shared higher purpose and energised by the autonomy and psychological safety (trust, respect, openness, etc.), greater levels of engagement and teamwork emerge, ultimately leading to increased levels of sustainable performance.

In short, learning capability is about learning to learn as a team. It is a function of *purposeful learning* coupled with *high-rate learning*. In the organisational learning literature it is a widely quoted fact that organisations that learn faster than their competitors outperform their competitors.

Indeed, it is not just the organisational learning literature that sets out this picture of open participative management that is free from command and control. Other bodies of literature, be it innovation, strategic change, adaptation, operational excellence and lean, either independently or by reference to systems thinking and/or organisational learning, give us the same message. If we want to create organisations that are resilient to disruptive change, we need to create a culture of organisational learning by creating an environment that is open and participative.

So, why is it that we have so many organisations still living in draconian ages, using outdated and archaic command-and-control management? It is no wonder that when we talk about performance measures, performance measurement or performance management people's eyes glaze over and they either want to change the subject or walk away and talk to someone more interesting. Just recently, I was attending an academic conference. At the conference dinner I sat at a table with a group of young academics. We started chatting about this and that and someone asked me what my area of research was. When I said performance measurement, there was a distinct *"Oh, that's boring – it's going to be a great evening, not!"* feeling around the table. As the evening progressed, it became evident that even this group of bright young academics saw performance measurement as a draconian command-and-control mechanism and did not appreciate that performance measurement and open participative management could co-exist.

Clearly we need performance measures and measurement systems to manage the performance of our organisations. But in the midst of the 21st century do we really need command-and-control-based management practices to operationalise these performance measurement systems?

My argument is that there is a better way. There is, in fact, clear evidence emerging every day that *where there is balance and harmony there will be performance*. We will explore this balance further in the next chapter.

Coming back to organisational capabilities, by now you should have a clear idea of the organisational capabilities that underpin long-term sustainable performance. As I mentioned in the previous chapter, the question I am usually asked is *"All well and good, but how do I operationalise this? How do I make it tangible so that I can focus management attention onto managing organisational capabilities?"* My usual response is covered in the next section.

TIME FOR REFLECTION

- Are we a learning organisation?
- Do we think about and manage the organisation as a series of interconnected systems?
- At a personal level, does everyone demonstrate commitment to learning and personal mastery?
- Are we flexible and open minded about our own mental models? Or are we too much set in our ways and our opinions?
- Do we have a shared higher purpose that extends beyond the financial and succeeding over competitors?
- Do we have an open, participative working environment where people feel psychologically safe, trust and respect one another, explore, experiment and innovate?

8.4 MANAGING ORGANISATIONAL CAPABILITIES AND CULTURE

We finished the previous section with a set of questions around how to operationalise organisational capabilities in practice. So far in this book we have introduced a set of capabilities which I would like to supplement with one final area of capability – *Organisational Culture*. Earlier, I also suggested that the literature around organisational capabilities was rather complicated and confused. I then went on to rationalise my own interpretation of this literature in the context of long-term sustainable performance and provided a list of organisational capabilities that we need to manage. At this stage, with the inclusion of organisational culture, my final list of organisational capabilities that we need to manage is as follows:

- Operational Capability.
  - Strategic capability.
  - Product leadership capability.
  - Operational excellence capability.
  - Customer intimacy capability.
- Dynamic Capability.
- Ambidexterity.
- Learning Capability.
- Organisational Culture.

The measurement and management of organisational capabilities is not a new challenge to management. During the 1970s, the concept first emerged in the information systems literature for managing the performance of the information systems function, resulting in the development of capability maturity models. Essentially, a capability maturity model is a statement of practices that describe a level of maturity of a capability area against a predetermined scale. The most commonly used capability maturity scale comprises five maturity levels:

- Uncertainty – basic practices poorly controlled and reactive.
- Awakening – repeatable practices that produce predictable outcomes.
- Enlightenment – defined practices that are tailored to organisational context.
- Wisdom – managed practices that are measured and controlled.
- Certainty – optimised practices that produce leading outcomes.

The relationship between maturity and performance is illustrated in Figure 8.7. As organisational capabilities develop, both in maturity and capacity, after a certain time lag their performance should also be improving. For example, for a basic-level capability in operational excellence the expected on-time

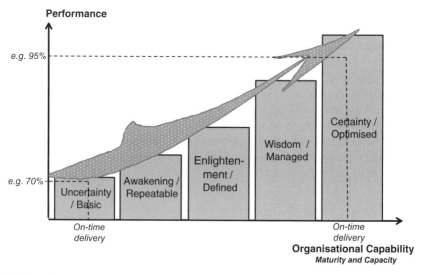

FIGURE 8.7   The capability–performance relationship

delivery performance would be significantly lower than an equivalent operation with world-class operational excellence capability.

Figure 8.8 shows an example of a maturity model where arrows are used to position a company's current and desired maturity level when an improvement is required. The circles are used to position the company's current maturity level where further improvement is deemed unnecessary.

As part of my research I have developed a series of generic maturity models that reflect the capability areas listed at the start of this section. These maturity models can be accessed through www.wiley.com/go/bititci. I have refrained from including these maturity models in the main body of the book as they are likely to change and evolve as our learning in the field advances.

However, at this point I should note that these are not the only maturity models available. There are many more maturity models available in the field. Whatever they are they tend to be generic in nature and will not fully reflect an organisation's particular needs. I would, therefore, recommend the use of generic maturity models, including those at www.wiley.com/go/bititci, with some caution. For the maturity models to be really impactful my recommendation is that you use the generic models as a basis but develop your own maturity models, using your own language and terminology, making them meaningful for everyone in the organisation. In this way you can ensure that you consider what 'good' looks like for your sector, market, region, etc. You can take into account your customers, competitors, suppliers, country, regional economic conditions and so forth, to develop a maturity model that is meaningful for your business, products, markets and economy.

	Uncertainty / Basic	Awakening / Repeatable	Enlightenment / Defined	Wisdom / Managed	Certainty / Optimised
Leadership	Management team working to conflicting objectives	Directive leadership towards a common operational vision that is communicated to all	Consultative leadership towards a common operational vision that is communicated to all	Coaching leadership style with leaders focusing on identifying improvement priorities	Coaching leadership style with leaders focusing on removing the barriers to enable teams to perform Strategising at all levels
Culture	Random fire fighting	Defined roles & structure Accountability Discipline	Defined policies Improvement	Processes teams, measures and continuous improvement	All processes are owned Performance focus at all levels Commitment to learning
Value Streams	Not recognised	Recognised but no clear responsibilities or measures	Recognised but with responsibilities and measures emerging	Individually managed with clearly defined responsibilities and measures	Optimised through integrated management supported with clearly defined responsibilities and measures
People	Functional Unaware Not being developed	Awareness of cross functional processes Development of key people	Cross functional teams Awareness Development of key people	Autonomous work teams Flexible workforce Communication forms Skills gap analysis and development	Training academies Apprenticeship programmes Skills gap analysis and continuous development
Business Processes Improvement	Not managed No formal improvement programmes	Some KPIs Short interval control 5S Visual management	Established process KPIs Short interval control 5S Visual management Emerging continuous improvement practices	All processes are managed Key processes are systematically improved Standardised tool box Common language Root cause analysis Lean tools	All business processes are continuously improved 4 BIKE events pa 12 Mini BIKEs pa Go-Do-IT for all key processes

FIGURE 8.8 Using capability maturity models to manage organisational capabilities

Having said that, some models are more transportable than others. As such, organisational culture and learning capability models are more widely applicable as generic maturity models compared with the product leadership model, which will need to be quite specific to the organisation's product/service. For example, I would expect the specifics of the product leadership maturity model for an engineering firm making complex pumps to be significantly different from that of a firm operating in the food and drink sector.

In any case, my research shows that maturity models serve two purposes. *First*, they enable organisations to manage their organisational capabilities by enabling them to more objectively assess and position their organisational capabilities and capability gaps. *Second*, they provide a platform for discussion and reflection amongst the management and wider team.

The latter point is quite significant. In a project funded by the European Union we used earlier versions of the maturity models introduced above to facilitate maturity assessments against organisational capabilities in 36 different organisations. The organisations varied in size from around 50 people to over 2000 people. They also varied in terms of sectors and regions across Europe. However, when we researched the value of maturity models the feedback was almost unanimous, reflecting the value of discussing, reflecting and learning, as exemplified by the following two quotes.

We have been in business for over 20 years. We have management meetings every month but all we talk about is our sales, profits, problem customers, suppliers, banks and so on. As a team this is the first time we had the opportunity to discuss how we manage. The differences in opinion were staggering. I learned a lot and I am sure others did as well.

Commercial Director

For me, the most valuable part was the opportunity to discuss with colleagues what we each think about our processes. It was useful to understand what others were thinking.

Managing Director

This brings us to the point where we need to discuss how best to use these maturity models. The previous discussion already hints at collective use of such maturity models to gain a shared understanding of the organisational capabilities and potential gaps in capability. In some instances I have seen a senior manager taking the models and doing a self-assessment against where he/she thinks the organisation is positioned. These are seldom constructive and helpful, as they reflect only one individual's view and their own mental model. Often, when they are persuaded to go through a facilitated discussion with colleagues to assess their organisation against a maturity model, they are surprised to find a considerably different (often less positive) result emerging.

Other organisations have tried different approaches. Some have asked each member of the management team to assess it individually and then come together to discuss the differences. This approach may work OK but tends to miss out on the rich discussion as two different members may have given a similar score to a particular capability area but for different reasons. This approach may give you results without having to get everyone together, but it is not as conducive to learning as it misses out on the *discussing together* and *reflecting together* elements of the learning cycle.

The bottom line is that these maturity models are useful and could add value to the organisation in two ways, as explained above. But they require an open and participative approach if their full value is to be realised. The best way of using them is through open workshops with the management team and other pertinent people in the organisation. Sometimes it may even serve to invite representatives from customers, suppliers, business advisers and other support organisations.

TIME FOR REFLECTION

- Are we concerned about our organisational capabilities?
- Do we ever ask ourselves how to continuously improve our organisational capabilities?
- Do we know where the critical gaps are in our organisational capabilities and do we understand how these constrain performance?
- Do we use maturity models to reflect on our organisational capabilities?
- Have the maturity models we use been tailored to the specifics of our own organisation? If they are generic ones, are they appropriate?
- Do we use maturity models to help us discuss, reflect and learn about our capabilities and the organisation as a whole?

8.5 SUMMARY

Organisational capabilities are fundamental enablers of long-term sustainable performance. In organisations, operational and dynamic capabilities develop as organisations learn. The better and faster an organisation is at learning, the faster its capabilities develop – underpinning long-term sustainable performance. An open, participative culture is essential for encouraging organisational learning. Vitally, it is the organisational capabilities and culture that determine how people interact with the processes that deliver performance. Evidence suggests that the best-performing companies worry less about performance and more about their organisational capabilities.

Maturity models provide one way of making organisational capabilities more tangible, measurable and actionable. Using maturity models, it is possible to create continuous improvement initiatives that are focused on developing the maturity and capacity of our organisational capabilities. Maturity models also serve as a vehicle to enable management teams to learn about each other, their organisational capabilities and the organisation as a whole.

REFERENCE

Senge, P.M. (1990) *The Fifth Discipline: The art and practice of the learning organization*, Doubleday: New York.

Organisations that learn faster than their competitors outperform their competitors ...

... maturity models help to accelerate learning and enable the development of organisational capabilities.

9

The People Component

Performance, particularly long-term sustainable performance, is all about people...

From the very outset this book has been about organisational controls. We started the book by claiming that *where there is balance there will be performance*. We then conceptualised performance as the function of *people operating processes*. Throughout the book, even when our focus was the *science* of performance measurement, we provided examples of how people interact with performance measures. From the discussions so far it is quite clear that there are two aspects to managing business performance:

- What we do to manage business performance – the rational 'processy' things we do about measuring, reporting and reviewing performance (i.e., technical controls).
- How we use the technical controls to manage the performance of the organisation (i.e., social controls).

In Chapter 2, when we provided an overview of the performance measurement literature, we conceptualised this in Figure 2.6 (repeated as Figure 9.1 here) and said that we would expand on it later in the book.

Our objective in this and the next chapter is to further explore the interplay between these two dimensions of organisational control.

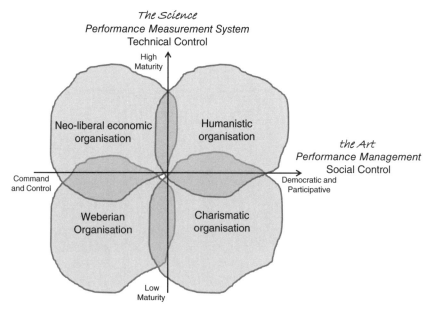

FIGURE 9.1 Managing business performance: technical and social controls

9.1 WHAT KIND OF ORGANISATION WOULD YOU LIKE TO WORK IN?

Try asking some colleagues, friends and family this question: *In an ideal situation, what kind of company would you like to work in?* Once you take out the product- and sector-specific factors, such as one that makes chocolates or one that sells expensive sports cars, and focus on the characteristics of the organisation you start to get a fairly uniform picture.

Figure 9.2 illustrates the outcome of several workshops involving over a hundred people who were asked to respond to this question with one or two words on a Post-It sticker. After a while people started repeating the same words or saying the same thing using slightly different words. The figure is a slightly sanitised and tidied-up version of what emerged from these workshops.

Naturally, different people will analyse, group and rationalise these statements differently. Figure 9.3 is my own grouping and rationalisation, based on the discussions and conversations we held with various groups of people during these workshops.

Of course, it does not come as a surprise to us that people want to work in organisations that offer all these factors; the key question is – as managers, owners and leaders of our organisations – how often do we ask ourselves the question *How well does our organisation fulfil these needs?* Even more pertinent, if these factors are so critical, should we be somehow trying to measure and gauge these factors that are largely vague, open to interpretation and intangible?

FIGURE 9.2   The kind of organisations people wish to work in

People want to work in organisations that…

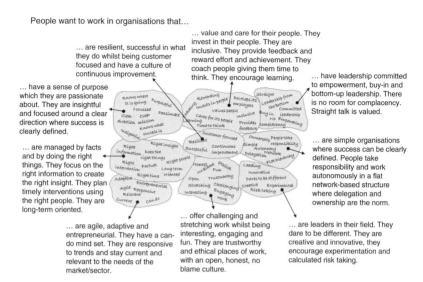

… are resilient, successful in what they do whilst being customer focused and have a culture of continuous improvement.

… value and care for their people. They invest in their people. They are inclusive. They provide feedback and reward effort and achievement. They coach people giving them time to think. They encourage learning.

… have a sense of purpose which they are passionate about. They are insightful and focused around a clear direction where success is clearly defined.

… have leadership committed to empowerment, buy-in and bottom-up leadership. There is no room for complacency. Straight talk is valued.

… are managed by facts and by doing the right things. They focus on the right information to create the right insight. They plan timely interventions using the right people. They are long-term oriented.

… are simple organisations where success can be clearly defined. People take responsibility and work autonomously in a flat network-based structure where delegation and ownership are the norm.

… are agile, adaptive and entrepreneurial. They have a can-do mind set. They are responsive to trends and stay current and relevant to the needs of the market/sector.

… offer challenging and stretching work whilst being interesting, engaging and fun. They are trustworthy and ethical places of work, with an open, honest, no blame culture.

… are leaders in their field. They dare to be different. They are creative and innovative, they encourage experimentation and calculated risk taking.

FIGURE 9.3 Analysis and rationalisation of the kind of organisations people wish to work in

Let's go back briefly to our earlier conceptualisation, where we said *people operate processes that deliver performance*. When we have good people working together to a common purpose but have bad, broken or dysfunctional processes, people can compensate for the broken processes and still deliver a level of performance that is acceptable. On the contrary, when we have a dysfunctional team, no matter how good our processes are, the likelihood is that at best we will get mediocre performance. Figure 9.4 illustrates this relationship; it is probably

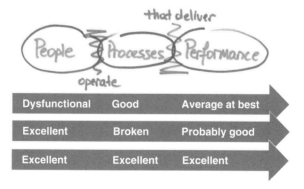

Dysfunctional	Good	Average at best
Excellent	Broken	Probably good
Excellent	Excellent	Excellent

FIGURE 9.4 The people–process–performance relationship

over-simplified but serves a purpose. The message here is that performance, particularly long-term sustainable performance, is all about people.

If people are the most critical aspect in delivering business performance, why is it that we spend so much time getting the processes right and so little time getting the people component right? We really need to understand what is wrong with current practices and understand what we need to do to get the people component right!

TIME FOR REFLECTION

- Do we know what kind of organisation our people like to work in?
- Do we know what kind of organisation we are?
- Do we care? Have we ever asked these questions?

9.2   THE PEOPLE COMPONENT

Sumantra Ghoshal (1948–2004), one of the leading management thinkers of our time, just before he passed away, drafted a very influential, hard-hitting and sobering article entitled 'Bad management theories are destroying good management practices' (Ghoshal, 2005). In this article he claimed that "*our theories and ideas have done much to strengthen the management practices we are all now so loudly condemning*". He went on to explain the rationale behind his arguments by highlighting some of the assumptions that underpin modern-day management practices and theories. One of his points was that a lot of the management theories are constructed on the assumption that managers cannot be trusted to do their jobs, which is to maximise shareholder value. Therefore, managers' interests and incentives must be aligned with those of shareholders; tight monitoring and control of people to prevent opportunistic behaviour is necessary. He suggests that, in management "*we have largely forgotten about the human component of organisations*".

Indeed, Ghoshal is not the only voice that is critical of modern-day management practices. The report entitled *Beyond Shareholder Value* (Williamson *et al.*, 2014) is also critical of the ways we manage our organisations. The report takes a macro view and suggests that "*if we are to build economies that work for all, we must address the endemic short-termism in our corporate culture and the narrow metrics by which success is judged*". It highlights the problems with the current economic model as stifling innovation; holding back investment; negatively impacting shareholder value in the long term; negatively impacting the environment; and creating inequality and economic imbalances. The report suggests that the problem is fuelled by over-emphasis on shareholders. The view is that whilst shareholders risk their investment, other stakeholders risk a lot more. Employees, for example, risk their livelihoods, pensions, families and overall well-being. Suppliers risk their own businesses, their employees and their personal livelihoods.

They also make some constructive recommendations as to how some of these imbalances and inequalities could be addressed. These include: diversification of decision-making boards; employees represented on boards; more women representation on boards, as they tend to take a more compassionate view; external and independent non-executive directors; voluntary stakeholder boards; reforming directors' legal duties; removing the requirement for quarterly reporting; changes to taxation rules (company and personal) to encourage long-term investment

In fact, whoever you talk to – be it employees of small and large companies, middle managers, CEOs and managing directors, public servants, academics or politicians – there is wide consensus that supports the need for reforming corporate governance, both at the micro (inside the firm) and macro (wider economy) levels.

However, my purpose here is not to go into a lengthy debate on what's right and what's wrong with our wider economic and governance structures. You can find plenty of that in recent books and government publications, as well as online. Suffice to say that in my own experience working with companies, helping them manage their performance, I find this view to be largely true but also rather ironic. Essentially, an organisation, by definition, is a network of individuals who have come together for a particular purpose. Without purpose there is no reason for the organisation. Without people there is no organisation. So, it is critical that in measuring and managing the performance of our organisations we do not forget about this human component.

After Ghoshal's words, as practicing managers or researching academics we need to do our own bit by recognising the people component in what we do. We really need to understand what motivates people and what we need to change!

9.3   WHAT MOTIVATES PEOPLE?

From our earlier discussions on the kind of organisations people would like to work in, the kind of factors that motivate people probably starts to become clearer. There are no surprises here really, what motivates us will, on the whole, motivate others. Factors such as fun, challenge, teamwork and autonomy are often quoted as job characteristics that motivate people. People often take jobs that are lower paid and in more arduous conditions because they are fun, more challenging and less tightly controlled.

EXAMPLE: CALL CENTRE

In a project that was funded by an economic development agency, our objective was to explore how we could move call centres higher up the value chain. One of the main concerns of the sector operating in this particular part of the world was the people attrition rate. Call centre employees (called agents) only lasted a few months on the job. When we were told of an exemplar call centre with low attrition rates we decided to visit the place. During the meeting with the management team we asked what their attrition rate was. This was a small call centre positioned in rural Scotland, which probably contributed to its relatively low attrition rate. The centre was employing about 230 people. The manager's response to our question was *"our attrition rate is really good, we rarely lose more than one employee per week"*. That is about 50 employees per annum, an attrition rate of approximately 22% – huge by any other industry's standards. They went on to say *"we usually get young people taking the job as a stop-gap before they move on to something better. We can understand that. But what we struggle with is that we sometimes have people leaving to go and work on a fish farm, out in the open, cold damp weather, going home stinking of fish every day, they get paid less but they say the craic[1] is better!"*

---

[1] Craic, the Irish for *good time*, but also widely used in Scotland with the same meaning.

Employee motivation and engagement is a big area of academic research and expertise. I will not attempt to go into any detail here, however, I will draw your attention to the book by Daniel Pink entitled *Drive – The surprising truth about what motivates us* (Pink, 2010). This also has an excellent YouTube video[2] that brings the key messages to life very effectively. The key message here is that there are six factors that we need to understand if we are to understand what motivates (and demotivates) people.

*First, **people are naturally motivated**. Although in some cases extrinsic motivations help, the biggest opportunity lies in tapping into the intrinsic motivation of people. I remember a conversation on this very topic with a retired senior manager from Shell (the oil and gas giant). His words will always stick in my mind: *"It is very easy to demotivate people, but it is really difficult to motivate them. Sometimes*

---

[2] www.youtube.com/watch?v=u6XAPnuFjJc

all you can do is get out of the way and let people get on with it". In my experience I have found this to be very true. I have seen managers recognising a motivation problem and trying very hard to resolve the issue but ending up making things worse, as demonstrated in the following example.

EXAMPLE: NEW MANAGER

A newly appointed manager of a department recognised that there were motivation and engagement problems in the workplace. To address the issue, a team-building day away from the workplace was organised. The reaction from the staff was that *"we are already busy and cannot afford to take time off to attend an off-site team-building event… it will put us under greater pressure"*. In response, the manager made attendance compulsory, which had the exact opposite effect to what he was trying to achieve in the first place. His determination to solve the problem exacerbated the problem.

Second, **rewards do not motivate people**. The call centre example above clearly demonstrates this flaw. Some people, instead of working in a warm cosy office earning more money, will choose to take a lower-paid job just because they enjoy it more. The traditional output- or productivity-focused reward mechanisms have a negative impact on intrinsic motivation, as exemplified below. This, in turn, leads to unintended and undesirable side-effects and encourages short-term and unethical behaviours. This is particularly true where the task/job has some knowledge content (i.e., the person has to use his/her ingenuity to innovate or solve a problem). Let's face it, today there are not many jobs without a knowledge content.

EXAMPLE: ACADEMIC 1

I was having a conversation with a senior academic colleague about academic performance measures, which are largely based on points collected, based on papers published, and his words were as follows: *"I used to like writing papers and I was good at it. Now I worry about writing papers. I am more stressed about it and I do not enjoy it any more."*

Third, **people need to work at the highest level**. We need to recognise that people are human beings. They think, they have feelings and they are creative. We need to tap into this potential and use them as problem solvers and innovators. We have to accept that someone needs to do the handle-turning work, but even the most repetitive and menial jobs can be enriched if we are prepared to tap into people's creative ingenuity and give them licence to innovate and improve.

Fourth, **people need autonomy**. According to Pink, independence and autonomy is our default setting. He suggests that people need autonomy over what they do, who they do it with, when they do it and how they do it. The very idea that people are managed starts interfering with this default setting, because it implies that some of this autonomy is being constrained.

Fifth, **people need to learn and get better at what they do**. Pink calls this *mastery*. The desire to get better at something you enjoy is a natural human trait. Intrinsically people want to get good at what they do, provided that they enjoy what they do. In the academic example above, the colleague had stopped enjoying writing papers. So the chances that he will continue to develop and refine his skills in this area have diminished significantly.

Some may argue that people are not always interested in getting better at what they do. I would argue that *most* people are interested in getting better at *something* they do. Our problem is that the thing they are interested in may be outside their work. It may be fishing, gardening, running or painting. If we can engage their attention and ignite their enthusiasm about their work, just think what can be achieved.

EXAMPLE: ACADEMIC 2

It was annual review time again and everybody was preparing their paperwork and attending review meetings. One senior academic colleague came to my office to blow off steam after his review meeting. He is a globally well-known figure, with a range of highly cited publications and a series of executive education programmes that generate significant income for his university. Here are his words: *"I was told my publications and industry engagement activities were well above expectations. I have generated over £200k in knowledge exchange income for the university, a lot more than what anyone else has done. But I am told that my main weakness is research grants. I have not had a research grant in my life; I have no experience of writing them and getting them. I enjoy what I do and I do not want to stop what I do."*

Here the danger is that we will be setting this colleague up for failure. An alternative approach to this would have been *"you are good at what you do with your executive programmes, how can we help you to make it even bigger?"* This, I think, would have served to motivate this particular colleague. Instead, all we did was to demotivate him. Eventually he left to join another institution.

*Sixth, **people need a higher purpose**.* This is not the first time we have mentioned the notion of higher purpose. Inherently, people want to contribute towards a greater good. They want to be part of something far bigger than they are. They need an altruistic purpose rather than one that is financially driven or succeeding over competitors. Again, some may argue that this is idealistic and that some people are in it for themselves. I think this is because we have failed to engage their attention on a higher purpose that ignites their passion. In some cases we may never do that. The person may be the wrong person for the job, but how do we know? Have we tried?

TIME FOR REFLECTION

- Are we placing sufficient management attention on the people component?
- Do we rely on financial reward mechanisms to motivate people?
- Do we use people at the highest level?
- Do managers get out of the way and let people get on with what they are good at?
- Do we support people to become masters at what they like doing?
- Have we given our people a higher purpose to contribute towards?

9.4 WHAT NEEDS TO CHANGE?

We are living in exponential times. As we move further into the 21st century, the pace of change is continuing to accelerate globally. We are seeing the global economic power base shifting towards emerging economies. Certain trends that were embryonic just a few years ago seem to be accelerating. We are witnessing the emergence of organisations that collaborate across global multicultural networks.

We are seeing greater degrees of transparency and openness, with information being shared openly across global social networks. It is becoming more difficult and indeed counterproductive to protect/hide our successes and failures.

We are seeing an increasing take-up of the service culture, with examples such as the aerospace giant Rolls Royce no longer selling jet engines but selling power-by-the-hour instead. This is similar to how we pay for electricity at home – as we need it, instead of having our own power station to generate it. Related to this, over the past 20 years we have witnessed a huge shift from manual work towards knowledge work. Today we have more graduates working in jobs that require more intellectual and cognitive skills, providing services, diagnosing and solving problems and innovating. We have less people working in factories doing repetitive manual work, even though our manufacturing output has increased. In effect we are using people at higher levels as problem solvers and innovators and replacing manual work with automation.

We are seeing more and more ground-breaking innovations emerging from small technology-based companies, universities and even from individuals working in their garages, rather than from large multinationals with big R&D budgets. Individuals and small organisations are collaborating, sharing ideas, co-developing and co-innovating using global social and professional networks. It seems that power is shifting from large multinational organisations to self-managing and self-organising networks of individuals. Just look at how Linux competes with Microsoft, powering one out of four corporate servers in the Fortune 500 companies, and how Apache has become the underpinning technology for almost all Internet sites.

And finally, we are seeing the growing importance of environmental and social responsibility. It is no longer sufficient to meet the minimum standards. Market and consumer expectations are that corporations, particularly large ones, are actively contributing to sustainability, be it environmental, social or economic.

Potentially, all these trends have far-reaching implications for the way we measure and manage the performance of our organisations. In their book, entitled *The Future of Management*, Hamel and Breen (2013) summarise succinctly the problems with traditional management paradigms under three headings, largely reflecting our earlier discussions and the views of Ghoshal and the *Beyond Shareholder Value* report. Hamel (2009) goes on to propose 25 grand challenges to overcome these problems. Table 9.1 summarises these problems and challenges.

When we analyse these problems and challenges we see a pattern emerging. Most of the problems can be attributed to highly developed technical controls that are being used in a command-and-control environment. In contrast, the challenges are about achieving a balance between technical and social controls.

The key messages emerging from these works is that we need to align our organisations to serve a higher purpose, a purpose other than profit or financial

TABLE 9.1 Problems and challenges for the future of management (based on Hamel, 2009; Hamel and Breen, 2013)

Problems with the traditional management paradigm		
Inertia	Incrementalism	Disempowerment
Too much power vested in too few individuals, i.e. over-centralisation	Too few individuals trained as innovators	Too many people in leadership positions who aren't really leaders
Monolithic structures	Allocational rigidities that lead to over-investment in incremental legacy programmes	Little discretion over job design
Too little genetic diversity at the top, i.e. a tendency to over-weight experience	Too little slack in organisational resources (time and money) to innovate	A lack of compelling sense of purpose that goes beyond shareholder value
Too little experimentation, i.e. not enough exploration and strategic variety	Too much emphasis on conformance and alignment	Persistent mismatches between interests and assignments
Too much emotional equity invested in legacy strategies	A lack of widespread accountability for innovation and a lack of clear innovation metrics	Too much bureaucracy, too little community
Too much influence derived from the budget resources individual managers control	Risk-averse behaviours leading to over-conservative resource allocation	Too few opportunities for real contribution and personal growth
	Industry orthodoxies encouraging 'baked-in' mind sets and processes	Leaders who are not truly accountable to the led

25 grand challenges to overcome the above problems	
1. Serve a higher purpose	13. Develop holistic performance measures
2. Fully embed the ideas of community and citizenship in management systems	14. Stretch executive timeframes and perspectives
3. Reconstruct management's philosophical foundations	15. Create a democracy of information
4. Eliminate the pathologies of formal hierarchy	16. Empower the renegades and disarm the reactionaries
5. Reduce fear and increase trust	17. Expand the scope of employee autonomy
6. Reinvent the means of control	18. Create internal markets for ideas, talent and resources
7. Redefine the work of leadership	19. Depoliticise decision making
8. Expand and exploit diversity	20. Better optimise trade-offs
9. Reinvent strategy making as an emergent process	21. Further unleash human imagination
10. Destructure and disaggregate the organisation	22. Enable communities of passion
11. Dramatically reduce the pull of the past	23. Retool management for an open world
12. Share the work of setting direction	24. Humanise the language and practice of business
	25. Retrain managerial minds

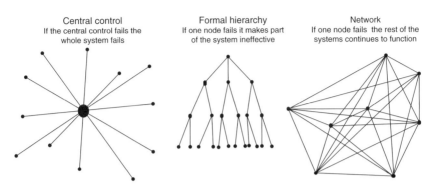

Central control
If the central control fails the whole system fails

Formal hierarchy
If one node fails it makes part of the system ineffective

Network
If one node fails the rest of the systems continues to function

FIGURE 9.5 Networks are more resilient and reliable than a single point or hierarchical control

gains. A purpose that captures everyone's imagination, stirs their passion and motivates them to become part of the big picture. Our performance measurement and management practices need to be balanced to serve this higher purpose. Everyone needs to understand that they do not exist in isolation (systems thinking), rather they are part of the whole. Performance measurement systems, balanced with open participatory management practices, will enable conversations between different stakeholder groups to aid the idea of community to emerge. Essentially, in order to build organisations that are as resilient as they are efficient, we need to rediscover the human component of organisations and achieve a balance between technical controls and social controls. We need to eliminate hierarchies and create organisations that comprise networks of people working towards a common purpose. A network is inherently more resilient than a single point of control or a hierarchy (Figure 9.5).[3]

Visual performance measurement systems used in open and transparent ways to engage people in a conversation about the performance of the organisation, balanced with open participatory management practices, gets us one step closer to the creation of democratic network-based organisations. They also serve to reduce fear and increase trust, where the leaders' work becomes the engagement of people in conversations about direction and performance, letting strategies and technical controls emerge from shared conversations. This dialogue enables organisations to learn, innovate and change faster than their competitors.

Recognising the universal competitive structure (Chapter 3), developing purposeful performance measurement systems that focus on value streams and business processes serves to eliminate complexity. This simplifies communication,

---

[3]For more on recent trends in organisational design, see Laloux (2014).

FIGURE 9.6   Control vs. autonomy

enabling a fear-free, open and trusting working environment to emerge that encourages democracy of information, experimentation and exploration, dramatically reducing the pull of the past. Balancing existing performance measures with things people value in organisations (fun, trust, caring, ethical, creative, etc.) serves to stretch management timeframes, addressing the short-termism problem.

Performance measurement systems that give us rich and relevant information, when balanced with an open participative culture, empower renegades and disarm reactionaries, as well as encouraging employee autonomy, helping to create a networked, market-based platform (rather like a bazaar). This serves to depoliticise decision making as well as enabling better optimisation of trade-offs.

In short, giving people a higher purpose and a system that enables them to control themselves, balanced with an open, safe and participative environment, provides the basis for unleashing human imagination and passion, opening minds and breaking traditional mental models and barriers (Figure 9.6).

With this I would argue that, if we are to manage the performance of our organisations successfully into the 21st century, we need to understand and strike a balance between two dimensions of organisational control, technical and social. Over the past 25 years I have worked in, worked for and worked with a wide range of organisations and people. This, together with my academic insights into the management literature in general and the performance measurement and management literature in particular, convinced me that until recently we have largely focused on developing and practicing technical controls with little attention being paid to social controls.

Whilst our research and practices developed our understanding of the technical controls into a science, our understanding of social controls remains largely a black art. Of course, some organisations are better at achieving this balance than

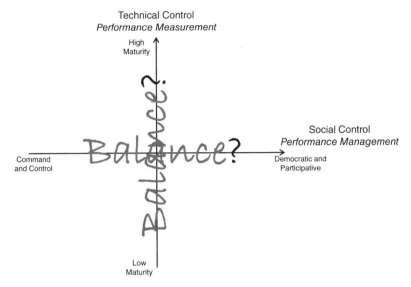

FIGURE 9.7   Balancing technical and social controls

others, as reflected in a recent conversation with three managers from the Irish manufacturing sector.

> I was invited to give a talk at an Irish conference on business excellence. My talk was about balancing organisational controls. After my talk three young managers approached me and we chatted over coffee. Their point was "*We get what you say but how do we do it? We know all about strategy, performance measurement, business improvement tools and techniques but we are not sure about how to do this cultural thing… when we get back to work tomorrow what do we do differently?*"

Generally, where there is balance and harmony there are happy people; where there are happy people (at home, at school, at sport or at work) there is performance. If we are to manage the performance of our organisations effectively, we really need to develop a profound understanding of this balance (Figure 9.7).[4]

---

[4]For more reading on the human component of organisations, motivation and organisational structures, the following sources may also be of some interest: Hock (1999), Sheth *et al.* (2003), Carney and Getz (2009).

TIME FOR REFLECTION

- Is our organisation suffering from inertia, incrementalism and disempowerment?
- Does our organisation serve a higher purpose?
- Are our people autonomous, working in networks towards a common purpose or are we still controlling, hierarchical and bureaucratic?
- Do we have an open, trusting and fear-free organisation?
- When we are designing and delivering change projects and improvement initiatives, are they designed as technical or social interventions?
- Do we have the right balance between technical and social controls?

9.5 SUMMARY

When it comes to measuring and managing performance, it appears that we have forgotten all about the human component of our organisations. What we measure and manage appears to have little to do with the kind of things people value in our organisations. If we manage only the things we can measure, we are in danger of treating our organisations like machines. Of course, in reality people are resilient and they will not let us forget about the people component – that is why organisations with a balance between technical and social controls appear to perform better. It appears that people prefer working autonomously in self-organising and self-managing networks towards a common purpose that is higher than financial gains. They value trust, a sense of community, social interaction, challenge and the opportunity to get really good at something over more materialistic outcomes. However, our management systems appear to take little cognisance of these factors. It appears that whilst our efforts have developed our understanding of the technical controls into a science, our understanding of the social controls remains largely a black art. Thus we need to understand how best to achieve a balance between social and technical controls.

REFERENCES

Carney, B.M. & Getz, I. (2009) *Freedom, Inc.: Free your employees and let them lead your business to higher productivity, profits, and growth*, Crown Business: New York.

Ghoshal, S. (2005) Bad management theories are destroying good management practices, *Academy of Management Learning and Education*, 4(1), 75–91.

Hamel, G. (2009) Moon shots for management, *Harvard Business Review*, 87(2), 91–98.

Hamel, G. and Breen, B. (2013) *The Future of Management*, Harvard Business Press: Boston, MA.

Hock, D. (1999) *Birth of the Chaordic Age*, Berrett-Koehler Publishers: San Francisco, CA.

Laloux, F. (2014) *Reinventing Organizations*, Nelson Parker: Brussels.

Pink, D.H. (2010) *Drive – The surprising truth about what motivates us*, Cannongate Books: Edinburgh.

Sheth, J.N., Sisodia, R.S. and Wolfe, D.B. (2003) *Firms of Endearment: How world-class companies profit from passion and purpose*, Pearson/Prentice Hall: Englewood Cliffs, NJ.

Williamson, J., Driver, C. and Kenway, P. (eds). (2014) *Beyond Shareholder Value*, TUC: London.

Where there is balance and harmony there are happy people…
where there are happy people there is performance.

Whilst our efforts developed our understanding of the
technical controls into a science, our understanding of the
social controls remains largely a black art.

Balancing Organisational Controls

Organisations that balance a well-developed, mature performance measurement system with open, participative and democratic management tend to perform better...

... we need to create humanistic organisations where we encourage team working, comradery and compassion.

10.1   WHAT IS THE RIGHT BALANCE?

This chapter is about balancing organisational controls. It is about achieving a balance between technical controls and social controls. In other words, it is about achieving a balance between the *science* and the *art* of managing business performance. To understand and make judgements as to the right balance, we first need to better understand the dimensions of organisational control.

I have already explained that the literature generally agrees on the two dimensions of organisational control, albeit possibly using slightly different terminology – such as *rational* and *technical controls* to describe mechanistic, 'processy' things we do to manage performance and *cultural* and *social controls* to describe the touchy-feely human dimension of organisational control. In this book, in the context of managing business performance, we called these dimensions the *performance measurement system* (i.e., the *science* describing *what* we do to manage performance) and the *performance management system* (i.e., the *art* describing *how* we manage performance).

Over the years, researchers in organisational studies and psychology fields have studied how organisations and people in organisations behave under different conditions. They developed a number of classifications, taxonomies and models that explain the behaviour of individuals, groups and organisations. One such classification, from Aston Studies,[1] groups organisations under four headings as follows (Donaldson and Luo, 2014; see Figure 10.1):

- Weberian organisations, where jobs are narrowly prescribed; work is closely supervised and governed by tight rules and standard procedures; the workplace lacks the emotional component; the performance measurement systems are usually not so well developed, where a small group of powerful bureaucratic managers act as judges following procedures. Quite often, the fear of discipline and job security drives performance.
- Charismatic organisations, where job enrichment, autonomous work groups, participation and industrial democracy are the norm; often a semi-divine leader lays down fundamental values, gives the vision, while the followers respond eagerly; the performance measurement systems are usually not so well developed, where a charismatic leader can ignore due process and makes decisions personally. Employees are usually engaged, they are team players, empowered by the vision. They work over and above the call of duty,

---

[1] Aston Studies represents the work of a group of organisational researchers from the Industrial Administration Research Unit of the Birmingham College of Advanced Technology, renamed Aston University in 1966.

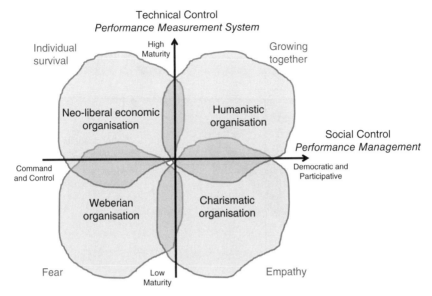

FIGURE 10.1   Managing business performance: technical and social controls and the drivers of performance

regardless of work–life balance. Quite often it is the empathy with the purpose and the leader that drives performance.

- Neo-liberal economic organisations, where principles of free enterprise are used to drive performance. The performance measurement systems are usually well developed and the senior managers' incentives are closely aligned with shareholders' interests. CEOs and managers are appointed on contracts with very specific performance indicators, with challenging targets that are closely monitored. There is usually tough internal competition and internal groups/divisions have to compete with outside providers. Employees are put in a weak position with casual, short-term and sometimes zero-hour contracts, with minimal commitments. Quite often it is the energy for individual survival and advancement that drives performance.
- Humanistic organisations, where there are well-developed performance measurement systems aligned with a shared purpose that often emerges from the values and views of the individuals; human relations, job enrichment, autonomy, participative working and industrial democracy are valued; diversity in gender and culture and equality in pay and stakeholder power are encouraged. In such organisations, quite often the driver of performance is the growth of the organisation as an entity working towards a common purpose.

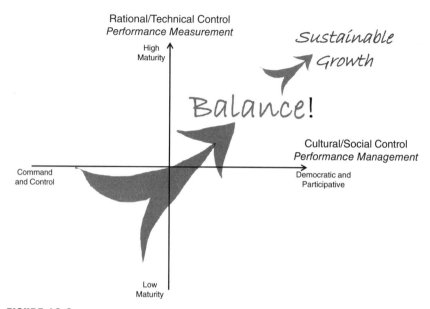

FIGURE 10.2 Balancing organisational controls for long-term sustainable performance

So what is the right balance? It is not difficult to guess by now that in my experience the organisations that balance well-developed performance measurement systems with democratic participative management practices perform better and grow faster than their counterparts; they are more resilient and innovative; they attract and retain the right talent. In short, they are good all-round companies to have around and to work in (Figure 10.2).

However, I should qualify this conclusion. The evidence that underpins this conclusion is largely based on established companies operating in developed western economies, where the knowledge content of the work is significant. Although I cannot claim that these conclusions are universally applicable, I am confident that they would hold true for many organisations worldwide, irrespective of the culture or the context they operate within. Still, there are always some exceptions!

10.2 WHAT HAPPENS WHEN WE GET THE BALANCE WRONG?

In this section I include several short examples, based on organisations I have observed and worked with, to illustrate what happens when we get the balance wrong.

EXAMPLE 1: AN UNDER-DEVELOPED PERFORMANCE MEASUREMENT SYSTEM COMBINED WITH A COMMAND-AND-CONTROL CULTURE

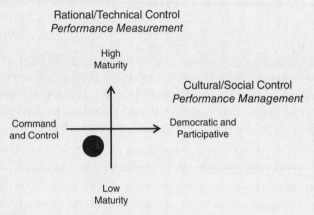

FIGURE 10.3 Position for company in Example 1

This is a company based in Southern Europe, manufacturing consumer goods for an international market. Products are sold through a network of distributors and retailers. The company is family owned and managed. There is no performance measurement system. The family monitors and manages the performance of the company based on management accounts and the knowledge they carry in their heads. There is no open sharing of information and there is little appetite for employee participation. The owner-managers usually tell people what to do and they do it. The company manufactures low-value products in high volumes that are sold directly to various hardware-store chains worldwide. Despite its apparent success, the company remains an SME with around 130 employees. To enable the family to concentrate on growth, during 2005 the company appointed two graduates, one focusing on managing and continuously improving operations and the other focusing on the development of new high-value products. Initially, the two graduate engineers had a good impact, with some early successes that included the introduction of lean and carbon-footprint-reduction projects and the development of new higher-value product ranges. However, despite their apparent success during the early stages, the two graduate engineers stayed with the company a little longer than two years then moved on to join other companies, just at the most productive point in their employment with this company. The reasons they quoted for moving on included wider responsibility, understanding the bigger picture and being part of a wider team. The company then went out to market and recruited another two engineers with a rather similar result. In fact, the product development engineer only stayed with the company for approximately nine months before moving on. Although the operations engineer stayed with the company for just over three years, he also eventually moved on.

In this company nothing essentially went drastically wrong but, despite their best intentions, they did not make the progress they wished. Over the past 10 years, since 2004, the company's growth has been negligible and the owner-manager team is still struggling to build a team of managers and engineers to give them the breathing space they require to grow the company.

EXAMPLE 2: AN UNDER-DEVELOPED PERFORMANCE MEASUREMENT SYSTEM COMBINED WITH AN OPEN PARTICIPATIVE CULTURE

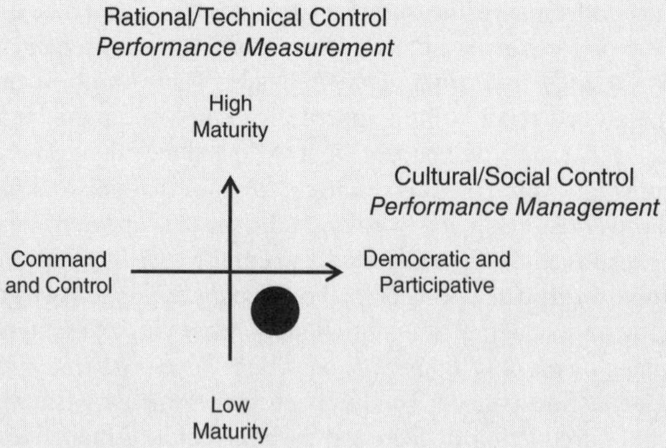

Rational/Technical Control
Performance Measurement

High
Maturity

Cultural/Social Control
Performance Management

Command
and Control

Democratic and
Participative

Low
Maturity

FIGURE 10.4 Position for company in Example 2

Our second example is an electronics manufacturer from Western Europe. Over the years the CEO – with his passion, charisma and industry contacts – was able to assemble a team of managers and engineers who were equally passionate about their product. Despite the lack of any formal performance measurement systems other than management accounts, the company grew steadily, innovating and launching market-leading products and services. It also diversified into complementary fields. At its peak the company had a global footprint and a business plan to double its turnover over the following five years. At this point the CEO decided to take life a little easier, taking partial retirement and appointing a professional managing director to head up the business in his absence. Virtually immediately cracks started to appear in the business. There were disagreements between the new MD and the senior management team with respect to new-product-development priorities, the functionality of new products, growth investments for new markets and technologies, manufacturing methods, acceptable quality levels and so on. When the company launched their next-generation products and services, they were inundated with quality problems and customer complaints. This also coincided with a largely unhappy workforce. Some key long-time-served personnel left the company. The quality problems became widely known amongst the company's customer community, significantly affecting its sales. This, coupled with the ongoing R&D costs and the additional costs incurred by the quality problems, sent the company from healthy profitability to a significant loss-making situation in a very short period of time. At this point their bank started to get nervous and ask questions about their investment. Fortunately there is a happy ending to this story. The incumbent management team acquired the company, but they had to significantly downsize the business and divest its interests to focus on its core products and services. Eventually, the business was grown and became part of a large electronics group.

Clearly the founding CEO – with his charisma and passion for the business and its products – was a key figure holding the team together. Perhaps it was bad luck that his departure coincided with a critical time when the whole world went into a financial crisis and major economies suffered a recession. But the fact that the business only recovered after a management buyout demonstrates the vulnerability of such charismatic organisations.

EXAMPLE 3: A WELL-DEVELOPED PERFORMANCE MEASUREMENT SYSTEM COMBINED WITH AN OPEN AND PARTICIPATIVE CULTURE

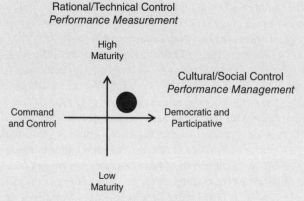

FIGURE 10.5 Position for company in Example 3

Our third example is a consumer electronics manufacturer. Although it is family owned and managed, it has a professional board to oversee the running of the business. In response to a previous downturn in business, the company had introduced a comprehensive performance measurement system organised to follow the flow of work through the business. The company has a discipline of reporting and reviewing measures on a daily basis. All the measures are organised on whiteboards located in a meeting room that is open for anyone to walk in and review at any time. Every day there is a 10 am meeting where key personnel attend to review performance. This is a stand-up meeting lasting no longer than 20 minutes, where the entire value stream is reviewed from marketing and sales, through procurement, manufacturing, distribution and customer service, to company financials. The meeting is usually attended by the senior managers as well as other people, as appropriate. For example, if the materials planner needs to raise an issue, he/she will attend the meeting and raise the issue, which will be discussed and the necessary course of action agreed. In effect, this is short-interval control of the business but not of the individuals. Over the past six years the performance measurement system in this company has evolved to reflect the lessons the company learned and they have refined their control systems. The company now has a new MD, the son of the founding CEO, who encourages the use of the performance measurement system but does not attend the meeting himself, unless he has been asked by the others to attend. The managers in the business value the system and want to use it to help them manage the performance of the business. No one is telling them they have to use it. There is a clear, open, confident and fear-free environment evident in the business. Over the past five years the company has launched several game-changing products, won industry awards and grown faster than its competitors.

EXAMPLE 4: A WELL-DEVELOPED PERFORMANCE MEASUREMENT SYSTEM COMBINED WITH A COMMAND-AND-CONTROL CULTURE

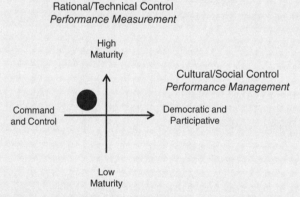

FIGURE 10.6   Position for company in Example 4

This particular company is a utilities provider, operating a number of customer service centres across Western Europe. At these centres they receive two types of call: *value calls* provide an opportunity to sell services to new and existing customers; *failure calls* arise when customers' requests are not satisfied correctly in the first place or customers experience a technical problem, which interrupts their service.

During 2008 the company was suffering from major customer service problems and was being criticised heavily in the media. The number of calls was on the increase, resulting in lengthy queue times for customers, fuelling their frustrations. Against a backdrop of falling revenues, productivity was deteriorating due to increasing call volumes, putting additional pressure on senior management, who were demanding immediate customer service and productivity improvements. Over the years the company had developed sophisticated performance measurement systems. It was able to monitor the productivity of each operator electronically by monitoring how many calls they were able to deal with and the average length of call times. Whilst productivity was reviewed on a daily basis, customer service was being reviewed on a monthly basis through customer feedback (complaints) and satisfaction surveys. Consequently, productivity received more management attention. Individual operator performance was monitored by managers and published in league tables. Operators that failed to meet their average target time of 8 minutes per call were reviewed and retrained, put on a personal improvement programme, warned and eventually dismissed. Needless to say, very few of the operators failed to meet their targets but when we interviewed them confidentially, the reasons became much clearer.

> "... if I have been on long calls and I start to fall behind target I just tell the next caller that they have come through to the wrong department and put them on the call queue again [for one of my colleagues to deal with]. This way I get my call completed under a minute and catch up on my target"

Imagine if you were holding on the phone for 20 minutes to talk to an operator and then you had to wait another 20 minutes to talk to someone else. How happy would you be?

> "... Sometimes we just have to tell callers that our systems are down and that they have to phone back in half-an-hour... I hate doing this but it is the only way I can make sure that I meet my targets"

I have personally experienced this phenomenon on more than one occasion and I am sure many of you have similar stories and experiences. In fact, the employees in this organisation were so unhappy that they went as far as setting fire to one of the premises so that they could have some time off.

Although our first and second examples also have their problems, our fourth example, unfortunately, reflects the behaviours and characteristics of many of today's organisations that combine a well-developed performance measurement system with a command-and-control culture. This, in effect, seems to create an environment where two things happen. *First*, all useful communications break down. *Second*, our personal goal becomes to protect ourselves from outcomes that may negatively impact our well-being and that of our families. We live in fear of being criticised and disciplined, and we go to extra lengths to ensure that the numbers look good even though deep down we do not like what we are doing. Although not all organisations are like this, the sad truth is that many private- and public-sector organisations, in many cases unintentionally, fall into this category. Actually, the literature places a lot of our education, healthcare and financial-sector organisations into the neo-liberal economic organisation category. The box below contains some more short examples that demonstrate what happens when we get this balance wrong.

> In some of our hospitals, to make the death-rate indicator look better, the hospital managers instruct doctors to discharge patients who are highly likely to die and send them home. When the patient dies at home it does not reflect on the hospital's death rate. How do they know that if the patient was cared for at the hospital they would not have survived?
>
> Some schools are preventing children from sitting examinations if they think they are likely to achieve a poor mark, thus dragging the school's performance rating down. How can they be so sure that some of these children were not going to get the results they needed? Also, they are preventing children from gaining a valuable experience even if they do not achieve the results the school is looking for.
>
> In some prisons they keep the number of violent incidents (a key KPI) to a minimum by segregating inmates and minimising contact between them. How is this type of intervention going to prepare these people for a better life in our society?

All of these examples indicate a common problem. It seems that when we have command-and-control management combined with highly developed performance measurement systems we create a dynamic where we do not trust people and monitor everything they do; there is fear and mistrust; and people do anything, even lie, to protect their personal interests. It appears that the purpose becomes survival by making the numbers look good, rather than making a contribution towards the overall purpose and performance of the organisation. Surely this is not sustainable!

The examples provided in this section demonstrate that there are a number of complex interactions between our performance measurement systems and how we go about using these measures to manage the performance of our organisations. *What we measure* (technical controls) and *how we use these measures* (social controls) appear to have an impact on the engagement of people and, ultimately, performance. It is thus important for us to understand these interactions.

10.3 UNDERSTANDING THE INTERPLAY BETWEEN PERFORMANCE MEASUREMENT AND PERFORMANCE MANAGEMENT

One important thing to understand here is that the axes of organisational control are not entirely mutually exclusive. What we do in one has an impact on the other. In concert, they impact on employee engagement and ultimately performance.

In this section I will demonstrate this interplay between performance measurement and performance management through a case study where I had the opportunity to conduct action-research-based *controlled experiments*. This approach allowed the research team to observe the complex interplay between performance measurement, performance management, employee engagement and performance.

The case study is a UK bank (*the Bank*) where employee engagement was a group-wide strategic initiative. At the time when the case study was conducted (2010), the Bank was of the opinion that their approach to performance measurement was having a negative impact on engagement levels. The following quotes reflect their thinking at the initial briefing.

"... initially (2004) we focused on measuring and managing productivity but this did not work, productivity deteriorated, customer service got worse and people were miserable... We then worked with consultants to focus more on customer service. This improved things a little but did not deliver the results we were looking for"

Head of Contact Centres

"... I believe our business is about people, we have people serving customers... I think the real issue is that our people are demotivated... it never used to be like this, my feeling is that over the past ten years we put more and more measures and controls in place, it feels like we are running a machine... people do not enjoy coming to work anymore, they do not smile or chat to each other... I think they feel like robots"

Operations Director

Subsequently, we undertook a controlled experiment with two distinctly different operational departments of the Bank:

Mortgage Services (MS) – responsible for receiving and processing mortgage applications. The key measures that drive activities in this department are productivity (i.e., the number of mortgage applications processed by each unit of resource), quality (i.e., the rigour with which each application is assessed) and customer satisfaction.

Account Management Services (AMS) – responsible for authenticating cheques received. The key measures that drive activities in this department are also productivity (i.e., the number of cheques processed by each unit of resource), quality (i.e., the rigour with which each cheque is authenticated) and customer satisfaction.

In 2001 the Bank implemented the Balanced Scorecard, which developed over the years. High-level goals and objectives were deployed to departments, teams and individuals. The measures used achieved a balance between financial, customer, process and growth perspectives. Visual displays of performance, targets and trends were widely used. Purpose-built performance measurement software underpinned the performance measurement system. Daily performance data was collected and used to produce performance reports. Amongst people at all levels there was a clear awareness of the causal relationship between processes, customer satisfaction and financial results. It was clear that the Bank had a well-developed, mature performance measurement system (i.e., technical controls) and key performance information – such as productivity, quality (errors), customer satisfaction (customer complaints) and employee engagement[2] – was being rigorously monitored and reported.

The teams from the two areas were split into a 'control' group and a 'pilot' group. The pilot groups (14 in MS and 16 in AMS) were facilitated by the academic team with no intervention from their management. The facilitation was focused around giving maximum autonomy and empowerment to the pilot teams by asking them *How would you change/design your job? How would you make your job better?* In other words, the intervention was in the social dimension. The changes in work practices, including changes to technical controls, were designed and implemented by the team members themselves, and then operated for six months to allow the changes to embed. Throughout, the academic team was constantly in touch with the teams receiving informal and formal feedback around the participants' jobs, organisation, customer satisfaction, performance and engagement.

---

[2]Employee engagement was measured using the two main components of engagement (job engagement and organisational engagement); from Saks (2006).

TABLE 10.1   Net change in performance outcomes

	MS pilot	MS control	AMS pilot	AMS control
Overall engagement	42% improvement	4% improvement	54% improvement	16% deterioration
Productivity	8% improvement	1% improvement	12% improvement	no change
Quality errors	7% improvement	no change	10% improvement	3% deterioration
Customer satisfaction	16% improvement	1% improvement	23% improvement	4% deterioration

Throughout the intervention both pilot teams learned about constraints and what was achievable (e.g., in MS the team planned to implement a flexible working arrangement, but concluded that this would not be feasible due to the structure of the work). In another case the team took away the targets, but then concluded that having a target to aim at created a positive focus and reinstated them.

The performance outcomes of intervention are summarised in Table 10.1.

Clearly, this intervention had a significantly positive impact. In contrast to the control groups, in the pilot groups we observed significant improvements across all measures, accompanied by a large change in employee engagement. So what really happened here? How was this possible?

When we look at the changes the teams made to the technical controls, it is somewhat surprising to see how few changes were made. All the measures and targets were retained. However, small changes made to the performance measurement system (technical controls) made a significant difference to how people engaged with their jobs and each other. The following summarises the changes made:

- In MS two changes were made. *First*, the frequency of performance measurement and review (that is the *interval of control*) was changed from daily intervals to weekly intervals. *Second*, the practice of publicly displaying individuals' performance in league tables was discontinued.
- In AMS also two changes were made. *First*, instead of measuring the performance of individual employees, the measurement system focused on the performance of the team as a whole (that is the *resolution of control*).[3] The practice of publicly displaying individuals' performance in league tables was discontinued.

So, how did these small changes result in such significant improvements in employee engagement and overall performance?

---

[3]Resolution of control – the unit of analysis at which performance against targets is set and reviewed (e.g., individual, team, function).

The answer is astoundingly simple. The social intervention we created by giving the team autonomy enabled them to make some small changes that enabled the teams to work as teams rather than as a group of individuals competing against one another. This is exemplified in the following before-and-after quotes collected from various individuals.

Before

"It is embarrassing when you are the bottom of the board and everyone can see it... it makes you feel ashamed and angry... especially when you know some people are making up their performance figures..." (MS Team Member)

"We name and shame low performers, it is not good..." (AMS Team Member)

"... a lot of people lie on their volume sheets... because there is competition between team members" (AMS Team Member)

After

"It is much better now, there is no fear of your name going up on the board... it has taken the focus away from me and is more on the team... my performance discussions are now between me and my team leader..." (MS Team Member)

"Process is more honest as people are not making up times for the volume sheets now" (MS Team Member)

"The pilot has resulted in encouraging teamwork – both giving and receiving help... this helps training of individuals... as a group we have more time to help people out..." (AMS Team Member)

It is clear that the employees were generally dissatisfied with the way performance information was used to create competition between team members. It appears that this practice was encouraging individualistic behaviours, misinformation and dishonesty within the teams.

Also, the management attention on productivity appears to be unbalanced, with less emphasis on quality and customer service. This focus was largely driven by the obsession around volume sheets that had to be completed by each individual on a daily basis. With this way of working it appears that time spent helping a colleague can have a negative impact on an individual's performance, thus further encouraging individualism and discouraging teamwork – as exemplified by the following quotes.

Before

"... there is too much focus on the volume sheets... you get penalised for helping people as this looks bad on your volume sheet" (MS Team Member)

"Management focus on quantity rather than quality... we are rushing to achieve targets so errors are being made" (MS Team Member)

"Time pressures are too much so we don't have time to do extra things" (MS Team Member)

"Different types of tasks have different times, so everyday can be different depending on what tasks you are doing but no one (managers) looks at the content of the work just the volume of work to do" (MS Team Member)

After

"... now we have more time to get the job done right first time instead of rushing it and getting it wrong and then someone needs to do it again when it comes back in a day or so" (MS Team Member)

"I seem to have more time to spend with my teammates... not just social-ising but also learning from them" (MS Team Member)

"I can now delegate tasks whereas before this didn't happen... the team seems to have more ownership of tasks" (MS Team Leader)

The removal of practices promoting internal competition, together with moderation of control from daily to weekly intervals, seems to have created a more relaxed environment where people feel less time pressure, they are able to focus on getting the job done right first time as well as taking on additional tasks previously undertaken by the team leader.

Likewise, it appears that the interval of control (i.e., weekly rather than daily targets and reviews) is more appropriate for the process that is being managed.

Here, as a result of the changes, the pilot teams are clearly feeling more relaxed and empowered. They are in control of balancing productivity, quality and customer service. They also take more ownership of tasks usually undertaken by team leaders (i.e., the more problematic and complex jobs), as well as taking more time to help and develop each other. In short, their jobs are enlarged.

There also appears to be an issue around trust and empowerment between management and the team. The team members, with an average service of 14 years, felt that they were not being trusted to do the jobs. The removal of practices that encourage internal completion, as well as relaxation of the resolution of control from an individual to the team level, resulted in a feeling of empowerment; a better balance between productivity, quality and customer service; reduced time pressures; and more time for support and training activities.

Before

"*... we are not trusted to do our jobs...*" (AMS Team Member)

"*We have years of experience but we still have no power over what we do... we can't even go to the bathroom without it going on your sheet... it's like being children*" (AMS Team Member)

After

"*People in the pilot are more keen to take on problems whereas people in the control area want to get rid of the problem... We are more empowered to solve problems*" (AMS Team Member)

"*Complaints have reduced as there is more chance to investigate fraud*" (AMS Team Member)

"*We now get more time to do updates; e-mails, compliance and training is up to date*" (AMS Team Leader)

A common theme that has been running through the above discussion is the perception of time pressure. Both pilot groups felt that the time pressures were not so much of an issue as before. It appears that changes have resulted in more time being created. It is believed that some of this extra time is real, for example created as a result of the elimination of volume sheets and a reduction in failure demand (i.e., getting more jobs right first time). However, at least some of this extra time is psychological, created by the removal of time pressures as exemplified by the

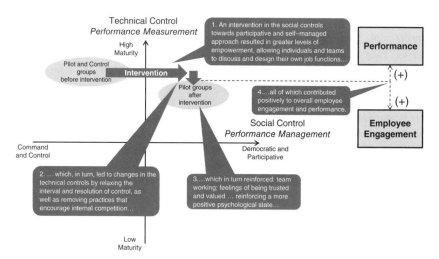

FIGURE 10.7 The interplay between performance measurement, performance management, employee engagement and performance

following quote from one of the senior managers "… *due to the pilot productivity improved, quality and customer service improved… so people are doing more work in the same timeframe and they are saying that they have more time to help each other and be involved in wider activities…*".

It is clear that the Bank had a well-developed (mature) performance measurement system, which was being used in a directive manner with prescribed activities and tight controls to create internal competition, positioning the Bank in the top-left quadrant of our framework. The findings demonstrate that an intervention in social controls towards a more democratic and participative approach has led to a few small changes in technical controls, by relaxing the interval and resolution of control as well as removing the emphasis on internal competition. This, in turn, has resulted in improved employee engagement and performance (productivity, quality and customer satisfaction). Figure 10.7 summarises the interplay we observed between performance measurement, performance management, employee engagement and performance.

10.4 BALANCING ORGANISATIONAL CONTROLS: DO'S AND DON'TS

It appears that in today's contemporary organisations we need performance measures; we cannot get away from them! However, it is also apparent that a performance measurement intervention, which is a tightening of technical controls,

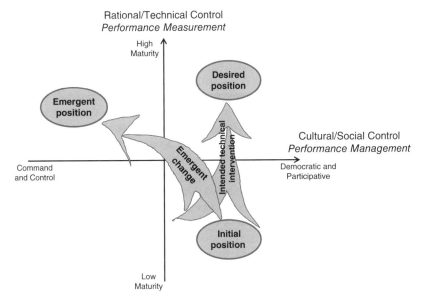

FIGURE 10.8 Emergent interventions in the absence of a balancing social intervention

could inadvertently result in a tightening of performance management practices (social controls) with negative impact on engagement and performance – unless supported by a purposeful social intervention. Figure 10.8 attempts to illustrate this dynamic. It implies that a technical intervention, such as the introduction of an improved performance measurement system, should be balanced with a social intervention if we are to avoid undesirable side-effects.

The inherent characteristics of the processes we are attempting to manage have an impact on the design of the performance measurement systems. Performance measurement systems designed without due recognition of these characteristics would have a negative impact on engagement and performance. People operating the process day in, day out are best placed to understand these characteristics. We should, therefore, educate and train our people and trust them to develop a performance measurement system that works for them. One that they value and want to use rather than one that the management wants to use to monitor employee performance. After all, what matters is that the process performs. We need to avoid creating a 'big brother watching you' feeling.

Another question that arises is whether we should be using performance measurement systems to make a judgement on individuals' performance. The minute we try to do this, the purpose of the system becomes one of monitoring and control rather than learning and improvement. If we want to learn and improve the performance of the process, the value stream and, ultimately, the business then we need to look at performance measurement as a tool that enables learning and growth. It is, therefore, fruitless to use performance measures to make a judgement on individuals' performance. Rather, we should be focused on designing performance measures that help people at all levels to learn about the process and manage the performance of the business. In short, we should learn to use performance measures in a formative mode rather than in a judgemental mode.

We should also ask ourselves if our performance measurement systems, or the way we use them, are creating internal competition amongst people. Whilst we need to recognise that creating an amount of internal competition is inevitable and indeed healthy, creating an environment where people feel they compete with one another every minute of every day is really not helpful. It simply encourages an individualistic behaviour and destroys any team spirit. In organisations, due to their structure, people feel that they are in competition for advancement and promotion in any case. It is pointless to reinforce this feeling any further. The Bank example in the previous section provided a very good illustration of how some small changes that eliminate league tables served to create a more positive environment for team working, caring and helping each other both in a professional and a social context.

There are numerous other examples of how performance measurement systems are destroying team working and encouraging individualistic behaviours, and academia is one of them. In Italy, for example, the impact factor of the papers an academic publishes are divided by the number of authors and then summed up to rate the quality of an academic's research. This encourages two types of behaviour. *First*, it encourages an academic to publish many mediocre papers instead of one game-changing paper in their career, because mediocre papers are a lot easier to publish. *Second*, it discourages them from collaborating with their academic colleagues, because having just one other author would simply half the points they get for that paper. I am afraid in the UK we are not much better, as publishing with a colleague from the same department or school is distinctly discouraged – the UK's Research Excellence Framework allows for only one of the authors to be credited for the paper. Consequently, people choose to collaborate and publish with colleagues from different institutions.

The nature of the performance measure can, at times, encourage an imbalance in management attention. For instance, in the Bank example above there was a distinct imbalance between productivity and customer satisfaction measures. Whilst both were being measured, the fact that it was possible to measure the productivity of each employee on a daily or even hourly basis attracted more management attention to managing productivity. In contrast, the customer satisfaction measure was being reported on a weekly basis for the entire team, consequently attracting less management attention. Creating an environment where people did not feel under pressure to deliver a particular number in a short time interval enabled the team to better manage this balance themselves. So, the tight controls were effectively skewing management attention.

Finally, it is more productive to design interventions considering both the social and technical dimensions of control. In some contexts, such as the Bank example above, a social intervention is all that may be required to fine-tune and optimise the existing performance measurement system. However, interventions that are purely of a technical nature, in my experience, are rarely sustainable. All they achieve is to create a Hawthorne effect, delivering some short-term gains which in almost all cases erode over time; in some cases performance deteriorates to levels lower than they were at the outset.

TIME FOR REFLECTION

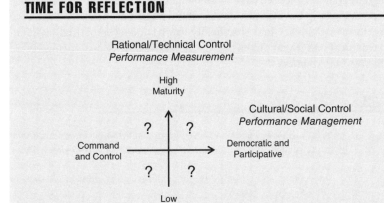

Rational/Technical Control
Performance Measurement

High
Maturity

Cultural/Social Control
Performance Management

Command
and Control

Democratic and
Participative

Low
Maturity

FIGURE 10.9 Where is your organisation positioned?

- Where does our organisation sit in the performance measurement versus management matrix?
- Do we have the right balance between performance measurement (technical controls) and performance management (social controls)?
- We may have a balanced set of performance measures (as in the Balanced Scorecard), but is our management attention balanced?
- Are most of our interventions technically focused without due attention to the social dimension?
- Do we purposefully design our interventions to achieve a balance between technical and social controls?
- Have we ever carried out or considered a social intervention by empowering our people and giving them some autonomy?

10.5 SUMMARY

This chapter has been about balancing organisational controls. We started by surmising that, if we are to create organisations that are capable of delivering long-term sustainable performance then we need to balance a well-developed, mature performance measurement system with open, participative and democratic management. In short, we need to create humanistic organisations where we encourage team working, comradery and a sense of belonging.

We then went on to demonstrate, through some examples, what can happen when we do not have the right balance. All examples are based on real organisations I have worked with, or at least observed, over time. I have kept their identities confidential to protect the innocent and to safeguard confidentiality.

Through these examples we have not only demonstrated what happens when the balance goes wrong but also demonstrated the impact of interventions on the behaviour of organisations. More specifically, we have conceptualised interventions into technical and social dimensions, which raises the question *How do we design effective interventions?*

REFERENCES

Donaldson, L. & Luo, B.N. (2014) The Aston Programme contribution to organizational research: A literature review, *International Journal of Management Reviews*, 16(1), 84–104.

Saks, A.M. (2006) Antecedents and consequences of employee engagement, *Journal of Managerial Psychology*, 21(7), 600–619.

Failing to achieve the right balance between social and technical controls results in bad things – like: poor customer service, misinformation, uninspiring work – which ultimately impacts on performance...

... we need to better understand how to design performance improvement interventions that deliver sustainable results.

11

Summary: The *Art* of Managing Business Performance

started this book with the quote *"where there is balance and harmony there is performance"* and conceptualised this as the balance between the *science* and the *art* of measuring and managing business performance. We defined the *science* bit as the rational or technical controls (i.e., the 'processy' things we do to manage the performance of organisations). In a similar vein, we defined the *art* bit as the social and cultural controls (i.e., the way we use the 'processy' bits to manage the performance of organisations).

In this part (Part Three) we explored the *art* of business performance management. We started Chapter 7 with a discussion on the drivers of performance with respect to a timeframe. We argued that *performance is timescale sensitive and what we do to improve performance for the short-term is not necessarily what we would do to improve performance for the medium- and long-term*. Whilst it is quite easy to deliver performance improvements in the short term by tackling cost drivers, this may not be a sustainable solution for the long term. We require a more mature approach to performance improvement for underpinning long-term performance by addressing value drivers in the medium term and capability drivers in the long-term. In this context we identified three fundamental value drivers: Product Leadership, Operational Excellence and Customer Intimacy. We also highlighted the importance of achieving a balance between having a focused business model that we deliver efficiently and effectively (exploitation) and our organisation's ability to anticipate opportunities and threats and change in strategic ways. We concluded this chapter by claiming that *the best-performing companies worry less about performance and more about managing their organisational capabilities that underpin performance*.

In Chapter 8 we claimed that *it is the organisational capabilities and culture that determine how people interact with the processes that deliver long-term sustainable performance*. We explored how organisational capabilities develop over time and we identified organisational learning as the core capability that enables other capabilities to develop through learning. We established *the necessity for an open, participative culture to enable organisations to learn*. We also introduced the concept of maturity models as a way of making organisational capabilities more tangible, measurable and actionable. We argued that *maturity models make it possible to create continuous improvement initiatives that enable the development of organisational capabilities*.

In Chapter 9 we stated that *performance, particularly long-term sustainable performance, is all about people*. We revisited organisational controls from a human perspective and explored what motivates people and the types of organisation people prefer to work in. We concluded that the modern management systems we use in our contemporary organisations largely lack the human component. We used Hamel's Framework for Management 2.0 to demonstrate the need to create a balance between technical and social controls. We identified that this balance needs to achieve an environment where people work autonomously in self-organising and self-managing networks towards a shared higher purpose, where trust, community, social interaction, challenge and mastery are valued. We concluded that *where there is balance and harmony there are happy people and where there are happy people there is performance*. We further concluded that *whilst our efforts to date developed our understanding of the technical controls into a science, our understanding of social controls remains largely a black art*.

Chapter 10 focused on *the balance between technical and social controls*. We introduced four types of organisation in the context of our measurement vs. management matrix. These were Neo-liberal economic, Weberian, Charismatic and Humanistic organisations. We proposed that in our contemporary, knowledge-based and innovative organisations, *the right balance is where we have well-developed, mature performance measurement systems (i.e., technical controls) that are balanced with open, participative and democratic social controls*. We gave examples of what happens when we get this balance wrong (such as uninspiring work, poor customer service, misinformation) and went on to explore the interaction between technical and social controls. We concluded that *we need to create humanistic organisations where we encourage team working, comradery and compassion*. Finally, we provided a summary of what needs to be done to ensure that the organisational controls remain balanced and concluded that *we need to better understand how to design performance improvement interventions that deliver sustainable results*.

Our overall message from this part is that all organisations need performance measurement. We just need to learn how to use them in open, participative and democratic ways!

TIME FOR REFLECTION

- Do we manage our organisational capabilities in a systematic way? In other words, do we have continuous improvement initiatives that aim to improve our capabilities?
- Do we purposefully try to achieve a balance between exploitation and exploration? When was the last time we did something to improve our ability to change?
- Do we ever think about social and technical controls? Or do we just do things and hope for the best?

- With respect to balancing technical and social controls, do we know where we are and where we want to be?
- Have we thought about how we should design our performance improvement interventions?

*All organisations need performance measurement systems.
We need to learn how to use them in open, participative
and democratic ways!*

PART
FOUR

Effective Interventions

12

Designing Effective Interventions

Let people decide what to change and how...!

C learly, the main aim of performance measurement and management should be to maximise the organisational purpose by ensuring that all its resources are orchestrated, in concert, to deliver its purpose effectively and efficiently. As people are the most unpredictable and variable resource, a performance management system needs to put people, at all levels, at the heart of its philosophy, enabling them to be part of the organisation and control themselves rather than being controlled. In previous chapters we have seen good and bad practices and developed an understanding of how some organisations use performance measurement and management techniques to engage, excite and enthuse people about their work and workplace. Usually, at this stage, the main questions in many people's minds are *Where do I start?* and *How do I get there?*

In this chapter my objective is to provide some guidance and tools to enable the business practitioner to design more effective interventions by striking the right balance between technical and social controls. In this context, understanding organisations as a system is an important first step for designing effective interventions.

12.1 A SYSTEMS APPROACH

In this section I do not intend to go to great lengths to discuss systems thinking; suffice to define a system as *a collection of interacting parts or actors in which the interactions result in system-level properties and behaviours not attributable to the sum of individual parts*. We can think about virtually anything as a system. For example a car, a human body, a company, a society are all systems. One may even argue that they are systems of systems. Let's expand on this to illustrate the point.

A car is made up of a chassis, a body, an engine, a transmission system, a braking system, an electrical system and so on. All cars have the same systems. There again, all cars are different. So, it is the interaction of these different parts or subsystems with each other that defines the behaviour of the car, be it performance, economy, comfort, aesthetics, etc. In a similar vein we can look at each part as a system. For example, the engine is a system itself. It has several parts that interact with each other to make it work. How well the engine works is not just a function of how well each part is made, but also a function of how each part interacts with the other parts in the system.

We can apply the same analysis to all other systems. A human body is made up of a circulatory system, a respiratory system, a nervous system, a digestive system, a sensory system and so on. Although each of these systems has a specific and important function, it is how these subsystems interact with each other that defines how well the human body functions.

All systems have boundaries. In the two examples above, the car and the human body, the boundaries are easy to define. However, this is not always the case. When we want to analyse a system to better understand its behaviour we need to take into account other parts and actors that initially may lie outside the system boundary. In other words, the boundary of the system usually depends on the purpose of analysis.

Let's continue with our car example. If we are a government agency and we want to classify cars according to their efficiency and emissions for tax purposes, we will draw our boundaries around each car as a technical system. We will subject each car to a standard test and measure its economy and emissions, and from this data we can develop a classification system. However, if we are an insurance company and we classify the same range of cars for risk-assessment purposes, we need to rethink our boundaries. We still have to look at the technical system (performance, safety, handling characteristics, etc.) but we also need to include in our system's boundary some social considerations that include the driver (age, sex, experience, driving track record), what he or she uses the car for (pleasure, commuting, business) and where he or she lives and works, as some areas are considered higher risk than others. So the system's boundaries change depending on the purpose of analysis.

If we want to understand the behaviour of a particular car on our roads, the most important and difficult part to understand and analyse is the driver and how he or she interacts with the car. The difficulty here is that however hard we try to understand the variables involved in trying to predict a driver's behaviour, we can only codify so much information (e.g., age, sex, experience, track record). Where people are involved in a system it becomes impossible to accurately predict behaviour. In the car example there are so many other factors that can influence the driver's behaviour at a given time – Is the driver in a bad mood? Has he/she had sufficient sleep? Is he/she distracted by a recent item of news? Is he/she suffering from flu? And so on… With so many variables that we cannot control, it becomes near impossible to predict the driver's behaviour. In the context of understanding and predicting the behaviour of the system (the car and its driver) the technical factors of the car, whilst still important, usually become a secondary consideration to the social factors of the driver.

The literature on systems thinking and analysis classifies systems as hard and soft systems. Hard systems are technical systems (e.g., a car), with well-defined components and interconnections between components with predictable behaviour. Soft systems are social systems (e.g., human- or animal-based systems), where components and the interconnections between components are not so well defined, with highly unpredictable behaviours. Put more simply: hard/technical systems, like machines and processes, are set up to perform reliably in the same way day in, day out whereas soft systems, like people, have a random element to them.

In fact, most organisations lie at the intersection of technical and social systems, with the social dimension providing the greatest challenge due to its unpredictable nature.

12.2 THE ORGANISATION AS A SYSTEM

Before we attempt to design a performance improvement intervention we need to understand our organisation as a system. All systems have a number of features, as illustrated in Figure 12.1.

The system exists within its operating *environment*, with other systems acting as *collaborators* and *competitors*. In this context, collaborators and competitors are not necessarily other businesses collaborating or competing with our own business – they could be other parts of our own business that concur or conflict with the intervention we are planning. We will expand on this point later in the chapter. The system itself has a *boundary*, and within the boundary there is a *structure* comprising *actors, parts and/or subsystems* that are *interconnected* with one another. The system has a *function* that transforms *inputs* to *outputs*. In transforming inputs to outputs the system serves a *purpose*. The system also has *clients*, who are beneficiaries or victims of the system. The system also has an *owner*, with the authority to change the system.

In Chapter 3 we provided a systems view of our organisational structure, defining it as a series of value streams and processes that serve these value streams. The universal competitive structure of an organisation as discussed earlier (Figure 3.13) is repeated below as Figure 12.2.

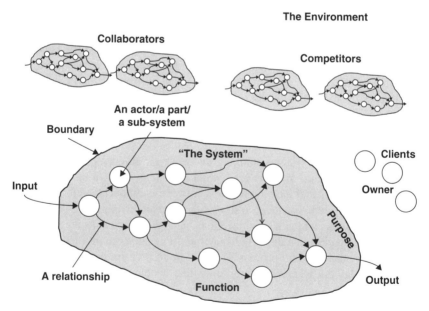

FIGURE 12.1   Features of a system

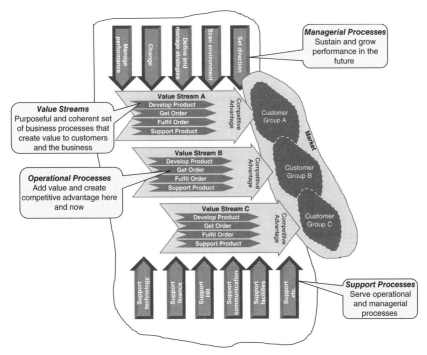

FIGURE 12.2 Universal competitive structure of an organisation (repeated from Chapter 3)

One thing to remember about systems is that they exist as interconnected and interdependent sets of activities. Rarely can we change one part of a system without affecting another part of the system. Sometimes, if we do not understand this interconnected nature of organisations, we can fall into the trap of making changes to improve one part of the organisation that may have positive or negative effects in other parts of the organisation, as exemplified by the two examples below.

ORGANISATIONS AS INTERCONNECTED SYSTEMS

Example 1

A large service-based organisation, having been criticised for having high administrative overheads in the HR department, decides to re-engineer the HR department. They study and re-engineer all the HR processes, reducing the cost of the HR function. However, these changes make the HR process in operational functions so inefficient that the overall cost of HR management to the organisation increases significantly.

Example 2

In a medium-sized engineering organisation they re-engineered the purchasing process, whereby the finance function had to approve each purchase order line by line instead of providing a blanket approval to the whole purchase order. This resulted in personnel in the accounts payable function spending a lot more time approving purchase orders, making the function appear inefficient. But when we look at the impact this had on the overall system, there was a net benefit. Management control over purchasing expenditure improved, the number of purchase order errors improved and the number of supplier credits reduced dramatically. In short, the increased effort in one function resulted in the organisation, as a whole, spending a lot less time trying to sort out the problems caused by purchase order errors, a clear benefit.

In this context, before we can design a performance improvement intervention, we need to be able to answer a number of questions:

- *Purpose*
    - What is the purpose of the intervention?
    - Does the purpose of the intervention concur with the purpose of the system?
- *System*
    - *Boundary*. What part of the competitive structure will the intervention be aimed at? Is it the whole organisation? Is it a specific value stream? Or is it a process within a value stream?
    - *Impact*. What is the likely system-wide impact of the intervention on other parts of the system?
- *Environment*
    - *Congruence/conflict*. What impact will the intervention have on other systems in the operating environment? Will it support collaborating systems? Will it compete with other systems?
- *Actors, clients and owners*
    - Do we know who all the actors, clients and owners are? Bear in mind that the actors are the individuals who will be responsible for making the system work, the clients are the beneficiaries or victims of the system and the owners are the individuals who can change the system. In this context one individual could be owner, client and actor all at the same time.

- *Congruence/conflict.* What impact will the intervention have on the personal interests and objectives of the actors, clients and owners?
- What needs to change in the system?
- How do we implement the change?

The answers to these questions will become important later when we design our interventions. The answers to the latter two questions – *What needs to change in the system?* and *How do we implement the change?* – are fundamental to designing the intervention and will require further scrutiny. The fundamental question we should also be asking ourselves at this point is **Who will decide** what needs to change and how?

12.3   WHO WILL DECIDE WHAT NEEDS TO CHANGE AND HOW?

In Chapter 10, when we looked at the interplay between technical and social control, we gave an example from a bank. To recap, in this case we had made a social intervention by giving the teams autonomy to redesign their work. They changed the interval of control from days to weeks, the resolution of control from the individual to the team, and they removed practices that create competition between team members. As a result, employee engagement and performance improved.

When I shared this experience with the CEOs of two different consultancy companies it became clear that the two consultancies had different philosophies on the way they approached performance improvement. One CEO's response was "*… that is interesting, we would have moved to hourly measures at individual level…*" (i.e., a tightening of technical controls). The other CEO's response was "*… we would have done exactly what you have done, but before we gave the team autonomy to redesign their own work we would have got them to interact with their customers so that they see the kind of effect the current process is having on the customers…*" (i.e., getting the team to experience the result of the system from the customers' perspective and then giving them autonomy to redesign the work). This is social intervention.

So we need to make a decision as to the kind of intervention we want to pursue. Fundamentally, the difference is a question of who decides what to change and how to implement that change. One approach is that the intervention is designed and led by someone outside the system. This may be the system's owner, clients or a third-party analyst/consultant. In practice, such interventions tend to focus on changing the technical controls of an organisation, usually by improving the maturity of technical controls. Another approach is when an intervention is designed by the actors of the system – that is, the people operating the process.

Going back to the bank case study, I often wondered what would have happened if we went in as consultants and made the same changes the team made. During the case study the pilot teams in the bank talked about making a lot more changes, some of which they ruled out as being impractical and others too expensive; some just got left by the wayside. All of this took considerable time (four months, actually), during which the team was communicating and more importantly learning. With hindsight we could probably have gone in and made the same changes within a week; the question is whether the changes would have been as effective.

The example of the UK-based engineering company from Chapter 7 (repeated below) is a case in point. Here the intervention was carried out over a week by a consultancy specialising in Kaizen Blitz, and the benefits of the intervention were short-lived. The conclusion was that the company was not ready for such an intervention.

A UK-based engineering company was featured in the press for outstanding performance improvement after a week-long Kaizen Blitz.[1] During this week significant changes were made to the way the company was manufacturing its products. The shop floor was tidied up, its layout was redesigned, lean techniques were used to control the flow of orders and materials through the factory – all resulting in significant improvements in quality, cost and lead times. However, I was somewhat surprised when I was asked to visit the company three months later as they had lost all the gains they had achieved and the performance had reverted to previous levels. The management's view was that the company was not ready for a Kaizen Blitz.

---

[1] A Kaizen Blitz is a rapid improvement workshop designed to deliver results within a few days. It is a way for teams to carry out structured problem solving and process improvement, in a workshop environment, over a short timeframe. Kaizen is the Japanese word for 'good change' and is now the established term for continuous improvement used in the lean management vocabulary.

Maybe, if the intervention was conducted as a social intervention, the results might have been more sustainable. In this case a social intervention would have comprised:

- Helping the people operating the process (the actors) to experience and understand the performance outcomes of the current system from the perspectives of different stakeholders (the clients).
- Educating them on process improvement tools and techniques.
- Giving them sufficient time to experiment and learn how best to use these tools and techniques in the context of their particular organisation.

- Letting the people operating the system (the actors) decide what changes to make as the system evolves and improves through this experimentation and learning.

Although such social intervention takes considerably longer to deliver results compared with technical interventions, the performance improvements are usually more sustainable. So my general rule is, where appropriate, let the people who operate the processes decide what to change and how to change.

12.4 TECHNICAL VS. SOCIAL INTERVENTION

The above discussion opens up another area of debate around technical and social interventions. We define technical and social interventions as follows.

A *technical intervention* is a process, technology or procedure change (i.e., a change in the technical controls). The following are typical technical interventions:

- Introduction of new performance measures.
- Implementation of a new ICT system.
- Changing a process or procedure.

A *social intervention* is a behavioural and cultural change that changes the way people are managed (i.e., a change in the social controls). The following are typical social interventions:

- Increasing or reducing levels of autonomy.
- Providing opportunities for education and self-development.
- Elimination of hierarchies.

In summary, technical interventions tend to be about changing *what* we do to manage the organisation. In contrast, social interventions are about changing *how* we manage the organisation.

However, as we demonstrated in Chapter 10, the two dimensions of organisational control are rarely independent. Making a change in one dimension has an impact in the other dimension. Thus, in designing our interventions we need to be mindful of what kind of intervention we want to make and the likely emergent path. It is my experience that a technical intervention that is imposed from outside (i.e., management, parent company, external consultant) is likely to create a shift in social controls towards command and control. Throughout my experience working with organisations I have seen and experienced this dynamic on many occasions. However, the opposite is also true, an intervention on the social axis, giving the people operating the processes more autonomy, is likely to result in a loosening of technical controls. Figure 12.3 attempts to illustrate these dynamics. It is, thus, useful to remember these when designing our interventions.

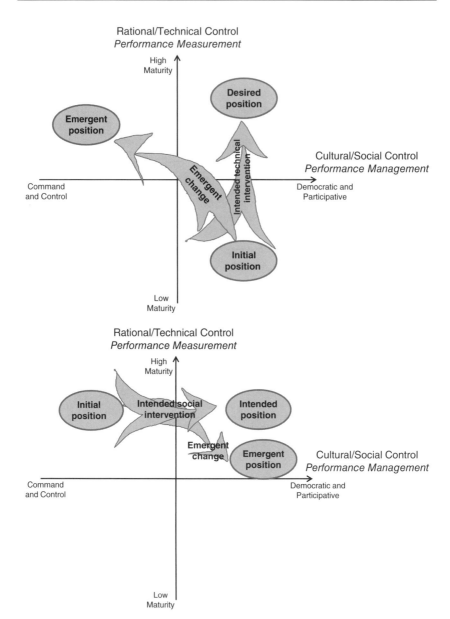

FIGURE 12.3 Likely dynamics between intended intervention and emergent result

However, in practice many interventions are conceptualised in the technical dimension with little consideration for the social consequences. Usually, management teams, based on their previous experience, decide what the intervention is going to be. It may be re-engineering a process, implementing a new ICT solution or implementing a Six-Sigma approach. The initiative is then rolled out as part of a change management process, where the whole purpose is to minimise and mitigate resistance to change. Whilst I am not condemning this approach, as I have seen and been personally involved in many that worked well, I feel we do not give sufficient thought to the intervention design at the outset. We should ask ourselves what kind of intervention is appropriate. The box below contains examples of different types of change.

EXAMPLE 1

The performance of a process is being constrained by the capacity of a bottleneck resource. The intervention is the introduction of an additional resource to alleviate the problem. This is clearly a technical intervention that requires little or no social intervention, other than initial conversations around the appropriateness of the additional resource.

EXAMPLE 2

A process is no longer fit for purpose and needs to be re-engineered to enable the process to better support the business objectives. Here the intervention is clearly a business process re-engineering intervention. We can approach this intervention in one of two ways.

First, we can hire a consultant to analyse the process and design an optimised process. We then implement the new process primarily as a technical intervention. However, we would need to balance this with a social intervention to ensure that the change is managed effectively.

Second, we can start with a social intervention. Here we work with the team – that is, the people who operate the process. We may start by raising their awareness that the current process is no longer fit for purpose. We may get them involved with the customers of the process so that they better understand what the customers are experiencing. We can give them some time to debate what is wrong with the process, what the potential solutions are and what needs to be done to resolve the problem. We may offer them some education on process improvement techniques without being prescriptive about how to use these techniques to redesign the current process. We then let the team decide how best to change the process.

In the second example, between the first and second approaches we may possibly end up with two very similar process designs. The first approach would be a lot faster but the ownership of the process will lie with the consultant and the management team who sponsored the intervention. The risk here is that it may suffer from the Hawthorne effect and may not be sustainable. The second approach, however, places all the authority and responsibility for the redesign of the process and its performance with the team. They have full ownership. The managers' and indeed, if necessary, the external consultants' role becomes one of coach and educator (social intervention) rather than that of an expert who has the technical solution (technical intervention). The second approach, although slower, will enable the technical solution to emerge from the team, thus enabling a more sustainable solution. What is more, the experience of working through the problem together – albeit with some guidance and coaching – will serve to develop the capabilities and culture of the team and thus the organisation.

In short, in designing interventions we need to achieve a balance between the technical and social content of the intervention. We also need to consider the likely impact of the intervention on the process and its performance, as well as on the underlying organisational culture and capabilities.

TIME FOR REFLECTION

- Do we understand our organisation as an interconnected system?
- When designing an intervention:
  - Do we know what part of the organisation it is aimed at? The organisation as a whole, a particular value stream or a particular process serving a particular value stream?
  - Do we know how the intervention will affect other parts of the system?
  - Who is going to make the decision as to what to change and how to change?
  - Do we think about the technical or social dimensions of the intervention and how best to balance these for the given context?
  - Do we have the necessary skills and experience to manage/facilitate the interventions?

12.5 WHAT TO CHANGE?

However we approach a given intervention, at some point a decision is made as to what needs to change. Again, looking at the organisation value stream or the process as a system we need to understand what needs to change in the system. Figure 12.4 illustrates the commonly understood virtuous circle for diagnosing, designing and implementing interventions, which is consistent with Deming's well-known Plan–Do–Check–Act and Six-Sigma's DMAIC[2] approach.

It is common practice to go through the diagnosis phase of this circle and identify several things that need to be changed to improve the performance of the system. Again, it is common to see companies making complicated plans with many projects, some in parallel and some in series, sometimes extending as far as five years. Whilst there is fundamentally nothing wrong with this approach, it is important to recognise that once you make one change to the system, the system changes. Thus, all other changes that were identified earlier may no longer be appropriate. So before we start making the next change we would need the changes already made to settle down, to study and diagnose the system again, and then decide what further change is necessary.

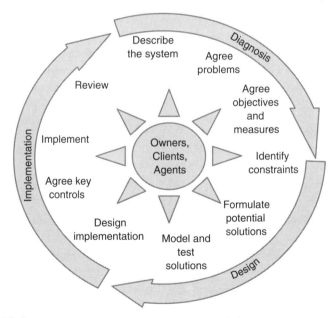

FIGURE 12.4   Designing interventions – the virtuous circle

---

[2]DMAIC is an abbreviation for Define, Measure, Analyse, Improve and Control and refers to a data-driven improvement cycle.

In fact, I have observed this apparently incremental behaviour in a number of companies but in strategic ways. One such company is Highland Spring Limited, now the UK's number-one bottled water company and at one time the UK's fastest-growing bottled water company. Their case study is documented in more detail in Bititci *et al.* (2010).

THE HIGHLAND SPRING STORY IN BRIEF

From the beginning the company had set out to become a brand leader in the UK and then a number of significant change initiatives ensued that under-pinned the company's growth and eventual success as the UK's number-one bottled water company. The journey started with a strategy review and the decision to position the company as a brand leader. The next project was a branding and product design process to ensure that the product and its packaging reflected the company's premium brand ambitions. Throughout, the company's mentality could be summed up as "*the objective is to become the UK's leading premium bottle company. We are on a journey. We do not have a grand plan. We will tackle obstacles one by one as they emerge*".

The next obstacle was that the company's order fulfilment process and supply chain were not delivering what was expected of a premium brand. So this was the next obstacle to tackle. The supply chain processes were re-engineered and a new company-wide information system was implemented to support all the company processes, including the supply chain. This was followed by several other projects that included instilling a continuous improvement culture on the shop floor, implementation of a shop-floor information management system, change of shift patterns, implementation of a sales and operations planning process, installation of a new state-of-the-art production system, re-engineering of warehouse management processes and implementation of new warehouse management systems, and a strategic supplier development programme. Today, this level of change continues.

From observing Highland Spring and other such companies, they have three simple (albeit unwritten) rules for selecting and designing their interventions:

- *First rule.* Have a higher purpose that stays constant over time.
- *Second rule.* Identify the most significant constraint that is preventing you from getting one step closer to your purpose and focus on alleviating that constraint.
- *Third rule.* Pursue one intervention at a time.

We have already covered the importance of having a higher purpose that stays constant over time (i.e., the first rule) in previous chapters. Essentially the higher purpose provides a valuable framework upon which all decisions about interventions and their priorities can be subordinated.

The second and third rules are about understanding that once we make a change to the system, the system is changed, and it would need to be re-studied and re-diagnosed to understand the new constraint. These rules are also about focus and speed. The objective here is to get one thing done, do it well and do it quickly. Get the change embedded and then move on to the next project. They recognise that all change initiatives consume resources. One scarce resource is people's time. They have to work on the 'day job' – designing products, managing production lines, operating machines, loading trucks, etc. – and they have to work on the 'project'. So, in terms of people's time, the change project is already in competition with the day job – if we introduced yet another project there is a good chance that it will also be competing for the same resources.

Whenever I am asked to work with a company on a major change initiative one of my favourite questions is to ask each functional manager/director the following question: *Apart from the 'day job', what improvement or development projects are you working on?* Once you have a list of all the projects, ask them to prioritise these projects. Try it in your own organisation; you will be amazed what comes out of the woodwork.

Figure 12.5 is an illustration developed from such a list. The top row represents all the functions and each coloured cell represents a unique project for that function (white cells are blank). The projects for each function are listed in order of priority, from the top down. Here, the specifics of each project are not important. What is important, however, is the number of projects the organisation is planning to deal with and how they relate to one another.

In total there are 19 different projects listed, some specific to a function, others cutting across a number of functions. The red cells represent the project I was asked to assist with. Notice that it is not a top-priority project in any of the functions. Considering that it was a company-wide project it was alarming that it was not even listed by two departments, both of which would have been central to the success or failure of the project. The projects coloured amber are those projects that would be competing for the same resources as the red project. The projects coloured green were considered to be complementary or not competing for resources, but still a significant distraction for the senior management team. So there was little chance for the red project to succeed and my first task was to coach the company to review and re-prioritise the projects, taking into account the potential competition between the projects and the day job of designing, manufacturing and installing sophisticated engineering systems. Needless to say, a number of projects were dropped and others cancelled. A few were combined and eventually the company decided to pursue three strategic performance improvement projects.

ENGINEERING	PROJECTS	PROCUREMENT	MANUF.	QUALITY	SALES & MARKETING	IT	FINANCE	HR
Monitor and improve on quality of internal documentation.	Re-launch NPI with milestone driven process.	Implement budgeted savings projects totalling 6% in 2004.	Achieve safety audit and identify safety concerns.	Continuous improvement (Office Kaizen) within transactional areas.	Identify product options and variants to include into eclipse.	Introduce an industry standard framework of operations for IT infrastructure.	Business/Power-Up/credit.	5S.
Develop new products to plan and configure sales process	Conclude a streamlined order handover and booking process and achieve buy-in.	Achieve white book targeted savings of £1m.	5S.	Establish a method of 'fleet Finance' (to be defined).	All product brochures to be re-branded.		Introduction of new Costing System (Approach) including EVM as part of BPU Project.	BPR.
Reinforce customer specification change and engineering change control processes.	Create Central Planning Team and procedures. Use CP Team to identify resource and capacity throughout whole business.	Create Central Planning Team and procedures. Use CP Team to identify resource and capacity throughout whole business.	Create Central Planning Team and procedures.	Re-work reduction and prevention.	Identify requirements for and deliver new product training through product champions.	Maximise reporting potential for eclipse/One World sales software.	Complete Finance standalone from WBS/MMF.	Implement cross-functional Continuous improvement and empower all employees, using 3Cs approach.
	5S.	Indirect Spend Savings Programme.	Remove all asbestos and PCB from the premises by April 2004.		Identify and create concern log for eclipse-related issues.	Undertake MAD training for all people managers and key personnel.	Identify and complete PIRs.	Produce required vs actual multi-skilling competence/skills training matrix and plan in each department.
Identify required training matrix and plan in each department.	Ensure our downblow business is developed to add bottom line value during 2004. Win at least one new job.				Implement 5S.	Implement 3Cs across all activities with an immediate emphasis on health and safety issues.	Align Chart of Accounts/Reporting.	Embed 5 Whys in all managers/supervisors/team leaders and selected problem analysis facilitators.
Support Quality awareness campaign in-house.	Establish site fault investigation and resolution team. Split present project management team into 'NPI' and 'Site Fault' teams.	Improve supplier deliveries.	Introduce customer specification change and engineering change control processes.	5S.	Five week Kaizen process improvement and KPI projects.	Undertake 5Y training and problem solving training for appropriate staff.	Achieve 100% Compliance Scorecard.	Quality awareness campaign in-house and supply base.
Lean Awareness in transactional areas.	Develop War Room teams as War Room is key method of delivering on customer and company commitments.	5S.	Implement cross-functional Continuous improvement and empower all employees, using 3Cs approach.	Vendor quality improvement.	HPI business plan development.	Provide full support to – BPU Standard Products and Central, Planning Organisation implementation.	Repositioning Finance to 'Banker' role.	Lean Awareness in transactional areas + refresher training in Manufacturing.
Review office safety procedures, use 3Cs and instil safety culture.	Implement cross-functional Continuous improvement and empower all employees using 3Cs approach.	Implement cross-functional Continuous improvement and empower all employees, using 3Cs approach.	Develop and implement a pull system that suits Central Planning and market requirements.	Quality Awareness Campaign.	Identify new product development requirements.	Develop effective business systems regarding Business Systems commitments to priority projects as determined by the project Improvement Register.	Education of Peers in Financial Awareness.	Transfer best practice within the Group.
5S.	Embed 5 Whys in all managers/supervisors/team leaders and selected problem analysis facilitators.	Produce required vs actual multi-skilling competence/skills training matrix and plan in each department.	Embed 5 Whys in all managers/supervisors/team leaders and selected problem analysis facilitators.	Identify safety concerns using the 3C board and risk assessment process.	Produce design briefs for agreed product development requirements.	Develop effective business systems, reporting early Business Systems involvement in company improvement activities.	Simplification of Payroll.	All people managers to go through Making A Difference training (HR1).
Transfer best practice within the Group.	Transfer best practice within the Group.	Embed 5 Whys in all managers/supervisors/team leaders and selected problem analysis facilitators.	Quality Awareness. Re-work reduction, quality at source including cell inspection.	Improve customer satisfaction through customer care.	Deliver agreed training programme.	Consolidate departmental 4S and attain 5S accreditation.	Improve Feeder Process Accuracy to Accounts Payable.	Develop and implement recruitment strategy. (HR2)
All people managers to go through Making a Difference training.	All people managers to go through Making a Difference training.	Quality awareness campaign in-house and supply base.	Lean Awareness in transactional areas + refresher training in Manufacturing.	Carry out PDPs, implement training needs within the function.	Identify reports requirement for sales tools.	Develop and implement a user charter for the infrastructure function. This to incorporate regular..	GRN Booking.	Design and implement system to capture training by function. (HR3)
Develop and support global sourcing of castings.		Lean Awareness in transactional areas + refresher training in Manufacturing.	Develop new products to plan and configure sales process.	Lean awareness in transactional areas and refresher training in QC.	Develop product metric to identify core and non-core business and options.	Develop proactive engagement and management with staff.	Budget Process.	Develop Strategy to meet T & D needs. (HR4)
		Re-organise supply chain management process.	Transfer best practice within the Group and selected partnership companies.	NCR process improvement.	Develop FAQs database for all core products.	Develop an improved 'Handshake' between Systems and Infrastructure function.	Foreign Entity Simplification.	Train Managers/Supervisors on Attendance Management (HR5)
		Reduce Supply Base by 20%.	All people managers to go through Making a Difference training.	C-Poka projects, Audit, Calibration, Customer Complaints and Corrective Action.		Ensure IT compliance with ISO 14001.	Travel and Subsistence Expenses.	
		All people managers to go through Making a Difference training.	Create skid assembly and test area.	Conduct machine capability studies in Manufacturing and develop programme of control.		Develop and implement an IT Disaster Recovery plan.	Linking and Reporting Currency Hedging (JASB9).	Develop Graduate Training Scheme. (HR6)
		Drive global sourcing of castings.	Combine skills to reduce demarcation in all areas.	Inspection records process improvement.		Transition IT infrastructure to position of minimal direct equipment sourcing.	Output Rules (Long Term Contracts).	Benchmark and develop Apprentice Training Scheme. (HR7)
			Design, implement and use a Sales to Despatch Order Booking System in Engineered.	Automated inspection linked to solid works.		Maximise potential for development of business focused customer and supplier portals.	Compliance to ISO9000:2001 (Mapping).	Assess and implement Psychometric testing provision. (HR8)
			Achieve TPM targets on selected machines and processes.			Develop a process for effective IT spend and forecasting monitoring and capex administration.	Inland Revenue and Customs & Excise (PPT).	Develop PDP Process. (HR9)
			Carry out SMED activities to selected processes.				Fixed Assets System linked to Maintenance, Capacity Planning, etc.	Assess and implement Standard Incentive Scheme. (HR10)
			Develop global distribution and global sales footprint.				Capex Approval / Post Completion Audit.	Develop and implement Strategy for Terms and Conditions. (HR11)
			Complete removal of cast iron flanges, pipework, etc., pressure systems including the boiler.				Formal Training for Entire Finance Team.	Develop and implement standard contracts and policies.
			Guarding of machines - Phase 2.				Data Ownership.	
			Improve goods received process.					
			Improve waste segregation company wide.					

FIGURE 12.5 Project priority list

At one point I was working with three different companies from three different manufacturing sectors, all about the same size, employing 250–350 people. One had 43 strategic projects, an extreme case, all of which were live and fighting for resources at the same time. As anticipated, none of the projects got delivered, the company performance deteriorated significantly and today the company is no longer in business. Another company had nine different projects, some of which were conflicting with other projects (a point we will expand on later). After conducting a strategic review of their projects, they combined some to eliminate conflict and postponed two. Eventually, they pursued four different performance improvement interventions in parallel and delivered all of them. However, all the projects were delivered over budget and significantly late. The third company was focusing on a single project at a time. It delivered most of its projects within budget and timescale. Today it is the number-one bottled water producer in the UK!

Here my analogy is as follows. Try pulling 20 hairs from your arm by grabbing all 20 at the same time and pulling them out slowly. It is painful! Alternatively, try pulling one hair at a time quickly. You hardly feel anything and you will probably get there faster!

In short, in deciding what to change, we should be focusing on the single intervention that is going to take us one step closer to achieving our purpose. It is about planning one intervention at a time and getting it done well and quickly. Then, let the system settle before we go forward and start looking for the next intervention.

12.6 FINDING THE TRIM-TAB

"Call me trim-tab" is the phrase engraved on the gravestone of Buckminster Fuller (1895–1983). Fuller, an American architect, systems theorist, author, designer and inventor, is frequently quoted on his use of trim-tabs as a metaphor for leadership and empowerment. In the February 1972 issue of *Playboy* Fuller said: "*Something hit me very hard once, thinking about what one little man could do. Think of the Queen Mary—the whole ship goes by and then comes the rudder. And there's a tiny thing at the edge of the rudder called a trim-tab. It's a miniature rudder. Just moving the little trim-tab builds a low pressure that pulls the rudder around* [and brings the whole ship around]. [It] *takes almost no effort at all…!*"

The trim-tab analogy captures an important feature of the systems approach. That is, a small intervention made in an almost insignificant part of a complex organisation could end up changing the behaviour of the whole organisation. The trick is knowing where the trim-tab is, or even how to find it.

The systems modelling and analysis literature offers many tools and techniques to enable us to understand and analyse a complex real-life system. In practice we tend to hear a lot about process mapping, which is good for demonstrating

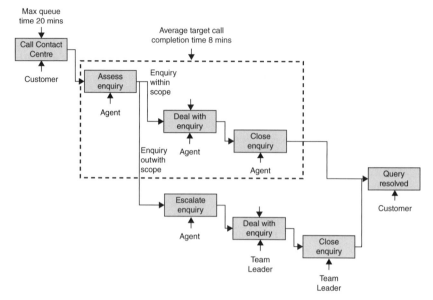

FIGURE 12.6 A process map for the call centre

the logical flow of the process but tells us very little about the real-life behaviour of the process. Figure 12.6 shows an example from a UK service company to illustrate this very point.

The process map illustrated in Figure 12.6 describes the operation of the customer contact centre of a UK utility services business. The company provides utility services to UK households and businesses. At the time of this intervention they were regularly criticised in the media for a very poor and deteriorating customer service. Simultaneously, their costs were escalating, putting additional pressure on their financial performance and ultimately affecting their share price.

The process map shown, although adequately describing the process, does not provide significant insight into the behaviour of the process. In contrast, the causal map of Figure 12.7 provides a much richer picture, but it is difficult to understand at first glance and needs some explanation.

Essentially the poor customer service is causing call volumes to increase, requiring additional agents to keep the queue times down. This adversely affects productivity and increases costs, attracting more management attention and tighter management of productivity. Agents' performance is monitored against target average call completion times of 8 minutes. Agents that fail to achieve the target are put on a Personal Improvement Plan (PIP) which is seen as a punishment exercise rather like detention at school, negatively impacting employee morale. Agents do anything to ensure that they are not on a PIP by playing the system.

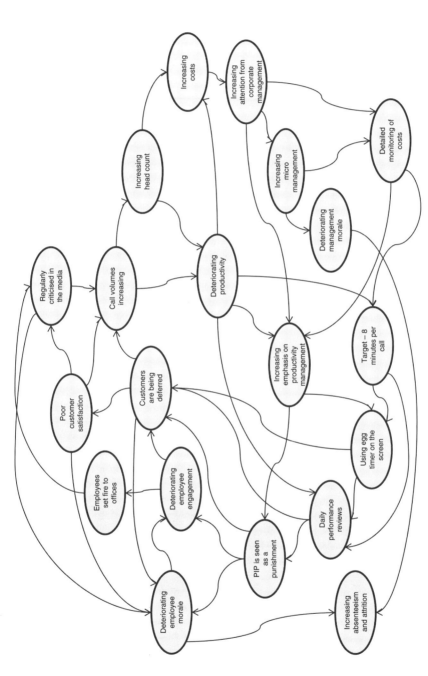

FIGURE 12.7 Causal map describing the behaviour of the process

Unhelpful practices discussed earlier, such as *telling the customer that they have been put through to the wrong department and putting them back into the same call queue* or *telling them that the systems are down and they should call back in 30 minutes* were commonplace. These practices just serve to increase the call volumes, exacerbating the productivity problems. The level of employee disengagement was such that at one point the employees even went as far as setting fire to the office building so that they could have a day off.

Today this organisation is transformed, but at the time it took some effort to convince the management to abandon the productivity measures and replace them with a *first call resolution* measure, which proved to be the trim-tab for this organisation. It took some analysis to demonstrate to the management that over 65% of the calls were failure calls, created by them as a result of not resolving the customer's issue at the first call.

Peter Checkland's Soft Systems Methodology (Checkland and Scholes, 1999) has been developed to deal with messy, complex systems that are difficult to understand through formalised representations, such as process maps. Rather they use rich pictures, similar to our sketches of the organisation in Chapter 3, to capture the organisation's behaviour from the different stakeholder perspectives.

Other organisations have developed innovative ways of capturing what actually happens along the formal processes (i.e., the hidden process). Figure 12.8 illustrates the lengths a large engineering firm went to, to uncover this hidden process. They used large-scale process maps on the floor and then they would role play along the process to illustrate what actually happens in reality.

FIGURE 12.8   Role playing along a large-scale process map

Whilst the process map depicted what appeared to be a robust and logical process, the role play surfaced a number of additional insights into the behaviour of the process in the real world. The following is a short extract from such a role-play exercise.

The order fulfilment process is being enacted. All the engineering and manufacturing has been done, the product is at the final test stage and the customer is about to fly in to witness the final acceptance test...

- **Mark** (Production Manager): Hi Jimmy (Sales Engineer), I just heard that we have problems with the final testing. We are trying to sort it out but we need more time. Any chance you can delay the customer a little bit?
- **Jimmy**: Oh darn, how long do you need?
- **Mark**: I need at least 6 hours, but to be on the safe side a day would be better. Can you delay him until tomorrow afternoon?
- **Jimmy**: He's flying in later this morning, I'll see what I can do.

  Later at the airport Jimmy is meeting the customer's engineer (Thomas)...
- **Jimmy**: Welcome to the UK Thomas. I thought that since this is your first visit to this part of the world I would take the liberty of booking us into the Golden Eagle hotel. I believe you play golf, so I am planning to take you out for a round of golf this afternoon. We'll stay at the hotel tonight and head down to the plant in the morning. Your test is scheduled for tomorrow afternoon and we can still have you on the evening flight out of here.
- **Thomas**: I thought the test was scheduled for this afternoon?
- **Jimmy**: To be honest I am not sure what happened here. I thought so as well, but the numpties[3] in planning have screwed up again...

---

[3] Scottish term for idiots.

It is virtually impossible to uncover this level of insight into the behaviour of the process using process mapping alone. At best it provides us with an insight into the rational system. However, as demonstrated above, most of our processes are influenced by people's behaviour. Thus, it is critical for us to perceive our value streams and processes as social systems. Consequently, it is important to get the people who operate the process to surface the real behaviour of the process through whatever means are necessary; only then do we begin to understand how the process behaves in reality.

Quite often it is difficult to identify what to change in the system. Sometimes the most obvious intervention fails to deliver the expected results, so we need to be prepared to experiment. More importantly, if we let the people who operate the process experiment with it they will eventually find the one change they need to make to dramatically change the behaviour of the whole system.

I frequently find that the best trim-tab is the people who operate the process, particularly in knowledge-intensive processes. If you trust them, invest in them, give them purpose and guidance and then let them loose they will find the trim-tab, delivering dramatic performance improvements.

TIME FOR REFLECTION

- Do we perceive our organisation as a system and understand the key constraints and barriers to performance?
- Is the intervention we are planning going to help us take a significant step towards our purpose?
- Does the intervention address the most significant constraint that is preventing us making a significant step towards our purpose?
- Are we pursuing more than one intervention at a time? If so, are we confident that these interventions are complementary and they do not compete for resources?
- Are we sure our intervention is going to deliver the expected impact? Have we found the trim-tab?
- Do we understand our value streams and processes as social systems rather than rational mechanistic processes?
- Do we have a track record of designing and delivering interventions successfully and quickly? If not, where did we go wrong?

12.7 SUMMARY

If we are to design effective performance improvement interventions we need to perceive our organisation as an interconnected system, which is connected to other systems in its operating environment. We also need to recognise that most of our value streams and processes lie at the intersection of technical systems and social systems. Whilst it is relatively easier to model and understand the rational behaviour of our business processes as technical systems, it is considerably harder to understand the behaviour of our processes as social systems. Social systems are messier and their behaviours are more difficult to predict.

In designing our interventions the first things we need to consider are the purpose of the organisation, the purpose of the intervention and the part of the organisation (system) the intervention is aimed at. The next thing we need to consider is the potential impact and consequences of the planned intervention on other parts of the organisation (system), as well as on its key stakeholders (actors, clients, owners). Only then can we start thinking about what needs to change and how to implement the change.

In designing our intervention a key question we need to ask ourselves is *Who decides what to change?* There are two competing options here. The first option is that the boss decides what to change and how to change, sometimes with help from an external consultant, and the change programme is rolled out. The second option is that the responsibility is given to the people who operate the process. They are given a clear purpose and some guidance but ultimately they learn from thinking, experimenting and reflecting together. The second option, although it may take longer to deliver the desired results, will almost certainly have a more sustainable effect. The key message here is that, whichever way we decide to go, in designing interventions we need to achieve a balance between the technical and the social content of the intervention.

Another key message is that once you make a change to the system, the system is changed. Thus, it is futile to plan a series of interventions. It is more effective and efficient to deliver interventions one at a time, let the system settle down, analyse the system and decide what to change next. Performance improvement interventions are most effective when we focus on a single intervention at a time, deliver it quickly and efficiently, and let the system settle before we start looking for the next intervention. In this way all our resources are focused on delivering the single most important intervention.

In many cases we only need to make a small change to the system to create a significant change in the behaviour of the overall system. However, in our socio-technical processes and value streams the trim-tab is often lost in the noise and complexity. Understanding the behaviour of our systems as a socio-technical system and engaging our people to surface the real behaviour of the system (i.e., the hidden factory/process/organisation) provides valuable clues as to what are the most impactful changes we could make. In my view, the best trim-tab is the people who operate the process. If you trust them, invest in them, give them purpose and guidance, they are capable of delivering dramatic performance improvements.

REFERENCES

Bititci, U.S., Mendibil, K. & Maguire, C. (2010) High value manufacturing: A case study in transformation, *Journal of Engineering Manufacture Part B, Institute of Mechanical Engineers*, 224(10), 1599–1644.

Checkland, P. and Scholes, J. (1999) *Soft Systems Methodology in Action*, John Wiley & Sons: Chichester.

Once you make one change to the system, the system changes… all other changes that were planned earlier may no longer be appropriate.

The best 'trim-tabs' are the people who operate the process… If you trust them, invest in them, give them purpose and guidance, they are capable of delivering dramatic performance improvements.

13

Delivering Effective Interventions

*Change programmes that have a clear purpose
and explicit links to overall performance
are more likely to succeed!*

I nterventions are only effective if they deliver the expected outcomes. But in many cases the expected outcomes are expressed either as short-term performance improvements or as people and management development objectives that are difficult to relate to long-term sustainable performance. Clearly it is important to ensure that the planned interventions are going to contribute towards overall organisational performance in the short- and long-term. It is, however, equally important to ensure that this relationship is explicit and widely understood across the organisation. Thus, communication of how the intervention is going to impact overall organisational performance is an important point we need to consider when planning and launching interventions. We need to ensure that everyone in the organisation is working towards delivering the same objectives and outcome.

In this chapter we will look at how to plan interventions that deliver performance improvements in the short term, whilst developing organisational capabilities for long-term sustainable performance. We will also explore how best to communicate, launch and review interventions to maximise the likelihood of their success.

13.1 BALANCING SHORT-TERM RESULTS WITH DRIVERS OF LONG-TERM SUSTAINABLE PERFORMANCE

In Chapter 7, when we looked at the drivers of performance, we talked about the different performance drivers for short-, medium- and long-term performance. In my experience, most externally driven performance improvement interventions fall into two categories. They are either focused on delivering short-term performance improvements, leaving long-term capability developments to chance, or they are management/people development and education programmes that attempt to develop a range of people-related capabilities with no clear or planned performance outcome.

However, our awareness of short-, medium- and long-term performance drivers (discussed earlier in Chapter 7) allows us to plan our interventions in a more informed manner. The following example tries to explain how this could be achieved.

> **BoxCo** (pseudonym) is a small company (48 people) producing packaging for take-away food shops. Typical products include pizza boxes, kebab boxes, fish and chip boxes. The owner is confident that he can expand the market from a current regional customer base to a national or even international market with significant

growth opportunities. But he says he does not have the time to do anything about this as he is far too busy dealing with existing operations. He even complained of having no life outside work.

When you walk around he is talking about how disorganised the facilities are. He complains about how everybody does things differently and how this can sometimes cause problems with communications, mistakes and customer service. He also complains about an expensive machine that seems to be the main constraint. He feels it takes too long to change over and it also has some reliability issues at start-up, with the machine jamming due to different people setting the machine up differently. You see various work-in-progress lying around, but it is not clear what is for which customer. The factory is generally untidy, with scraps of cardboard lying about. There is no clear, observable workflow path.

After your walk around you ask the owner what keeps him awake at nights. His response is escalating costs, together with increasing price pressure. He says that what he sells is a commodity and his customers generally go for the lowest-cost supplier. Towards the end of your meeting he gets restless and as he is walking you out he complains about how he makes all the decisions. He says it is going to be another late night.

Although this is a story of one particular company, I have seen several others just like this, particularly with owner-managed SMEs who struggle to grow. Clearly there are some immediate issues that need to be tackled. An operations improvement-type intervention using some of the lean tools would serve the company well to get the operations under control and eliminate some of the quality and customer-service issues. For example:

- A 5S[1] project would help to tidy up the factory floor and promote visual management by labelling and identifying some of the products.
- A shop-floor layout project could improve the workflow through the factory, making products easier to follow through the manufacturing process (although this would probably be addressed as part of the 5S intervention).

---

[1] 5S is the name of a workplace organisation method based around five Japanese words that are loosely translated into English as sort (seiri), set (seiton), shine (seiso), standardise (seiketsu) and sustain (shitsuke). For further reading, see Hirano (1995).

- A SMED[2] project to improve the change-over times on the bottleneck machine would help release additional capacity to the whole system. The SMED project would also establish standard operating procedures for setting up that could be used to train all operators. This would serve to eliminate the machine-jamming problems, creating additional capacity.
- A performance management process based around performance measurement systems, as discussed in Chapter 5.

All of these interventions will make a difference in the short-term and will release some additional capacity for growth. But they will not resolve the fundamental problem of this company, which is centred around its organisational capabilities and culture. At best, the above interventions will help to improve the operational capability. They will do nothing to help create the headroom needed to develop new customers, markets and products. The owner clearly feels that he is stuck in a corner, but he is not thinking strategically about how to get the company out of that corner (strategic capability). He clearly sees the opportunity to grow but he does not have the capacity, and perhaps even the knowhow, for turning some of the opportunities into orders (customer intimacy capability). He has not even mentioned product development (product leadership). Whilst new product development could be an option for differentiating BoxCo in the marketplace, the existing products could be developed further to improve their functionality and/or manufacturability – all serving to improve the competitive position of BoxCo.

What would you do faced with a situation like this? The challenge here is that if you went in and offered to *develop the company's competitive capabilities for long-term sustainable performance* you would most likely be shown the door and told never to come back! The owner-manager's mind is clearly occupied with short-term operational issues. Although he clearly sees some of the opportunities, and he is also aware of his personal circumstances, they are in the background. We need to start by joining the conversations in his head and designing an intervention that addresses the issues he thinks are important. However, in doing so, we need to think about how we could leverage the short-term interventions to start addressing the organisational capabilities essential for long-term sustainable performance. Figure 13.1 outlines what such an intervention could look like for BoxCo.

Clearly, the owner-manager of BoxCo is concerned about short-term results. We need to get him to worry about underlying capabilities. He needs to understand that by focusing on underlying capabilities, the results will look after themselves. But he is a small company, he probably has cashflow concerns, he can't afford to

---

[2]Single-Minute Exchange of Die (SMED) is a method for reducing set-up or change-over times associated with manufacturing and service processes. For further reading, see Shingo (1985).

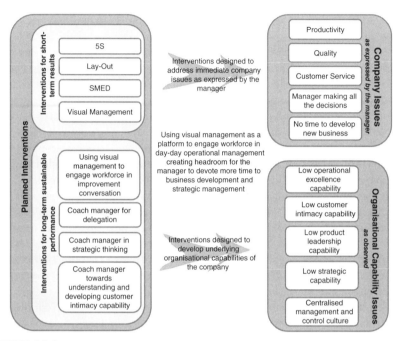

FIGURE 13.1 Planning interventions: balancing short-term results with drivers of sustainable performance

see whether the results will look after themselves. So, this is not going to happen overnight. It is essential that we develop an intervention that delivers what he wants and needs in the short-term. But it also needs to start laying the foundations for developing the organisational capabilities. We need to start working on the way he thinks, we need to get him to start thinking strategically, but we will not be able to do that if he gets sucked in to operational issues. So we need 5S, SMED and layout improvement-type interventions, together with a visual performance measurement and management board (such as a war-room), to engage the workforce in a conversation about the performance of the organisation. Once the workforce starts to understand what this is all about, they can then take ownership of some of the day-to-day operational management, freeing the manager to devote more time to business development and strategic management. But we will have to coach the manager in this direction. Left to his own devices he is unlikely to start delegating and empowering. Without this social intervention we will end up driving the whole organisation further into a command-and-control culture as the manager will start using the visual management system as a command-and-control tool, potentially spending even less time on business development or strategic management, something we want to avoid at all costs.

In effect there are two phases to this intervention. *Phase one* is a technical intervention to address some short-term issues that keep the manager awake at night. As part of this phase, we will help the company implement a visual performance measurement system. *Phase two* is a longer-term social intervention where we coach the manager and other staff so that they learn how to make use of the performance measurement system. Remember, our ultimate aim at the other end of this journey is to arrive at a destination where there is a sense of calm and confidence, with the daily operations virtually running themselves. This will enable the owner-manager to spend more time on strategic business development.

However, in my experience most of our interventions focus on delivering the first phase and only pay lip service to the second phase. Quite often I see companies engaging external help to deliver the technical element of the intervention, typically delivered over 10–20 consulting days, spread over two to three months. But learning how best to use the new system takes time and ideally requires light-touch coaching over longer periods. Although some companies are better at learning than others, I still find that phase two may take anything between six months and a year, and sometimes a little longer, to ensure that the right practices are embedded into the culture of the company.

The key message from this section is that in planning our interventions we need to balance short-term gains with long-term performance drivers (i.e., the development of organisational capabilities). This involves planning interventions informed by where the organisation is with respect to these capabilities, and where we expect them to be as a result of these interventions. At BoxCo current performance was clearly an issue, they demonstrated low operational capabilities

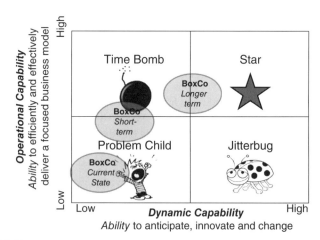

FIGURE 13.2 Expected effect of the planned intervention on BoxCo's organisational capabilities

(i.e., strategic, operational excellence, product leadership, customer intimacy) as well as low dynamic capabilities (i.e., they knew the opportunities and threats but were not able to do anything about them). In our 2×2 matrix we could position them as a Problem Child and would expect this position to improve significantly as a result of this intervention. In the short-term we would expect to observe a more significant improvement in operational capabilities but, given time and sustained intervention, we could look forward to observing their progress towards being a Star. Figure 13.2 illustrates the expected dynamic.

TIME FOR REFLECTION

- In planning our interventions do we think about balancing short-term results with drivers of long-term sustainable performance (i.e., organisational capabilities)?
- Do we understand what keeps the client of the intervention awake at night? Do we think about how best to join the conversation in his/her head when planning interventions?
- When planning interventions do we think about the short-, medium- and long-term impact of our interventions on the organisation's performance and capabilities?
- Do we know what short-, medium- and long-term impact we are expecting?
- Are we able to review whether we are doing the right things?

13.2   PLANNING AND MONITORING INTERVENTIONS

In the opening paragraphs of this chapter we emphasised the importance of linking the intended outcome of an intervention to overall business performance, whatever the nature of the intervention. We also emphasised the need to be explicit about these linkages for clear and concise communication of what we are trying to do and why. In earlier chapters (Chapters 2 and 5) we demonstrated the use of strategy maps for linking learning and growth objectives to internal process and customer-related performance measures, and ultimately to the financial performance of the business. Whilst the strategy map approach provides a good visual means for depicting these relationships, they do not provide a useful way of accounting for time. That is, an intervention takes time and its impacts on the business are rarely immediate. In the BoxCo example, the planned interventions are unlikely to turn into improved productivity, reduced costs and increased sales immediately. It will take some time for the new practices to bed in and operational improvements to be visible, and then the financial results will improve. There is always this time lag. With operational-productivity-improvement-focused interventions this time lag may be relatively short. Other interventions, such as developing customer intimacy capability or customer service improvement, the customers need to see a noticeable and sustained improvement before they place more business with the company.

I am sure there are myriad ways of doing this, but one of the best examples I have seen for mapping interventions to expected performance outcomes is illustrated in Figure 13.3.

This illustration is effectively a strategy map linking learning and growth interventions to financial objectives through internal process and customer objectives and metrics. Reading from bottom up, the interventions, as they progress, will result in improved organisational capabilities (shown here as red, amber and green). These, in turn, will deliver improvements in internal process and customer-facing performance metrics, ultimately delivering improvements in financial performance.

Although this illustration oversimplifies the significant amount of analysis required to confidently predict how planned interventions are expected to impact the future performance of the organisation, they serve two critical purposes. *First*, they provide a means of communication at all levels, including people inside the organisation, shareholders, investors and banks. *Second*, having such a document on visual display acts as a constant reminder of which interventions are currently live, what is happening, which interventions are due to start and so on. This enables management teams to review the status and impact of the planned interventions at appropriate levels and intervals. In some organisations where we implemented strategy walls (see Chapter 5), we used this structure instead of the classic strategy maps along with project monitors (also in Chapter 5) to enable review of each project in the context of overall impact. These were used to communicate and review the progress of each initiative in the context of overall company performance at various levels. In some cases, daily stand-up meetings incorporated the project reviews. In other cases, the progress and impact of performance improvement initiatives were reviewed at a weekly management meeting using the same (or a very similar) approach. In other cases, with large initiatives, a project steering committee used the same approach to review the progress of a project in relation to its expected outcomes and impact. In one particular case the CEO of a venture capital organisation used this approach to conduct monthly reviews with the management teams of the companies in his portfolio. These reviews were mostly focused on questions such as how the initiatives were going; what could be done to help them progress faster and better; were there any barriers slowing or preventing progress; what could be done to remove these barriers; were we likely

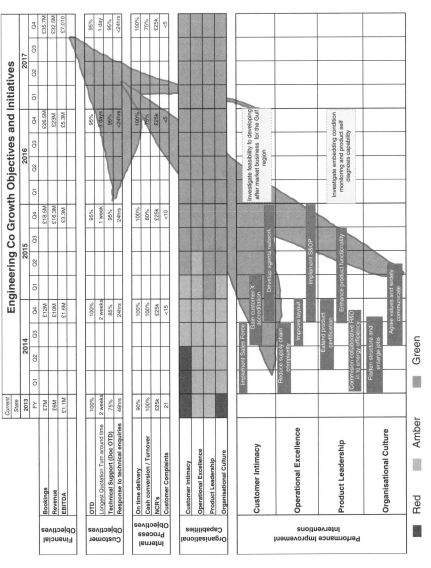

FIGURE 13.3 Mapping interventions to performance

to realise the expected impact; what could be done to improve the impact; were we trying to do too much at one time; should we reschedule the interventions to minimise competition for resources; if an intervention was not delivering were we doing it right; what is the right thing to do; should we do something else instead; and so on.

Across all the performance improvement interventions that worked well and delivered the expected outcomes, these reviews took place in an open and supportive style. The management teams, steering committees and investors, in conducting the reviews, were more interested in three things. *First*, how they could help to make the interventions progress better. *Second*, asking questions to make the project teams think along divergent paths about the company's purpose, objectives and the interventions they were pursuing. *Third*, facilitating the team to converge towards a unified decision as to how best to progress.

In short, to be effective, performance improvement interventions need to be planned and reviewed effectively in order to maximise the likelihood of delivering their expected outcomes. Our intervention plans need to relate to where the organisation is in terms of overall performance, as well as how the intervention is expected to impact on performance and when. Regular reviews of interventions, in the context of performance, are critical to success, but these need to be conducted in an open and supportive manner. Here the purpose is not to scrutinise if the team is doing a good job but to help the team achieve their objective. After all, the more positive experiences we create for people participating in these interventions the more they will want to be involved and engaged in them.

13.3 JOINED-UP THINKING

In planning and delivering projects, what is important to remember is that our interventions will be on a single system. Even though each intervention may appear to be aimed at separate parts of the system, they will almost certainly affect one another. In fact, I have experienced this phenomenon quite often. At times it appears that different interventions, aimed at improving the performance of one part of the system, are working against each other. In some cases it may even come across as if one part of the organisation is trying to sabotage an intervention in another part of the organisation. Sounds familiar?

EngineeringCo, a large UK-based engineering company, designs, manufactures and installs complex engineering solutions for the oil and gas and mining sectors. They have a single strategic intervention running, which is focused around re-engineering of the end-to-end order fulfilment process from Winning Order, through Engineering, Sourcing, Manufacturing, Installation and Commissioning. They work very hard for several months in cross-functional teams to review their existing processes and define a new efficient and effective process. However, to enable the new process, new information systems are required. A review concludes that the current ERP system will not be able to cope with the demands of the new process and a new ERP system is required. A team is then constituted to develop a requirements specification; review available software solutions; select and facilitate the implementation of a new ERP system.

A requirements specification is compiled and signed off by all departments. It is then issued to selected suppliers and responses gathered. A short-list of suppliers is compiled and just as the detailed reviews of each software solution are being conducted, one of the design engineers announces that the engineering department is upgrading their CAD (Computer Aided Design) systems and implementing a new PDM (Product Data Management) system. Further investigation reveals that the new CAD system and PDM system are being implemented in response to the earlier business process engineering initiative. However, a failure to communicate between the engineering team and the ERP team cost the company three months in lost effort as both teams had to go back and reconsider their approach and requirement specifications.

A lack of joined-up thinking at best slows intervention projects down, causes frustration and escalates costs. At worst it can result in complete failure of the intervention, however well it has been designed. Having a single plan that integrates all interventions with company objectives, such as that discussed above, is a good start for avoiding such costly mistakes. However, having a joined-up plan is not sufficient if we do not use it to continuously review and coordinate between interventions. In the EngineeringCo example there is potential for this sort of conflict between several interventions.

When it comes to improvement projects and interventions we are all very guilty of treating them as standalone, mutually independent work streams. We quite often follow good project management practices and create steering committees for each large intervention. With all the best intentions, in order to avoid overloading people, we often create steering committees that are mutually exclusive, further compounding the problem of managing projects in isolation from one another.

One way of avoiding such potential conflicts is through regular reviews of the interventions, where project teams (or at least the project managers) of different interventions are present. The challenge here is to create a simple and effective communications mechanism that enables different teams and project managers to communicate effectively and efficiently. At the end of the last section we concluded that performance improvement interventions, to be effective, need to be reviewed regularly. Here I would argue that, in addition to regularly reviewing each intervention, interventions need to be collectively reviewed in order to minimise the likelihood of unintentional conflicts arising between them.

13.4   MILESTONES: ONE BIG STEP AT A TIME

Another way of avoiding such conflicts is to reduce the number of interventions we pursue at a time. Earlier, in Chapter 12, we discussed the benefits of such an approach and how different interventions compete for resources. In Chapter 5, we also introduced an idea around creating company milestones and tackling one project at a time. Planning one intervention at a time and delivering it quickly and efficiently is certainly the best way of engaging everyone in the organisation to work towards a common purpose. This is especially so if we are creative with the way we name the intervention to reflect the intended outcome. The examples we quoted earlier in Chapter 5 include '*Simple to install*' and '*Simple to buy*'. Other examples could include '*A better place to work*' (capturing the social dimension of the intervention), '*20% cheaper to manufacture*' and '*15% more energy efficient*' (associating a milestone with a significant improvement in performance).

Looking at all the things we need to do, and thinking about what we are trying to achieve, enables us to group or integrate apparently different interventions under a common purpose, as illustrated in Figure 13.4 for EngineeringCo.

In this case, the example is not trying to do anything different. It is just expressing what the company is trying to achieve in a more purposeful way. Each milestone indicates what will be achieved in a certain timescale, such as: by the end of the first year the company will be better at selling products and will be a better place to work in; by month 18 it will be 20% more productive; by the end of the second year it will increase its global reach and it will have products that are 20% more efficient. Creating such milestones provides a common purpose, aids in communication and reduces the apparent complexity of what needs to be done. It can also simplify the review process.

13.5   MAKING IMPROVEMENT PART OF THE DAY JOB

Another common issue to consider when delivering performance improvement interventions is the apparent conflict between the day job and the improvement project (i.e., the intervention). Many workplaces still suffer from the day job vs. project syndrome, as people see improvement projects as a separate additional

Engineering Co Growth Objectives and Initiatives

		Current State	2014				2015				2016				2017			
		2013 FY	Q1	Q2	Q3	Q4	Q1	Q2	Q3	Q4	Q1	Q2	Q3	Q4	Q1	Q2	Q3	Q4
Financial Objectives	Bookings	£7M				£12M				£18.5M				£26.5M				£35.7M
	Revenue	£6M				£10M				£16.3M				£23M				£32.5M
	EBITDA	£1.1M				£1.6M				£3.3M				£5.3M				£7,010
Customer Objectives	OTD	100%				100%				95%				95%				95%
	Longest Quotation Turn around time	2 weeks				2 weeks				1 week				3 days				1 day
	Technical Support (Doc OTD)	75%				85%				95%				95%				95%
	Response to technical enquiries	48hrs				24hrs				24hrs				<24hrs				<24hrs
Internal Process Objectives	On time delivery	90%				100%				100%				100%				100%
	Cash conversion / Turnover	100%				100%				80%				75%				75%
	NCR's	£25k				£25k				£25k				£25k				£25k
	Customer Complaints	21				<15				<10				<5				<5
Organisational Capabilities	Customer Intimacy																	
	Operational Excellence																	
	Product Leadership																	
	Organisational Culture																	

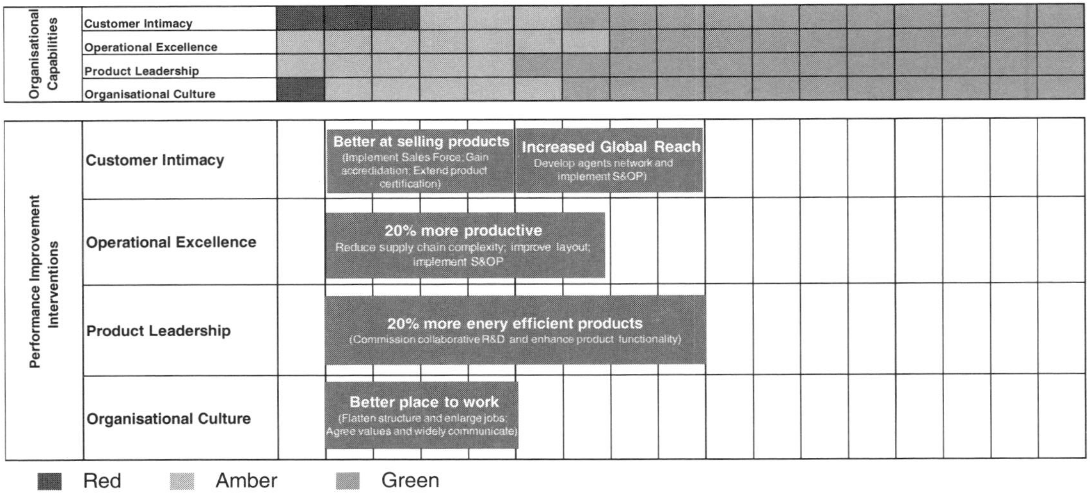

Performance Improvement Interventions

- **Customer Intimacy:** Better at selling products (Implement Sales Force; Gain accreditation Extend product certification) — Increased Global Reach (Develop agents network and implement S&OP)
- **Operational Excellence:** 20% more productive (Reduce supply chain complexity; improve layout; implement S&OP)
- **Product Leadership:** 20% more energy efficient products (Commission collaborative R&D and enhance product functionality)
- **Organisational Culture:** Better place to work (Flatten structure and enlarge jobs Agree values and widely communicate)

Legend: ■ Red ■ Amber ■ Green

FIGURE 13.4 Milestones creating meaningful purpose

piece of work to the job they have been engaged to do. One way of changing this is by ensuring that an improvement objective is integrated into the day job. In a small service manufacturing business that specialised in contract bottling and packaging for the Scottish whisky industry we achieved some remarkable results by including a monthly improvement target of £10k savings into the team's objectives. Here we were trying to implement process improvement across the manufacturing facilities. We had a process improvement specialist working hard trying to identify cost-saving opportunities and implement changes, but we were not getting anywhere fast. The message from the manufacturing team was that *"we get what you are trying to do... just get out of our way and we'll do it"*. So an agreement was reached, the team had a monthly cost savings target of £10k and the process improvement specialist was retained to act as a consultant/resource to the manufacturing team. For the following months the manufacturing team rarely failed to hit the target savings. In one year the company increased its profitability by 13% solely through this approach. Another company, operating in the food and drinks sector, used measures such as *number of hours saved* and *percentage reduction in defects* as KPIs in their regular performance measurement systems. In short, as well as measuring the flow of work through their processes, they were also measuring the improvement rate. It appears that using improvement rates as a measure of performance does indeed serve to embed continuous improvement into the day job.

It appears that one of the best ways of integrating improvement (continuous or radical) is through integrating project reviews of interventions with the regular performance reviews as discussed earlier in Chapter 5. This ensures that all parties are aware of what is happening to business performance and what is happening in each intervention. More importantly, everyone is constantly reminded of the relationship between interventions and performance. In short, everyone is informed and everyone will learn something. The trick is to make these reviews short and sharp. People often get bored with long, drawn-out meetings that become talking and moaning shops but achieve very little else. The purpose should be to focus on exceptions; communicate how each intervention/project is progressing; discuss issues, barriers and concerns; agree actions and move on.

TIME FOR REFLECTION

- Do we clearly link our performance improvement interventions to overall performance? Are these easy to understand and communicate?
- Do we conduct regular reviews of our interventions? If so, is the purpose of the review to help and support the teams delivering the interventions?

- Are our interventions creating positive experiences for those involved? Do people want to get involved and be engaged in our interventions?
- Are our interventions joined up or do we manage them as independent projects?
- Have we got too many interventions? Have we thought about what we are trying to achieve and expressed our interventions as purposeful milestones?
- Culturally, is improvement – be it incremental, continuous improvement or working on a transformational project – seen as part of our everyday job?

13.6 SUMMARY

Generally we are not very good at planning and monitoring the delivery of the performance improvement interventions we have so painstakingly researched, analysed and decided upon. In many cases our interventions are concerned with a single timeframe, mostly focusing on short-term results. Rarely do we ask ourselves how we can deliver short-term results whilst simultaneously developing the underlying capabilities of the business for longer-term sustainable performance. Understanding our current state with respect to organisational capabilities and planning, our interventions, with due consideration, will enable us to balance short-term results with longer-term sustainable performance.

Visualising our interventions and their expected impact on overall performance provides a powerful tool for planning, communicating and reviewing the progress of our interventions. In most cases there is a time lag between delivering an intervention and the top- and/or bottom-line impact of that intervention. Using time-based strategy maps allows us to capture this time lag and visualise our interventions in an integrated way. They also provide the basis for managing our interventions in a joined-up way to minimise the potential conflicts between different interventions. Integrating our interventions into purposeful milestones helps us to minimise the complexity of our planned interventions, improving communications and creating clarity. Also, it is good practice to regularly review the progress of our interventions. Integrating reviews of intervention projects with regular performance reviews provides excellent opportunities for collective reviews of our interventions, as well as embedding improvement (incremental or radical) into everyday work, thus further reducing the likelihood of conflicts between projects. Balancing the short-term with the long-term requires a clear plan. Communicating this is not straightforward; indeed, it's pretty challenging to get the appropriate level of buy-in and understanding. What is perhaps most important, however, is that we keep on communicating, reviewing and re-prioritising as the plan unfolds. This is the only way we can learn!

REFERENCES

Hirano, H. (1995) *5 Pillars of the Visual Workplace*, Productivity Press: Cambridge, MA.
Shingo, S. (1985) *A Revolution in Manufacturing: The SMED System*, Productivity Press: Stamford, CT.

It is essential to make improvement, incremental or radical, part of the day job.

Continuously communicating, reviewing and reprioritising, as the plan unfolds, is the only way we can learn!

Epilogue

Where there is balance and harmony there is performance.

14.1   IT'S ALL ABOUT BALANCE AND HARMONY

It is amazing how writing down your thoughts and experiences enables you to see new patterns and develop new insights that you have not thought of previously. At the outset, in planning this book, my intention was to write about the essential balance between the *science* and the *art* of managing business performance, balancing the 'processy' things we do with the people component. Having now written the book, I have come to realise that sustainable performance is about balancing a number of competing forces. Indeed, it is crucial that we achieve a balance between the technical controls and the social controls in the way we manage our organisations. But there are other forces we also need to balance.

In designing performance measurement systems we need to achieve a workable balance between simplicity and complexity. Over the past 20 or more years I have seen some complex performance measurement systems that no one wanted to use, as well as some very simple systems that did not provide sufficient information for the management to take any action. We need to be able to achieve a workable balance between simplicity and complexity if we are to create performance measurement systems that provide us with actionable insights into the behaviour of our business processes and value streams.

We need to create a balance between our operational and dynamic capabilities. Whilst having well-developed operational capabilities enables us to efficiently and effectively deliver a focused business model, this can also prevent us from quickly and efficiently responding to changes in the world around us – unless it is supported by equally well-developed dynamic capabilities. Similarly, having well-developed dynamic capabilities without equally well-developed operational capabilities is also counterproductive. In this situation we end up reacting to opportunities and threats with innovative responses but without the ability to deliver effectively and efficiently.

We also need to create balance between short-term and long-term results. Whilst it may be tempting to focus on and deliver results quickly in the short term, we need to make sure that these are not achieved at the expense of longer-term sustainable performance. Similarly, focusing on the long-term results whilst ignoring the short-term implications is also counterproductive. We do need to be able to do both and balance our actions accordingly.

We also need to achieve an appropriate balance in the technical and social dimensions of our interventions. On the one hand technical interventions may deliver quick results, but if our people are not fully on board they are rarely sustainable. On the other hand, if we have the right people with the right direction and motivation, we could be amazed at what they achieve. But it is not often that we find ourselves in these situations. Thus, it is crucial that our performance improvement interventions have the right balance between the technical and social factors.

On a personal note, my mother and grandfather had it all worked out and a couple of their teachings have stuck with me to this date: "… *everything in excess is harmful, it is important to strike a balance…*". Here my mother was referring to achieving a balance between studying vs. partying, friends vs. family, consuming alcohol vs. not consuming alcohol and so on. My grandfather, who was a landscape architect, used to say "… *in nature everything needs to be in balance* [meaning water, sun and earth]. *When they are in balance gardens live and grow in harmony. If the balance is not right there is no harmony, they just die*".

14.2   LEARNING THE RIGHT BALANCE

When it comes to organisations I really do not think there is a one-size-fits-all answer to the question *What is the right balance?* As each one of us has to learn how to achieve balance and harmony in our personal lives, our organisations also have to learn what the right balance is for them. I believe that being a learning organisation is the key message that underpins everything I have said in this book. You may have noticed that I have refrained from telling you which measures to use – a question I am asked quite regularly when I run my performance measurement and management workshops. This is because I know that one set of measures that works for one organisation may not work for another.

Also, when we were talking about organisational capabilities, you may have noticed my recommendation for each organisation to develop their own maturity models for each capability area. At the end of the day, even if you end up with very similar models, the fact that you took the time out to think, discuss and reflect what 'good' means for your organisation, sector or industry shows what you have learned.

Although organisations can learn from the experiences of other organisations, real learning and profound knowledge only develop as a result of doing something and reflecting on its results. Just recently I have come across a gem of a company with the axiom '*fail faster*', which reflects the open and participative learning culture they have managed to create in the organisation. They actively encourage everyone to try new things; the more they try the more they learn what works and what does not, and the faster they improve. Notice that the axiom '*fail faster*' is the exact opposite of "… *you'd better watch yourselves, I don't like failure…*", a message commonly delivered by many bosses. Even if you do not explicitly say this, your behaviour and actions can easily convey this message without you even realising it.

In short, if we want to create sustainable organisations that are able to grow and flourish, we need to achieve balance and harmony in our organisations by learning to fail and learning to learn.

14.3   WHERE DO WE START?

A common question I am often asked by people who have attended my seminars and read the first drafts of this book is "*OK, we get all this but where do we start?*" Unfortunately, I do not have an easy answer to this. The only way I can answer this question is by asking another – *Where are you right now?*

If you have read this book and had a go at reflecting on the points I raised in the 'Time for reflection' boxes, you probably have a good idea of where you are right now. But the question still remains – *Where do you start?*

You should start by making a list of all the immediate issues that keep you and your people awake at night (i.e., the burning issues). You should also be able to identify the key gaps in your organisational culture and your organisational capabilities. You could always try using the generic capability maturity models at www.wiley.com/go/bititci but, as I said before, it would be better if these were your own models. Now, armed with this information, you should be able to start charting a course of action that will help you address the short-term issues and develop your organisation's capabilities and culture. But you should not try to do this alone; involve your team and your people. The more you open up, the more ideas and engagement you will get. For me, the first step should always be an open discussion to identify the burning issues and the key gaps in your organisation and culture.

In most cases, I honestly do not think that we purposefully set out to create command-and-control-based organisations. They just emerge that way. Reflecting on Desmond Morris's book *The Naked Ape* (Morris, 2010), I cannot help but think that creating hierarchies and controlling our subordinates is in our genetic make-up. This is probably stronger in the male population, as we often refer to alpha-male behaviour in our organisations. Somehow we need to learn to get our people involved; give them direction; trust them and let them go.

Don't get me wrong. I am not suggesting that we turn our organisations into mystical hippie communes. However, we do need to achieve a workable balance between the *science* and the *art* of managing business performance.

REFERENCE

Morris, D. (2010) *The Naked Ape: A zoologist's study of the human animal*, Random House: New York.

*Our organisations have to learn what
the right balance is for them.*

The Book in a Nutshell

*Where there is balance and
harmony there is performance.*

15.1 PART ONE – INTRODUCTION

This book has been about the *science* and the *art* of managing business performance. Having started the book with an overview of how the theory and practice of performance measurement and management developed, we concluded that theory follows practice. In other words, as the operating environment changes – politically, economically, socially, technologically and environmentally – managers respond to these changes by innovating new ways of measuring and managing performance that are more appropriate for the emerging context. Researchers then observe these practices, they analyse what mangers do, what works and what does not, why and in what context. Eventually they use the emerging insights to theorise about management. These models and frameworks are used by different organisations in different contexts, and further analysis of these leads to more insights, new understanding, refined models, frameworks and theories. In summary, *performance measurement and management is a live subject where practice leads theory*.

Over the years the theory of performance measurement has developed from *performance measurement* to *performance management*. That is, from **what to measure** to **how to use these measures to manage the performance of the organisation**. Today, with increasing rates of change, globalisation and connectivity, we are witnessing the emergence of new forms of organisation where people network externally as they do internally. In short, we are living in a period of exponential change, when the nature of work and the rules of competition are changing. The big question is: **Are today's performance measurement and management practices fit for the contemporary organisations and societies of the 21st century?**

Fundamentally, performance measurement and management is about organisational control. With this shift from performance measurement to performance management, over recent times our conceptualisation of performance measurement has been changing. Where in the past we saw performance measurement as a technical or mechanistic control mechanism, today we are more concerned with how we use performance measures to engage our people in a dialogue about the performance of the organisation. In short, we are more concerned about the balance we achieve between technical controls and social controls (i.e., the *science* and the *art* of managing business performance).

15.2 PART TWO – THE SCIENCE

Today, most organisations – with many customers, markets, products and services – are complex systems. Complexity is one of the most significant constraints of performance, as people operating in different parts of the organisation perceive the organisation differently. This results in everyone having a different view as to what is important and what is not. However, when we look at what organisations do rather than how they are organised, we see a common structure emerging. That is, all organisations exist to service a demand. They operate with different products and services, serving different customers in different markets, who use varying criteria to make buying decisions. So, organisations create value through business units that focus on particular product and customer groups. We call these focused business units that create value, value streams. In this context a value stream is defined as a purposeful and coherent set of business processes, aligned with delivering value to a customer or specific group of customers whilst creating value for the business. Therefore, *unless we have a clear understanding of how each value stream competes in the market and what its critical success factors are, here and now and in the future, we cannot effectively manage the business performance as a whole*.

At the most fundamental level, *each value stream comprises a set of four business processes: Develop Product, Get Order, Fulfil Order and Support Product*. For each one of our value streams to be competitive we need to be better than our competitors across all four of these processes. Furthermore, these four core business processes are supported by other managerial and support processes that are critical for effective and efficient operation of each value stream here and now (i.e., today), as well as in the future. The emerging anatomy represents the *universal competitive structure of an organisation* that is inherent in all organisations, industrial and service as well as public and private.

Many organisations do not understand the value streams and business processes that underpin their competitive structure. Managers need to unify their diverse perceptions of the organisation and collectively recognise and manage this universal competitive structure if they are to effectively manage the performance of their organisation.

In managing business processes and value streams, *the purpose of the process* and *the flow of work through the process* are the two most important things about a process. The purpose of a process should align with the competitive priorities of the value stream. In turn, the work flow through the process should harmonise with the purpose of the process. Materials, products, information and customers can all flow through the process. Hence, in managing our processes we need to understand what flows through the process and we need to be particularly sensitive to how customers interact with the process.

Processes, whether operational, support or managerial, are rarely consistent. Natural variation within the underlying capabilities will inevitably cause a certain degree of variation in all processes. Our task, as managers, is to understand these capabilities and try to manage this variation. *The lower the variation the more consistent the process performance.* Also, it is important to remember that our capabilities are hugely affected by the capabilities of our suppliers, partners and customers. It is, thus, important to understand our capabilities in the context of the whole value system.

We use performance measures and comparisons all the time in our everyday lives, there is no getting away from them. What we need to do is design effective performance measurement systems. In designing performance measurement systems, we first need to focus on the value stream. For each value stream we need to focus on two things, the purpose of the value stream and the work flow through the value stream. Whilst our performance measures should be kept as simple as possible, it is also important that they communicate the rich information that is required to enable people to make a decision. It is quite common to have performance information indicating that something is wrong, but with no further information on potential causes the team cannot make a decision. The trick is to create performance measurement systems people value and want to use. Creating visual scorecards and dashboards in war-rooms, integrated with strategy walls/boards, is an effective way of getting people engaged in a conversation about the purpose and performance of an organisation. Regular performance reviews should be an important part of the managerial routine in all organisations. However, the purpose of these reviews should not be to check and make a judgement on people's performance; rather, it should be about communication and collective learning.

Clearly, measurement is important. We need to measure the right things, we need to display these measures to communicate rich and valuable information, and we also need to conduct regular performance reviews. *However, how we use these measures (i.e., the art of managing performance) is even more important for the future performance of our organisations. After all, the purpose of a performance measurement should be to engage people in a conversation about the performance of the organisation. Hence, we need to create performance measurement systems that people value and want to use!*

15.3 PART THREE – THE ART

Performance is timescale sensitive. What we do to improve performance for the short-term is not necessarily what we would do to improve performance for the medium- and long-term. When we talk about business performance we are all very guilty of using lagging performance metrics that tell us what has happened in the past. Instead, we should be more concerned with the future performance of the organisation. Questions such as *Are people happy? Is the place well organised? What do the customers think?* are quite common but rarely feature in our performance measurement systems. In managing the performance of our business it is quite easy to increase its value in the short-term by simply stripping away capability. We can cut all sorts of costs and make the numbers look good at the end of the year. But this is not sustainable. For sustainable medium-term growth we need to be concerned with three capability areas: Product Leadership, Operational Excellence and Customer Intimacy. If we can understand how our organisation is positioned in comparison with our competitors or the market average, then we can start thinking about how we can invest in developing these capabilities. For longer-term growth, however, we also need to be concerned about becoming an adaptive and dynamic organisation. More explicitly, an organisation that is able to deliver a focused business model efficiently and effectively, whilst simultaneously identifying opportunities and threats, developing innovative responses and changing with minimum pain and disruption. In short, *it is the organisational capabilities and culture that determine how people interact with the processes that deliver performance*.

As managers we need to understand the fundamental organisational capabilities that underpin our performance. Investing in the organisational capabilities today will mean improved performance in the future. Even though the literature on organisational capabilities is somewhat confused, there are some useful models emerging. There are a few pertinent points that one needs to remember. Organisational capabilities are not mutually exclusive, rather, they co-evolve as organisations learn from their and others' experiences. So, organisational learning is an important capability that underpins all other capability areas. It is now a commonly quoted and accepted fact that *organisations that learn faster than their competitors outperform their competitors*. The conditions that encourage organisations to learn are also well understood. An open, participative, democratic, trusting and fear-free culture encourages people to communicate openly, share ideas and concerns openly, experiment and share insights, all enhancing the organisation's learning. Whilst maturity models help to accelerate learning and enable the development of organisational capabilities, the key organisational capabilities that we need to focus on are:

- *Operational capability.* The ability to define a focused business model and deliver it efficiently and effectively. This includes:
  - Strategic capability.
  - Product leadership capability.
  - Operational excellence capability.
  - Customer intimacy capability.
- *Dynamic capability.* The ability to sense opportunities and threats; evaluate and anticipate their significance; develop innovative responses; change with minimum pain and disruption.
- *Ambidexterity.* The ability to achieve an appropriate balance between operational and dynamic capabilities.
- Learning capability.
- Organisational culture.

Try using the maturity models from www.wiley.com/go/bititci to evaluate your organisation in these capability areas. But beware; these generic maturity models are limited at best. It is always better to use these as the basis and develop your own maturity models.

Performance, particularly long-term sustainable performance, is all about people. However, in our theories and frameworks for managing the performance of organisations we seem to have forgotten about the people component. When we ask people to describe the characteristics of the organisations they would like to work in, we get a wide range of factors. The sad truth is that very few of these characteristics actually feature in our performance measurement systems. We know that performance measurement and management is about organisational control. Earlier we conceptualised performance measurement and management as technical and social controls, respectively. It appears that *whilst our research and practices have developed our understanding of the technical controls into a science, our understanding of social controls remains largely a black art.* However, it is clear that unless we achieve the right balance between these technical and social controls we are always in danger of undermining the performance potential of our organisation. Clearly, if we are concerned with knowledge-based, innovative and creative organisations, which we all should be, we need to achieve a balance between well-developed, mature technical controls and open, participative social controls. In short, *organisations that balance a well-developed mature performance measurement system with open, participative and democratic management tend to perform better. We need to create humanistic organisations where we encourage team working, comradery and compassion* (Figure 15.1). The problem is that, today, there are many organisations that have not managed to find this balance. In fact, they are quite rare. *Failing to achieve the right balance between social and technical controls results in bad things, like poor customer service, misinformation, uninspiring work – which ultimately impacts on performance.* So, we still have some work to do to help most of our organisations find this balance. We need to better understand how to design performance improvement interventions that deliver sustainable results.

15.4 PART FOUR – EFFECTIVE INTERVENTIONS

Interventions are rarely effective if we do not understand and conceptualise our organisation as an interconnected system. Only then can we start thinking about what needs to change and how. However, another important consideration is *who decides what to change*. Often, interventions that are designed by people outside the organisation (system) – such as the parent company, senior management or a consultant – are technical interventions. They expect to make a policy, process or procedural change that would lead to a significant change in the behaviour

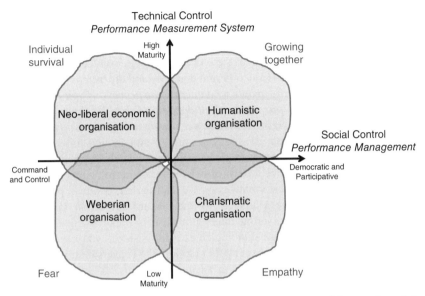

FIGURE 15.1 Managing business performance: technical and social controls and the drivers of performance

and, therefore, the performance of the system. However, as we all know, this rarely happens. All interventions have a technical and a social dimension. Once again we often forget about the social dimension; at best it becomes a bolt-on to our technical intervention, guised as *management of change*. In designing our interventions we once again need to achieve a balance between the technical and the social dimension of our interventions. Sometimes purely social interventions, *letting the people decide what to change*, deliver unprecedented performance improvements.

Another point about systems is that once you have changed one thing in the system, the system is changed. You need to study the system again to understand its new behaviour. So, the three basic rules for designing effective interventions are: (1) ensure that the intervention serves a higher purpose that stays constant over time; (2) identify the most significant constraint that is preventing you from getting one step closer to your purpose and focus on alleviating that constraint; (3) pursue one intervention at a time.

One other thing about systems is that there is usually a small change you can make, known as the trim-tab, which significantly changes the behaviour of the whole system. Whilst more popular approaches such as process mapping enable us to describe what the system does, they rarely tell us why the system behaves as it does. Approaches such as Soft Systems Methodology and role playing enable organisations to develop a much better understanding of why the system behaves as it does. Quite often it is difficult to identify what to change in the system, so we need to be prepared to experiment. More importantly, if we let the people who operate the process experiment with the process, they will eventually find the one change they need to make. I frequently find that *provided the 'sciency' bits are in place, the best trim-tab is the people who operate the process. If you trust them, invest in them, give them purpose and guidance and then let them loose they will find the trim-tab, delivering dramatic performance improvements*.

Change programmes that have a clear purpose and explicit links to overall performance are more likely to succeed. In designing and delivering interventions it is also important to achieve a balance between short-term results and drivers of long-term sustainable performance. As we said earlier, people's perceptions are different. What may be a concern to one person may be an insignificant point to another. So, in delivering interventions, it is important to understand what the key stakeholders are thinking. It is a lot easier if you can join their conversations as opposed to expecting them to join the conversation in your own head. Whichever way we look at it, if an intervention is not going to make a contribution towards the bottom- or top-line performance it is not worth doing. So we need to ensure that the expected impact and timescale of our interventions are made explicit. This is best done through visual, time-based strategy maps that illustrate how and when an intervention is expected to impact on organisational capabilities, operational and customer-facing performance, and eventually overall performance. Once again, regular reviews of interventions is critical to success, but these need to be conducted in an open and supportive manner – where the purpose is to help the team to achieve their objective. After all, the more positive experiences we create for people participating in these interventions, the more they will want to be involved and engaged in them.

When we have too many parallel interventions the likelihood of conflict arising between them increases. Naturally there will be some conflict for resources, which is not helpful. But what is even more destructive is when the two different improvement projects are trying to change the same bit of the organisation. This is destructive and serves to discredit both interventions. One way of ensuring some joined-up thinking is to ensure that intervention reviews are integrated and all parties participate in the collective conversation. Here any such conflicts can be identified and resolved before they become a problem. The best way of avoiding this problem is to minimise the number of interventions. Sometimes merging a number of small interventions into a larger purposeful change programme helps to overcome this problem, as well as serving to mobilise people towards a common purpose.

Finally, all too often working on improvement projects is seen as a separate activity from one's normal job. People often talk about their *day job* and *projects*. One way of achieving this is by integrating improvement-related measures into the performance measurement systems people use to do their daily work. This gives us technical control. Another pertinent factor is to engage people in a conversation about the interventions they are involved in as part of the routine performance reviews. This approach, over time, helps to embed a culture where improvement projects, incremental or radical, are embedded in the day jobs of people at all levels.

15.5 CONCLUSIONS

Overall, if we are to effectively manage the performance of our organisations we need to be concerned with creating a platform for long-term growth. To achieve this we need to achieve a balance between various things:

- *First*, we need to achieve a balance between technical controls and social controls in the way we manage our organisations.
- *Second*, in designing our performance measurement systems we need to achieve a balance between simplicity and creating an information system that provides us with actionable information.
- *Third*, we need to achieve a balance between focusing on short-term results and longer-term drivers of performance.
- *Fourth*, in designing and delivering our interventions we need to achieve a balance between the technical and the social dimension.

In short, we need to balance organisational controls!

Appendices

A

Overview of Popular Performance Measurement Models and Frameworks

A.1 DuPONT MODEL

This is one of the original performance measurement systems that was developed by Du Pont, the American chemicals giant, and is based on cost accounting theories and practices. Du Pont developed a structure by linking accounting measures and financial ratios – such as Return On Net Assets (RONA), Return On Investment (ROI) and Return On Equity (ROE) – to more operational indicators and measures.

RONA is commonly used to evaluate the effective use of assets by measuring the ratio of profit margins (net income) to asset turnover (average total assets). ROI is used to evaluate the efficiency of an investment by comparing the ratio of profit and investment cost. ROE is the ratio of net income to shareholders' equity, which shows the amount of profit generated from the money invested by shareholders.

One of the advantages of Du Pont's model is its structure, which integrates financial measures with operational indicators. In contrast, the main drawback is that it is mainly focused on financial measures and has been criticised for being myopic and short-term oriented.

Figure A.1 illustrates DuPont's RONA tree.

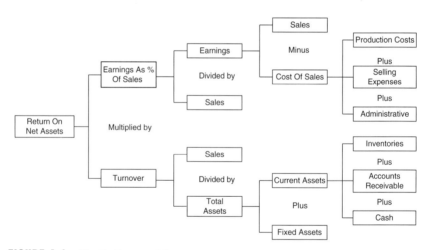

FIGURE A.1   The DuPont model

A.2 THE PERFORMANCE MEASUREMENT MATRIX (PMM)

The PMM was developed by Keegan *et al.* (1989). It integrates financial and non-financial internal and external facets of business performance, as illustrated in

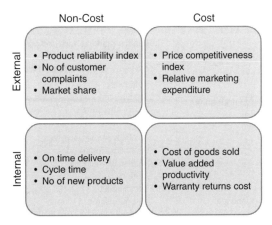

FIGURE A.2   The Performance Measurement Matrix   .

Figure A.2. The main strengths of PMM are its simplicity and integrated structure. The main criticisms of PMM include a lack of structure and detail, particularly in relation to making the links between different business dimensions more explicit, as in the Balanced Scorecard.

A.3   THE PERFORMANCE MEASUREMENT QUESTIONNAIRE (PMQ)

The PMQ was created by Dixon *et al.* (1990) to serve as a decision tool for managers. Essentially, it is a structured questionnaire that audits the compatibility of a firm's performance measures in relation to its improvement aims and objectives. The questionnaire analyses alignment, congruence, consensus and confusion – helping maintain consistency between the firm's strategy, improvement actions and measures. Essentially it is different from previous frameworks and models as it does not attempt to provide a framework for designing a performance measurement system, rather it is a tool for auditing the appropriateness of a performance measurement system.

A.4   THE RESULTS AND DETERMINANTS FRAMEWORK

The Results and Determinants Framework (Fitzgerald *et al.*, 1991) has a structure composed of six performance dimensions classified under two categories: results and determinants (Figure A.3).

	Dimension of performance	Types of measure
RESULTS Lagging indicators	Competitiveness	Relative market share and position Sales growth Measures of the customer base
	Financial performance	Profitability Liquidity Capital structure Market ratios
DETERMINANTS Leading indicators	Quality of service	Reliability responsiveness Aesthetics/appearance Cleanliness/tidiness Comfort Friendliness Communication Courtesy Competence Access Availability Security
	Flexibility	Volume flexibility Delivery speed flexibility Specification flexibility
	Resource utilisation	Productivity Efficiency
	Innovation	Performance of the innovation process Performance of the individual innovations

FIGURE A.3   The Results and Determinants Framework

The results category covers financial- and competitiveness-related perfor-mance measures. The framework conceptualises these measures as lagging indi-cators that reflect the ultimate objectives of an organisation. The determinants category includes performance measures for service quality, flexibility, resource utilisation and innovation, which are conceptualised as leading indicators.

A.5 THE STRATEGIC MEASUREMENT ANALYSIS AND REPORTING TECHNIQUE (SMART)

SMART, which is also known as the Performance Pyramid, was developed to eliminate the disadvantages associated with traditional, financially focused per-formance measurement systems (Cross and Lynch, 1989). This pyramid integrates the strategic objectives and operational performance dimensions through a four-level structure (Figure A.4). Whilst the right-hand side of the pyramid reflects

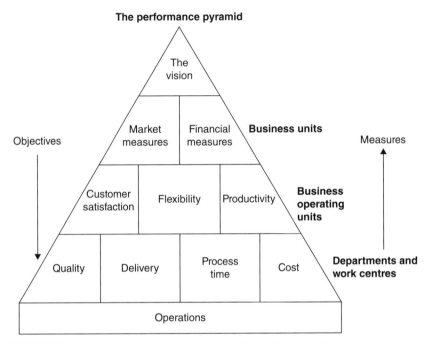

FIGURE A.4 The Strategic Measurement Analysis and Reporting Technique

internal efficiency measures, the left-hand side of the pyramid reflects external effectiveness measures.

A.6 THE CAMBRIDGE PERFORMANCE MEASUREMENT DESIGN PROCESS

The Cambridge Performance Measurement Design Process, illustrated in Figure A.5, was developed in order to improve the design of performance measurement systems (Neely *et al.*, 1996). The process is documented in the form of a workbook, which is available from the Institute for Manufacturing.[1]

The main contribution of this work is to show how all internal, external, financial and non-financial elements are integrated with the strategy to create a coherent performance measurement system. The framework can assist with identifying conflicting performance measures whilst maintaining a balance between external and internal measures.

---

[1] www.ifm.eng.cam.ac.uk/resources/strategy/getting-the-measure-of-your-business/.

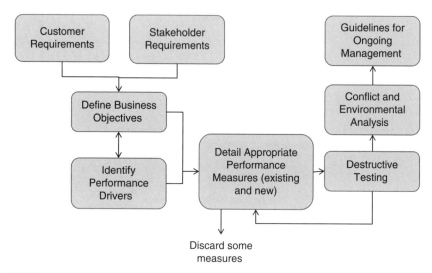

FIGURE A.5   The Cambridge Performance Measurement Design Process

A.7   THE PYRAMID OF ORGANISATIONAL DEVELOPMENT

Developed by Flamholtz (1995), the model links organisational capabilities (culture, system and resources) to success in the markets using six factors: corporate culture, management systems, operational systems, resource management, products and services, and markets (Figure A.6). As a model it is much broader than performance measurement systems, which it incorporates as a management system.

A.8   INTEGRATED PERFORMANCE MEASUREMENT SYSTEM (IPMS) REFERENCE MODEL

The IPMS reference model (Bititci *et al.*, 1997) was developed to quantify and model the relationships between performance measures. This system comprises a reference model and an audit method. The model integrates stakeholder requirements with performance measures through: differentiating competitive characteristics of different business units; deployment of stakeholder requirements through the entire organisation; external monitoring and competitive positioning; key business processes and associated performance measures (Figure A.7). It also includes normative planning and active monitoring through the usage of leading measures.

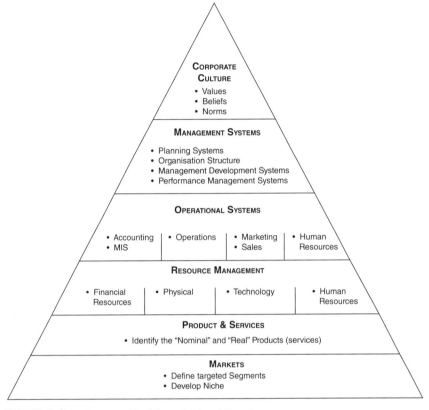

FIGURE A.6   The Pyramid of Organisational Development

A.9   THE BUSINESS EXCELLENCE MODEL OF THE EUROPEAN FOUNDATION FOR QUALITY MANAGEMENT (EFQM)

The EFQM's Business Excellence[2] model is a framework, which links the key performance results of an organisation to its processes and leadership. Referring to Figure A.8 and working from right to left:

- Long-term sustainable performance (key performance results) is a function of satisfied people (people results), satisfied customers (customer results) and a positive impact on the society (society results).

---

[2]www.efqm.org/the-efqm-excellence-model.

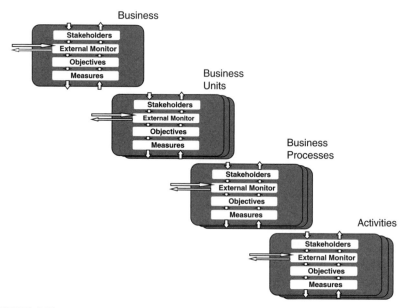

FIGURE A.7   Integrated Performance Measurement System reference model

- These results in turn are enabled by well-developed and mature processes that are
  - resourced with good people with appropriate education, training and attitudes;
  - directed by appropriate policies and strategies;
  - supported by appropriate partnerships (e.g., suppliers) and other resources.
- All the results and enablers, in turn, are enabled by appropriate leadership.

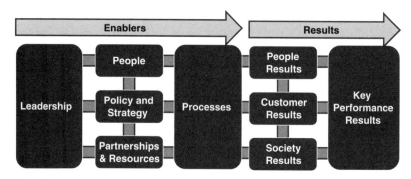

FIGURE A.8   The EFQM Business Excellence model

The EFQM Business Excellence model, despite being criticised for its vagueness, has been popular and widely adopted across Europe and modified in other regions of the world – for example the Australian[3] and the Singapore[4] Business Excellence frameworks, amongst others.

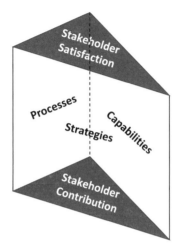

FIGURE A.9   The Performance Prism

A.10   THE PERFORMANCE PRISM

Developed by Neely *et al.* (2002), the Performance Prism (Figure A.9) links Stakeholder Contribution (the bottom face of the prism) with Stakeholder Satisfaction (the top face of the prism) through Processes, Strategies and Capabilities (i.e., the three vertical faces of the prism). Essentially its key message is that performance results (i.e., stakeholder satisfaction) are a function of stakeholder contribution orchestrated through strategies, processes and underlying organisational capabilities. Each facet of the prism intends to create a focus around a key question:

- Who are the stakeholders of the organisation and what are their requirements?
- What strategies are required to ensure the needs of our stakeholders are satisfied?

---

[3] www.saiglobal.com/Improve/ExcellenceModels/BusinessExcellenceFramework.
[4] www.spring.gov.sg/Building-Trust/Business-Excellence/Pages/business-excellence-overview.aspx.

- What processes have to be put in place to allow the strategies to be delivered?
- What capabilities are required to operate the processes?
- What contributions do the stakeholders need to make to ensure that the required strategies, processes and capabilities are in place?

REFERENCES

Bititci, U.S., Carrie, A.S. & McDevitt, L. (1997) Integrated performance measurement systems: A development guide, *International Journal of Operations & Production Management*, 17(5), 522–534.

Cross, K.F. and Lynch, R.L. (1989) The SMART way to define and sustain success,. *National Productivity Review*, 9(1), 23–33.

Dixon, J.R., Nanni, A.J. and Vollmann, T.E. (1990) *The New Performance Challenge: Measuring operations for world class competition*, Dow Jones-Irwin: Homewood, IL.

Fitzgerald, L., Johnson, R., Brignall, S., Silvestro, R. and Voss, C. (1991) *Performance Measurement in Service Business*, CIMA: London.

Flamholtz, E. (1995) Managing organizational transitions: Implications for corporate and human resource management, *European Management Journal*, 13(1), 39–51.

Keegan, D.P., Eiler, R.G. and Jones, C.R. (1989) Are your performance measures obsolete? *Management Accounting*, June, 45–50.

Neely, A., Mills, J., Gregory, M., Richards, H., Platts, K. and Bourne, M. (1996) Getting the measure of your business. Manufacturing Engineering Group, University of Cambridge, Cambridge.

Neely, A.D., Adams, C. and Kennerley, M. (2002) *The Performance Prism: The scorecard for measuring and managing business success*, Prentice Hall/Financial Times: London.

B

Common Performance
Measures

There are too many measures to create an exhaustive list of all the possible measures we might need and want to use. However, over the years some measures have emerged as more popular or commonly used than others. In this section my objective is to provide an overview of these more common performance measures. In the following sections I have organised the measures according to the four perspectives of the Balanced Scorecard, with a brief explanation of each measure. Further on in this appendix I have also provided overviews of performance measures from three different sources which I have found useful, namely the Advance Performance Institute, Oliver Wight International and the Supply Chain Operations Reference (SCOR) model. However, I am sure there are many others.

B.1 FINANCIALLY FOCUSED MEASURES

- *Revenue/turnover*. The income that an organisation receives from its normal business activities, usually from the sale of goods and services to customers.
- *Market share*. The organisation's revenue or unit sales expressed as a percentage of the market total. Many companies, particularly SMEs, have problems defining/identifying the total size of the market they serve.
- *Profits*. Surplus generated after deducting business expenses from revenues.
- *Profitability*. Profits expressed as a percentage of revenues. More profitable businesses will return higher profit figures for a given revenue.
- *Cash-to-cash cycle time*. Measure of the cashflow required to finance the running of the business – that is, the time taken from paying for raw materials to getting paid for the sale of the product which contains that raw material.
- *EBITDA – Earnings Before Interest, Tax, Depreciation and Amortisation*. Essentially a business profitability measure, but widely used for valuing a business.
- *ROI – Return On Investment and RONA – Return On Net Assets*. Measures of the returns a business generates on its investments. RONA is the preferred choice for capital-intensive businesses (e.g., process industries); ROI is the more common measure.

B.2 CUSTOMER-FOCUSED MEASURES

- Customer satisfaction
  - *Customer satisfaction index*. Usually a measure based on a customer satisfaction survey.
  - *Customer complaints*. Usually expressed as a number of customer complaints received in a given period of time (e.g., a week, month, quarter, year).

- *Net Promoter Score (NPS)*. The likelihood of a customer recommending your business to another potential customer.
- *Customer retention rate*. The likelihood or number of customers returning for more business; a measure of customer loyalty.

- **Delivery reliability**
  - *On-time delivery to request*. A measure of product/service delivery performance in relation to the delivery date/timescale as requested by the customer.
  - *On-time delivery to promise*. A measure of product/service delivery performance in relation to the delivery date/timescale as promised to the customer.
  - *On-time-in-full delivery*. Sometimes also known as perfect order fulfilment (i.e., orders delivered on time to the correct address in correct quantities with no documentation errors).

- **Speed and flexibility**
  - *Delivery lead times*. Time taken from receipt of customer order to delivery of product or service. Essentially a measure of delivery speed.
  - *Response times*. Speed of response to customer enquiry (e.g., quotations, return of calls, etc.).
  - *Fill rates*. Percentage of orders that ship directly from stock. Although it measures the speed at which an organisation can fulfil an order, it is essentially a measure of an organisation's ability to plan stock levels to meet anticipated demand.
  - *Flexibility*. The ability to accommodate changes in customers' requirements.

- ***External quality***. Many different measures all attempting to quantify the number or percentage of defects and failures experienced by the customer. In some industries they are also known as 'escapes' (i.e., those products that managed to escape the internal quality controls).

- ***Price competitiveness index***. Measures the competitiveness of sales price as a percentage of the market or competitors' average sales prices (e.g., 110% would mean prices are 10% above the market or competitors' average).

B.3   INTERNAL PROCESS-FOCUSED MEASURES

- **Sales process**
  - *Margin attainment*. Measures planned margins vs. attained margins.
  - *Conversion rate*. Measures the effectiveness of your sales process in converting enquiries, tenders and website visits into orders.
  - *Forecast accuracy*. Measures expected/planned demand against actual demand realised.

- *Sales contribution.* Measures planned vs. actual net sales value after marketing and sales costs.
- **Product development process**
  - *Time to market/product development cycle time.* Measures the average time taken to develop new products from concept to launch.
  - *Design re-use.* Measures the use of components, designs and IP in new products. Higher design re-use is usually associated with faster development cycle times.
  - *Plan/schedule adherence.* Tracks whether a development project is on schedule, both in terms of activity completion and project budget.
  - *Profitability tracking.* Measures how well new products are achieving their planned revenue and profitability projections.
- **Resource productivity and process flow**
  - *Cost of goods sold.* Usually expressed as a percentage of revenue; measures how effectively raw materials are being managed. It is a function of the effective utilisation of raw materials with minimum waste, as well as the effective management of buying prices.
  - *Value-added productivity.* Usually based on headcount or salary bill, expressed as a percentage of revenue. It essentially measures the contribution made by each employee. Although *salary bill as a percentage of revenue* is the more popular measure, to compare the productivity of organisations working with significant salary differences (e.g., UK vs. India), sometimes *head count as a percentage of revenue* becomes more meaningful.
  - *Inventory turns/inventory days of supply.* Measures how efficiently (quickly) we are turning/consuming inventory – the quicker the better.
  - *Net asset turns.* Usually expressed as a percentage of revenue; measures how effectively investment in assets is used to generate revenue.
  - *Management costs/total supply chain management costs.* Also expressed as a percentage of revenue; measures how effectively overheads are being used. Would also include the cost associated with processing internal and external quality and warranty problems.
  - *Value-add ratio.* The time consumed by value-adding activities vs. total time.
  - *Change-over time.* The time taken to change over a process (usually a manufacturing processes) from one product to another.
  - *Overall Equipment Effectiveness (OEE).* A measure of the overall effectiveness of equipment; expressed as a function of actual availability, speed × quality rate vs. theoretical values.
  - *Tact time.* Measures the pace of output from a process (drum beat) – for example, one product/order/call every 8 minutes.

- **Internal quality**
  - *Quality rates.* Many different internal quality measures (including PPM) measuring the defect rates from a process.
  - *First-pass yield.* A measure of getting jobs right first time throughout the process.
- **Planning**
  - *Forecast accuracy.* Accuracy of sales forecasts vs. actual demand.
  - *Schedule adherence.* Ability of operations to deliver to plan/schedule. Sometimes also known as schedule hit rate.
  - *Inventory turns/levels.* Measures how effectively inventory is being used to service demand.
  - *Inventory accuracy.* A measure of the accuracy of inventory records used for planning purposes. Usually measured and expressed as a percentage of actual inventory values (i.e., inventory record vs. physical inventory).
  - *Supplier performance.* Similar to customer-focused measures but from the customer's perspective; measures the cost, quality and delivery performance of suppliers.

B.4   LEARNING AND GROWTH-FOCUSED MEASURES

These are the most critical and elusive measures. They are critical because today's learning underpins tomorrow's performance. They are elusive because they tend to focus on skills, capabilities, attitudes and behaviours that are more difficult to quantify and measure using objective performance measures. Some of the most commonly seen indicators include:

- **People satisfaction**
  - People satisfaction index.
  - Average years of service.
  - People retention.
- **People engagement**
  - Motivation.
  - Empowerment.
  - Participation in external networks (e.g., professional or trade associations).
  - Ownership (e.g., participation in share ownership).
  - Engagement score.
- **People development**
  - Number of multi-skilled/cross-trained employees.
  - Personal goal achievement.

- Development/training hours.
- Development/training spend.
- **Attractive place to work**
  - Number of employment enquiries.
  - Diversity.
  - Quality of work environment.
  - Health promotions.
  - Training investment.
- **Health and safety**
  - Lost-time accidents.
  - Reportable accidents.
- **Improvement and innovation**
  - Participation in improvement (e.g., number of suggestions).
  - Number of improvement initiatives.
  - Number of cross-functional projects.
  - Improvement rate of various KPIs.
  - Innovation rate.
- **Communications and knowledge sharing**
  - Communication planning.
  - Internal communication rate.
  - Strategic communication rate.
  - Knowledge management.

However, even though the above indicators provide some form of insight into the learning and growth aspects of the organisation, they do not provide a meaningful measurement framework for measuring the underlying capabilities of the organisation. See Chapter 8 for more information on organisational capabilities and how to assess/measure these capabilities.

In addition, there are a number of models and frameworks that provide explicit guidelines on performance measures. The following sections include some of the more popular ones that I have come across throughout my work.

B.5 ADVANCED PERFORMANCE INSTITUTE AND BERNARD MARR'S 25 MEASURES THAT EVERY MANAGER SHOULD KNOW

Bernard Marr is an author and consultant who specialises in performance measurement and management. His book, entitled *Key Performance Indicators (KPI): The 75 Measures Every Manager Needs to Know* (Marr, 2012) lists 75 key business performance measures that all businesses should consider. He highlights the 25 most important KPIs (see Table B.1).

TABLE B.1   The 25 most important KPIs, as listed by Marr (2012)

Customers	Financial performance
▪ Net promoter score	▪ Revenue growth rate
▪ Customer profitability score	▪ Net profit
▪ Customer retention rate	▪ Net profit margin
▪ Conversion rate	▪ Gross profit margin
▪ Relative market share	▪ Operating profit margin
	▪ Return on investment
	▪ Cash conversion cycle
Internal processes	**Employees**
▪ Capacity utilisation rate	▪ Staff advocacy score
▪ Project schedule variance	▪ Employee engagement level
▪ Project cost variance	▪ Absenteeism Bradford factor
▪ Earned value metric	▪ Human capital value added
▪ Order fulfilment cycle time	▪ 360-degree feedback score
▪ Delivery in full, on-time rate	
▪ Quality index	
▪ Process downtime level	

Visit www.ap-institute.com or www.linkedin.com/pulse/20140729071337-64875646-the-25-kpis-every-manager-must-know for further information on these measures. The Advance Performance Institute website provides valuable information on a range of popular performance measures.

B.6   OLIVER WIGHT INTERNATIONAL AND THE ABCD CHECKLIST FOR BUSINESS EXCELLENCE

Oliver Wight International is a US-based business improvement specialist with an international footprint. Their A Class checklist for business excellence first started life as the ABCD checklist for classifying MRPII (Manufacturing Resources Planning) implementations. It then went on to evolve from a checklist for operations excellence to a checklist for business excellence. Currently in its sixth edition (Oliver Wight International, 2005), it provides a series of statements by which an organisation can audit its key business areas. The checklist includes a number of performance measures, including:

- ▪ Sales Plan Performance (by product family, product or item).
- ▪ Quality (PPM, etc.).
- ▪ Manufacturing costs.
- ▪ Velocity.

- Engineering/Product Development Schedule Performance.
- Production Plan Performance.
- Master Schedule Performance.
- Supplier Delivery Performance.
- Item Master Accuracy.
- Supporting Data Accuracy.
- Inventory Record Accuracy.
- Inventory Location Accuracy.
- Bill of Material Accuracy.
- Routing Accuracy.
- Master Schedule Accuracy.
- Materials Plan Accuracy.
- Capacity Plan Accuracy.

Visit www.oliverwight.com/checklist.htm for a comprehensive list of KPIs, further information on the A Class checklist and on Oliver Wight International.

B.7   SUPPLY CHAIN OPERATIONS REFERENCE (SCOR) MODEL

The SCOR® model is a globally recognised framework for supply chain management. It links business processes, performance metrics, practices and people skills into a unified structure.

It organises the key supply chain management processes and metrics into a number of levels, with level 1 being the highest. Level-1 processes include: Plan, Source, Make, Deliver, Return, Enable. Level-1 performance measures include:

- Perfect order fulfilment.
- Order fulfilment cycle time.
- Upside supply chain flexibility.
- Upside supply chain adaptability.
- Downside supply chain adaptability.
- Overall value at risk.
- Total cost to serve.
- Cash-to-cash cycle time.
- Return on supply chain fixed assets.
- Return on working capital.

Visit www.apics.org/sites/apics-supply-chain-council/frameworks/scor for further information on the SCOR model and its performance measures.

REFERENCES

Marr, B. (2012) *Key Performance Indicators (KPI): The 75 measures every manager needs to know*, Pearson: Oxford.

Oliver Wight International (2005) *The Oliver Wight Class A Checklist for Business Excellence*, 6th edn, John Wiley & Sons: New York.

Index